Fredrick L. M

A Life on the Color Line, 1861–

Fredrick L. McGhee

A Life on the Color Line, 1861–1912

PAUL D. NELSON

Foreword by

DAVID LEVERING LEWIS

MINNESOTA HISTORICAL SOCIETY PRESS

www.mnhs.org/mhspress

Manufactured in the United States of America.

10 9 8 7 6 5 4 3 2 1

ISBN: 978-1-68134-024-1

∞ The paper used in this publication meets the minimum requirements of the American National Standard for Information Sciences—Permanence for Printed Library Materials, ANSI Z39.48-1984.

Library of Congress Cataloging-in-Publication Data
is available upon request.

To my father, C. Richard Nelson,
and my wife, Paula Osborn

Fredrick L. McGhee

A Life on the Color Line, 1861–1912

Foreword		ix
Introduction		xv
Acknowledgments		xxv
1	Up from Slavery	3
2	Making Headlines	13
3	Our Perfect Freedom	25
4	Shelter in the Mighty Storm	39
5	Trials and Tribulations	50
6	Law Enforcement	66
7	All Else Is the Sea	80
8	Crossing the Rubicon	96
9	The Italian Murder Case	112
10	Heart and Soul I Believe	122
11	The Raverty Murder	133
12	Home	147
13	Niagara	157
14	The Civil Rights Cases	168
15	Who Was Fred McGhee?	176
16	I Will Need No Monument	186
17	The Lottery of Life	193
	Epilogue	205
	Notes	209
	Index	227

Foreword

The introduction to *Fredrick L. McGhee: A Life on the Color Line, 1861–1912* is a textbook study in communicable enthusiasm. That Paul Nelson is not a biographer by profession is incidental. He has the instincts of one—the keen discernment, the dogged determination, and the professional's love of a good story. It appears that Nelson sensed from the moment of peradventurous discovery the importance of this long-dead Minnesota attorney of whose existence he had been utterly innocent. Fredrick Lamar McGhee practiced law in St. Paul for twenty three years, the first African American admitted to plead before the state supreme court, one of the most successful criminal lawyers of his time and place, so well respected that whites sought his counsel as avidly as blacks. When McGhee died in 1912 at nearly fifty-one, his record of professional and civic achievement within the state was, irrespective of race, exceptional. Beyond Minnesota's borders, McGhee was celebrated as one of black America's most representative men of distinction. No less an authority than William Edward Burghardt Du Bois, the embodiment of black civil rights and professional probity, lamented McGhee's passing as a terrible loss. "Why," adopted Minnesotan Paul Nelson asked himself, "why haven't I heard of this guy?" In his pursuit of the answer to his question, Nelson came to appreciate that McGhee was the "most accomplished, effective, and interesting black Minnesotan of his time—indeed, of any time." "Thus began one of the greatest adventures of my life."

F. L. McGhee (Fred McGhee, as he was universally known) belonged to the generation of the 1860s, the women and men either emancipated during the Civil War or born free in its immediate aftermath. Reconstruction—"Black Reconstruction," the white South called it—was overthrown just as most of them reached adulthood. By the end of the nineteenth century, Fred McGhee's generation confronted civil rights conditions in the South that made a mockery of the protections guaranteed under the Fourteenth and Fifteenth Amendments. In the North, racial discrimination in housing and employment rapidly worsened. If they were generally spared the violence that was omnipresent below the Mason-Dixon Line, black people were excluded from theaters, restaurants, public parks, and colleges and universities where their presence in some northern cities had formerly elicited few objections from the majority population. The years from 1890 until the nation's entry into the First World War marked a period of legal and customary oppression of black people so pervasive and intense as to deserve the designation "the Nadir" by an African American historian writing on the eve of *Brown v. Board of Education*. From his Mississippi birth in 1861 to his Minnesota demise in 1912, Fred McGhee's life spanned the history of black people from Emancipation through Reconstruction to the Nadir. In fifty-one fully lived years, his biography exemplifies what could be achieved by a black person under the regime of white supremacy, and, irrespective of talent and character, what could not.

Barely resettled from Chicago in the city, Fred McGhee captured the attention of St. Paul's citizens by winning presidential clemency for Lewis Carter, a black soldier convicted of raping a white woman. In that same year, 1890, the state of Mississippi rewrote its constitution in order to complete the elimination of its Negro citizens from the ballot, thereby commencing the revision of constitutions in one southern state after another. Where there had been 130,344 registered African American voters in Louisiana in 1896, a mere 5,320 remained on the rolls four years later. In 1900 only some three thousand out of a male voting-age population of 181,471 were still registered in Alabama. Two years after his coup in the Lewis Carter Case, black voters efficiently corralled by McGhee helped in capturing the St. Paul city hall for the GOP. McGhee was to be bitterly disappointed when the position of third assistant to the City Attorney was given to a white lawyer by the local GOP. As his people were being deprived in the South of ability to defend themselves through the ballot, McGhee believed that the Republican Party their great leader Frederick Douglass had warned them never to abandon had now begun to abandon them. Black Democrats before the New Deal were even more rare than black Catholics. In 1893 Fred McGhee became both a Democrat and a Catholic, stumping for William Jennings Bryan three years later and forming an intellectual and enduring personal bond with Archbishop John Ireland, St. Paul's great Liberal Catholic prelate. Speaking of the political decision, Nelson writes that "McGhee must have understood the profound implications of his act."

It seems altogether likely that McGhee was among the handful of political clairvoyants of the Nadir (Archibald Grimke, William Monroe Trotter, and, on occasions, W.E.B. Du Bois, were other premature Democrats) who divined the balance-of-power potential of the black vote once the GOP's monopoly over the race's loyalty was broken. His religious conversion appears to have been motivated by a somewhat analogous reasoning. Profoundly influenced by charismatic Archbishop Ireland, whose racial ideals were as enlightened as his theology was progressive, McGhee foresaw African American converts playing a vital role in the great Catholic-inspired transformation of American society. Only a person of unusual ability and magnetism could have sustained his position of racial leadership after departing the party of Lincoln and the Protestant faith of his community. McGhee not only retained his standing among St. Paul's people of color, he greatly augmented his authority. That augmented standing became evident to much of the population of the Twin Cities in 1902 when Minnesota's outstanding criminal attorney presided over the fifth annual meeting of the National Afro-American Council in St. Paul. More of a troubled work-in-progress than the premier leadership forum it pretended to be, the council was of sufficient real and prospective importance, nevertheless, to draw Ida B. Wells, T. Thomas Fortune, Du Bois, and Booker T. Washington himself to St. Paul.

The historic St. Paul meeting exposed the ideological fault lines beneath the African American leadership class. Although prey to mounting doubts about the prevailing doctrine of racial accommodationism, McGhee had remained publicly supportive of Booker Washington and his large cohort of sympathizers until the southern educator's naked display of power politics at the St. Paul meeting. Convinced that an appearance of unity was now far less important than an effective civil rights policy, McGhee was one of the first prominent leaders to break with the southern educator. Ever since the electrifying address delivered at the Atlanta and Cotton States Exposition in 1895, Washington's pledge on behalf of southern black people of withdrawal from politics and surrender of civil rights in exchange for jobs and fair dealing from southern white people had all but obliterated the civil rights assertiveness of the previous decades. As the Negro was now a problem to be solved in and by the South, the white North, released from all residual moral, political, and constitutional obligations to monitor race relations, was offered the opportunity to invest in Henry Grady's New South of cheap, obedient labor. One year after the Atlanta Compromise came *Plessy v. Ferguson* in which the U.S. Supreme Court ratified a two-tiered citizenship based on race—equality based on separation.

As Paul Nelson reminds us, it is McGhee that Du Bois, in a moving obituary, was to credit for the impetus leading to the formation of the Niagara

Movement, the beleaguered little organization that threw down the gauntlet of full civil rights for black people at St. Paul. Something must be done to counter the obsequious policies flowing from the Atlanta Compromise, Du Bois recalled McGhee urging. Within the year, public opposition to what was called the "Tuskegee Machine" had coalesced. In April 1903, A.C. McClurg of Chicago published Du Bois's *The Souls of Black Folk*, the book that would begin the transformation of race relations in America. In July of that year, the radical journalist William Monroe Trotter would cause a national scandal in a Boston church when he and a dozen others denounced Booker Washington as he waited to be introduced to the overflow audience. In the main, Fred McGhee's biography complements the group profile of Washington's most prominent critics. Born between 1855 and 1875, most were urban northerners (whether originally from elsewhere or not), college-educated, and professionally accomplished as physicians, lawyers, preachers, morticians, and teachers along with a few businessmen, journalists, and civil servants—known as "quality folk", "representative Negroes" and, increasingly, as the "talented tenth" that took its marching orders from Du Bois. In a population of some nine million people of color, they were numerically infinitesimal—several hundred families in the North and perhaps several dozens in the South. Yet their influence on the politics of race was to prove astonishingly large.

Fred McGhee was among the first to sign the "Call," the June 1905 document summoning those who opposed the policies of the Bookerites to a meeting in Buffalo, New York. The prose was Du Bois's, the sentiments fully reflected McGhee's. The fifty-nine signatories pledged themselves to "aggressive action on the part of men who believe in Negro freedom and growth." They condemned the "present methods of strangling and honest criticism." Du Bois would describe McGhee and the twenty-eight men (and one adolescent male) who joined him on the Canadian side of Niagara Falls in July for three days of deliberations as "educated, determined, and unpurchasable." Ironically, this first collective demand by African Americans for full, immediate citizenship rights in the twentieth century had taken place on Canadian soil because of the eleventh-hour refusal of the Buffalo Hotel to honor the group's reservations. Fittingly the new Niagara Movement's "Declaration of Principles" vibrated with high indignation. Once again, the language was Du Bois's, but he spoke for all the Fred McGhees in black America who were resolved to regain the rights that the white South and now the complicit North had all but nullified. "We refuse to allow the impression to remain that the Negro assents to inferiority," they announced:

The Negro race in America stolen, ravished and degraded, struggling up through difficulties and oppression, needs sympathy and receives criticism; needs help and is given hindrance, needs protection and is Given mob-violence, needs justice and is given charity, needs leadership and is given cowardice and apology; needs bread and is given a stone. This nation will never stand justified before God until these things are changed.

In order to change these things, McGhee would work untiringly with Du Bois and the others to build a force resourceful enough to survive the crushing might of the Tuskegee Machine and, ultimately, powerful enough to be heard through the country. When Fredrick Lamar McGhee died in St. Paul of overwork in 1912, the Niagara Movement, to which he gave unstintingly of his time, talent, and money, had been superseded by the two-year-old organization that would gradually achieve the objectives of the Declaration of Principles. McGhee had envisaged something like the National Association for the Advancement of Colored People immediately after the fateful National Afro-American Council meeting in his hometown. He had rejoiced at the founding of the NAACP and his great and good friend Du Bois would imbue that new organization with a principled militancy and fierce intelligence that McGhee himself had displayed throughout his singular life.

DAVID LEVERING LEWIS
New York, September 2001

Introduction

When Fredrick L. McGhee died in September 1912, he was eulogized in the pages of *The Crisis* by no less than W. E. B. Du Bois. Knowing what I know now about the friendship and professional partnership between the two men, it's not surprising that Du Bois assumed the role of memorialist. Du Bois had openly and often praised McGhee as "brilliant" and written in the first public declaration of the goals of the Niagara Movement—the forerunner to Du Bois's NAACP—that "the honor of founding the organization belongs to F. L. McGhee, who first suggested it."[1]

The obituary carried the requisite recounting of McGhee's accomplishments, from his birth "in Mississippi on the eve of the Civil War" to his final years when he became "one of the great criminal lawyers of the Northwest." But Du Bois could not limit his tribute to a mere listing of facts. "McGhee was not simply a lawyer," he wrote:

> He was a staunch advocate of democracy, and because he knew by bitter experience how his own dark face had served as excuse for discouraging him and discriminating unfairly against him, he became especially an advocate of the rights of colored men. He stood like a wall against the encroachment of color caste in the Northwest.[2]

Du Bois's high estimate of McGhee's importance did not diminish over time. When Fred's widow Mattie died in 1933, more than twenty years later, Du Bois wrote an obituary for her, again published in *The Crisis*, but began the tribute by remembering the significance of her late husband:

> When the Niagara movement was contemplated, and we were trying to find in the United States a few colored men who dared to stand up and ask plainly and unequivocally for the full manhood rights of American Negroes; the right to vote, the right to travel without insult, the right to education, college as well as elementary and industrial,—when we looked about for these men, among the fourteen who eagerly volunteered, was Fredrick L. McGhee of St. Paul.[3]

So why have you never heard of Fredrick McGhee? I have spent nearly ten years trying to figure out the answer, and the question has never really changed.

But I should confess that until one day in 1993, I had never heard of McGhee either. It began when I noticed a copy of David Levering Lewis's *W. E. B. Du Bois, Biography of a Race* in the new arrivals section of the Merriam Park branch of the St. Paul Public Library. The book had gotten excellent reviews, so I took it home. Lewis first mentions "Frederick L. McGhee, a Minnesota attorney," on page 306, and then a few pages later states that after graduating from law school in 1885, McGhee "set up practice in St. Paul, Minnesota, to become one of the city's most successful criminal lawyers." This stopped me. I knew just enough St. Paul history to believe that the presence of a successful black criminal lawyer in our provincial city of pale complexion over one hundred years ago should have been too amazing and wonderful to be forgotten. That was the first time I asked myself the question: Why haven't I heard of this guy?

In search of an answer, I went first to the Minnesota Historical Society, where a research librarian brought me a file folder. Inside I found a few clippings and photos. The librarian also directed me to a nearby card catalog, the Minnesota Biography File, eighty-four old-fashioned wooden file card drawers filled with thousands of three-by-five-inch index cards of biographical information about Minnesota residents. The single Fredrick McGhee card, typewritten many years before (and since replaced) gave his basic dates and places. One item caught my eye: It said that McGhee had been born in Aberdeen, Mississippi, and also died there.

This struck me as unlikely: Why would a man born into slavery return to his birthplace to die? I began looking in newspaper microfilm for notices of McGhee's death, and quickly verified that he had died in St. Paul. I knew something the Minnesota Historical Society (MHS) didn't. Of course, all I had really done was find a typographical error, but I didn't see it that way at the time. I decided to see what more I could learn about Fred McGhee that MHS did not know.

Thus began one of the greatest adventures of my life. I had no thought then of writing a book, nor any particular research plan. I just went to the microfilm of *The Appeal* newspaper and began trolling. As things turned out, this first step, so casually taken, gave form to all that followed. *The Appeal,* published weekly during McGhee's life in Minnesota, chronicled the social, religious, and political doings of black St. Paul and, to a lesser extent, Minneapolis. McGhee appears in its pages hundreds of times, and his friends, family, and clients hundreds more. I reviewed every available issue from 1885–1916 or so, and went back to it time and time again, consistently finding new material; or, to be more precise about it, old material that I had overlooked or misunderstood. Without *The Appeal* and its preservation by the Minnesota Historical Society, the Fred McGhee story could not be told.

McGhee left no personal papers, no diary, no memoir, no sheaf of letters, nor did his wife and daughter. He has no descendants to preserve family lore. What has survived is a large and scattered record of his public life, along with occasional glimpses into his private world.

Some biographers and writers on biography counsel against undertaking a biography under such circumstances; the sources simply do not allow the reader to get inside the subject's head. Fortunately, I did not know about such counsel when I began to think of writing McGhee's life story. Had I known, I don't think I would have agreed with this conventional wisdom, and now having completed a biography I believe such counsel to be wrong. When the subject is sufficiently important, it is better to tell the story incompletely than not at all. Fred McGhee led a public life. So far as I can tell, he did not talk much about himself. He demonstrated his interests, allegiances, and convictions through his deeds. If I may indulge in speculation, I believe he would have wanted to be remembered and judged by his acts and nothing else.

Fortunately, his public acts were so many and so well covered by the press that McGhee left a record large enough to fill a steamer trunk and thousands of hours. The six daily newspapers of St. Paul and Minneapolis took considerable interest in McGhee from his first days forward. He made good copy. What's more, the papers covered local news in a depth of detail unimaginable today. Stories about criminal trials routinely included paragraph upon paragraph of verbatim (or purportedly verbatim) testimony. Afternoon papers often published two stories daily—one of the previous day's doings, another of that morning's. During election seasons the St. Paul dailies covered several precinct rallies every day and quoted the speakers. McGhee showed up hundreds of times in such stories. Also, the *St. Paul Daily Globe* covered local black politics surprisingly well, not regularly but when big events took place, and of course Fred McGhee was usually prominent. The sheer volume of such coverage helped enormously in assembling a portrait of McGhee. Little by little he revealed himself.

McGhee created a record, too, in the files of every court case in which he participated. Most of these still exist and are easily accessible at MHS and elsewhere. The contents are usually scant and disappointing, just the barest record. Only rarely did I find transcripts of testimony, and never what I hoped for most, a transcript of one of his closing arguments. Still, the court files were useful as confirmation of or a check against the newspaper accounts, which sometimes wandered a little distance from the truth.

To the extent that my inquiries followed a pattern, it went like this. Trolling through *The Appeal* microfilm I would read of a case, usually a criminal case, of McGhee's. I would then check the daily press, which, because *The Appeal* was not always precise about dates and places and even names, sometimes meant scanning a few weeks worth of five different dailies. Then I would look for the district court file. If the case went to trial and McGhee's client was convicted, I searched for information about the prisoner in the Stillwater prison records. Thus, a single line in *The Appeal* could lead to hours upon hours of searching through other sources. When I had pursued the lead to the end, I would go back to *The Appeal* and pick up where I had left off. The newspaper thus gave my research a reliable and comforting axis. No matter how far I spun off in pursuit of a lead, I knew I could come back to *The Appeal* and reorient myself.

Assembling a chronology of Fred McGhee's life proved a huge undertaking—putting it in context, larger still. The combined tasks took me on a fabulous journey of learning—through slave and census records of eastern Tennessee; the Civil War and its aftermath in Mississippi; Knoxville during Reconstruction; African-American society in 1880s Chicago; the early African-American church in St. Paul; the lives of Archbishop John Ireland, W. E. B. Du Bois, Booker T. Washington, T. Thomas Fortune, William Jennings Bryan, and others; the Negro Catholic Congresses; the amazing network of African-American weekly newspapers a century ago; the African-American response to the Spanish-American War; crime and criminal procedure in turn-of-the-century Minnesota; the Brownsville incident and Teddy Roosevelt on race; the Elks, Odd Fellows, and Prince Hall Masons, the United Brotherhood of Friendship and Sisters of the Mysterious Ten; death certificates, real estate records, probate files, and the archives of the Josephite Fathers; styles of African-American protest, discourse, and entertainment; and the history of civil rights organizing leading up to and including the creation of the NAACP. This world, or these worlds, were Fred McGhee's; unknown to me before I began this project.

Exploring those worlds and chasing down Fred McGhee wherever I could find him was endlessly interesting. Adventure may seem too strong a word for slow, solitary work that takes place mostly in libraries; yet, as I look back on my search for Fred McGhee it seems full of thrills—leads pursued, documents discovered, questions answered, familiar faces appearing suddenly in old photos, mysteries resolved.

Some thrills were tangible—finding McGhee's grave, for example; or opening a century-old court file to see for the first time Fred McGhee's autograph and to hold in my hand a paper he had held; or walking the land he had owned in Wisconsin.

Some satisfactions came slowly and only after persistent effort. In the late 1890s, for instance, McGhee and his wife became involved in a loud controversy over a popular dance called the cakewalk. It was a detail, a passing thing, but I felt compelled to get to the bottom of it. To do so required finding out precisely what the cakewalk looked like and where it came from, an inquiry into nineteenth century black dance forms whose path confounded me for a long time. (A chance find in a remainder bookstore helped a lot.) Then I had to try to understand the context in which such a dispute could arise, a question tied up with race, class, and class division in black America, popular entertainment, and the black image in the white mind. Only after I had written, rewritten, and rewritten again my account of the controversy did I become satisfied that I understood the events. The satisfaction is real, but the few paragraphs that produced it cost many days of effort.

Every now and then a knotty problem seemed to resolve itself in a moment of epiphany. I knew from an early biographical sketch that McGhee had been born on the John A. Walker farm in Monroe County, Mississippi, just as the Civil War began, and that as a teenager he lived in Knoxville. But how and when did the family leave Mississippi? I mulled the question for years, paging through journals of Mississippi history and the long 1870s congressional investigation of Ku Klux Klan activity in northern Mississippi. I contacted the Monroe County Historical Society. Hours of slogging produced nothing, and I finally concluded that this part of the story was lost. But the question continued to smolder somewhere until one day, unbidden, it flared and emitted a beam of clarity: slaves often escaped with invading (or retreating) Union troops. *Had Union armies passed through Monroe County?* It suddenly occurred to me that I probably had the answer in my own dining room, in Shelby Foote's *The Civil War.* A check of the index, then the text, then the citations put me on the right path, a four-block walk to the Macalester College library and its complete compilation of military documents from the war. Within a couple hours and without leaving my neighborhood I learned how and when slavery had ended for Fred McGhee and family, down to the very date. I understate when I call this a thrill.

Sometimes even a criminal case can be solved in a library. McGhee once represented a physician accused of manslaughter in a botched abortion.

Neither the press accounts nor the court file made the case clear. The doctor and the boyfriend denied involvement. The victim was dead, but I found a copy of her dying declaration in the records of the Washington County, Minnesota, medical examiner. She did not know the name of the doctor who had performed the abortion, but she remembered a detail of the building where he had his offices—the name and floor of a business next door. A quick check of a city directory resolved my doubts. Did the jury rule correctly? I, and only I, now knew the answer.

Luck blessed me more than once. I found a great story by physical accident; the excessive spinning of a microfilm handle. Searching the newspapers for coverage of the 1900 election, I found an important speech given by McGhee for William Jennings Bryan. This was wonderful, so I decided to check the next day's paper as well for any follow up coverage. In my enthusiasm I overspun the handle of the microfilm reading machine and went a few pages further than I intended. The spinning stopped on the opinion page of the *Pioneer Press*, and there appeared before my eyes an editorial blasting McGhee for supporting Bryan. Then I found editorials in other papers, stuff I would never have thought to look for, material that helped me understand how prominent a public figure McGhee had become. Pure luck.

Luck helped me resolve another mystery, too. I developed the habit of checking for Fred McGhee's name in every book of African-American or Minnesota history that I came across, just in case. One of the most difficult stories to uncover had been the complete sequence of events that led to McGhee leaving the Republican Party. Why had McGhee been removed as a Republican presidential elector in 1892? After many hours of searching I discerned the general outlines of it, and some details, enough to relate, but not enough to be completely satisfactory. I could not get to the bottom of that. Months after the book had been accepted for publication I bought a copy of Peg Meier's *Bring Warm Clothes*, mostly because I collect books of old photographs. Out of habit, I checked the index, and to my amazement found McGhee. The index entry sent me to an editorial about McGhee published in the *Svenskarna Amerikanska Posten* in 1892 that gave me a key to resolving the mystery. Once again, fortune favored this endeavor.

Over the months and years as I compiled McGhee's life I enjoyed an ever-growing sense of wonder at his accomplishments. As if rising from slave to trial lawyer were not enough, McGhee achieved distinction in every endeavor he tried. He did not merely speak; people hailed him as an orator. When he joined an organization, he soon led it. If he had a part, it was a starring role.

When he had friends, mentors, and rivals, they were giants: Edward H. Morris, John Ireland, Booker T. Washington, W. E. B. Du Bois. Fred McGhee devoted himself to law, politics, civil rights, and religion. In all four he rose about as high as a Midwestern black man in turn of the century America could go. He found time, somehow, for other things, too—he did charity work, appeared in amateur theater, wrote articles, gave book talks, organized clubs, meetings, dinners, debates, mock trials, and picnics, sponsored visiting artists, followed boxing and football, fished, presided over children's events at the parish, and must have done a thousand other things that left no record. He led an extraordinary life.

I developed the conviction that Fred McGhee was the most accomplished, effective, and interesting black Minnesotan of his time—indeed, of any time. He achieved local fame as a lawyer and political leader, and national prominence in African-American politics and civil rights. Yet he had been nearly forgotten. Why? After ten years of research and writing, the question I first posed, "How come I never heard of this guy?" has not changed. In spite of all that I have learned, the best I can do is guess at an answer or, to put it more accurately, at a handful of partial answers.

Most popular interest in post-Emancipation black America has centered around the great figures of the time, Frederick Douglass, Booker T. Washington, and W. E. B. Du Bois. These titans deserve all the attention they get, and they also fit conveniently into what might be called the "great man" approach to African-American history. What is more, one can tell a great deal of the bigger story through them, as David Levering Lewis so ably does in his biography about Du Bois, the first volume subtitled, *Biography of a Race.* Scholars have done a lot of very good work on the themes of African-American struggles and progress during McGhee's time, but it is to be expected that this work does not much reach or interest the general public. One partial answer, then, to the question of McGhee's obscurity is he was simply lost in a field of history of limited interest and dominated by larger-than-life personalities.

One might say that we are fortunate to have as much of this history available to us as we do. With just a little bit of effort one can find very good biographies of T. Thomas Fortune, William Monroe Trotter, and Ida B. Wells Barnett, all contemporaries and collaborators or rivals of Fredrick McGhee. McGhee ranks with them as leaders in the early fight against Jim Crow, but he is far from alone in his obscurity. Relatively few in the general public have heard of Fortune, Trotter, and Wells Barnett; even fewer know or have reason to know about their collaborators, people such as Professor Kelly Miller,

Bishop Alexander Walters, Edward H. Morris, Emmett Scott, and many others in addition to McGhee. There are many fascinating stories to be told of these faithful, optimistic, American strivers. Another partial reason why McGhee has been forgotten is that telling stories like his takes a lot of work, and scholars just haven't got around to it yet.

Where he lived had something to do with it, too. Though Fred McGhee exercised national leadership, he did it from St. Paul, far from the centers of controversy and decision centered on an axis running from Tuskegee to Washington, New York, and Boston. McGhee remains, therefore, primarily a regional figure. Regional and local history, though compelling, fascinating, and essential to the development of national and world histories, is not a very big business. The number of people who make a living, or even an income, teaching or writing Minnesota history probably wouldn't fill a minivan. Amateurs do much of the work that does get done.

Why is there so little popular memory of McGhee even in St. Paul? Part of the answer must be that no descendants remained in the city to carry on his name and legend. Surely, another part is that he lived at the wrong time. He did not live to see any of his civil rights causes succeed, and success is better remembered than failure. Still another share of the cause of McGhee's invisibility is that that's the way things are: many worthy people, seen as great in their times, have been forgotten.

And Fred McGhee was a great man. Not on the scale of George Washington or even Booker T. Washington, but on a scale that is more accessible to ordinary people. He rose from rags not to riches but to prosperity, from obscurity not to fame but to renown. He did this by developing qualities familiar to all of us: persistence, ambition, and belief in something bigger than himself.

McGhee achieved wonders. He became a lawyer despite little education, then Minnesota's first black attorney, then so successful a lawyer and politician that he was Minnesota's first celebrated African American public figure. Working from St. Paul, a distant outpost of black America, he became so forceful a national civil rights leader that Booker T. Washington had to fight him and W. E. B. Du Bois rely on him. McGhee made himself a national leader, too, among African-American Catholics and Democrats.

He did all this not by great deeds but by tens of thousands of small decisions: to take on one more case, chair one more meeting, give one more speech, raise one more dollar, shake one more hand. McGhee probably would have denied that he had any special talents. He simply acted on his beliefs. He believed in the future of his people, in the American Catholic Church, in William Jennings Bryan and the Minnesota Democratic Party, in the U.S. Constitution, and in the power of citizen organization.

Fred McGhee provides a fascinating example of the middle class striver of the first post-Emancipation generation. There were tens of thousands like him—optimistic, faithful, patriotic Americans doing what had never been done before, turning a slave people into a free one, their stories rarely told. So it is not at all surprising that Fred McGhee's story has gone unwritten until now. It is perhaps more astonishing that it will be told at all. No one is more surprised than I am. By a stroke of fate Fred McGhee beckoned to me from across the decades at a moment in my life when I was able to follow him. It has been a pleasure and a privilege. May he never be forgotten.

PAUL D. NELSON
St. Paul, September 2001

Acknowledgments

Many people helped me in this endeavor, often providing information, leads, or encouragement without which I could not have completed the task. I will thank some of them by name here. I want to thank, too, people whose names I will never know, those responsible for compiling and maintaining the libraries and archives where fragments of the Fred McGhee story have been preserved for decades, awaiting me.

I did most of my research at the Minnesota History Center, where newspapers, court files, census records, prison records, city directories, photographs and other marvels are preserved and made easily available to anyone, including amateurs like me. Other libraries held other treasures: those of the University of Minnesota, Macalester College, and the University of St. Thomas, here in Minnesota, and Howard University, the University of Massachusetts, the College of Holy Cross, the National Archives and the Library of Congress as well. I found essential information also in the files of the Ramsey and Hennepin County courts, the Ramsey County Recorder, and the Minnesota Department of Health. The Saint Paul Public Library interlibrary loan services helped me get my hands on microfilm from distant places. My thanks to the people of all those institutions.

Patrick Anzelc of the Archdiocese of Minneapolis and St. Paul gave me a boost early in my research for which I will always be grateful—he found me Fred McGhee's grave. Bob Booker of the Beck Cultural Center in Knoxville provided me wonderful stuff about Knoxville College and that city's black history. Steve Cotham, head of the McClung Historical Collection of the Knox County Library, spent hours, unbidden, digging up invaluable data about the McGhee family from census and probate records I would never have known to check, plus astute analysis of what he had found. Father Peter Hogan, S. S. J., sent me many marvelous pages from the archive of the Josephite Fathers in Baltimore. David Levering Lewis of course (and unknowingly) set this whole thing in motion with his biography of W. E. B. Du Bois, and also gave me crucial encouragement along the way. Father Kevin McDonough made the records of St. Peter Claver parish available to me. Dave Riehle, a St. Paul amateur historian, sent me several newspaper bits about McGhee, most of them pure gold. Linda Seidman of the W. E. B. Du Bois Papers at the University of Massachusetts, Amherst, made those papers available to me and helped me use them.

Finally, and most important, I wish to thank my wife, Paula Osborn. For the better part of a decade she supported the family and tolerated my ravings while I pursued Fred McGhee. In short, she made this book possible.

Fredrick L. McGhee

A Life on the Color Line, 1861–1912

The problem of the Twentieth Century
is the problem of the color-line.
W. E. B. Du Bois
The Souls of Black Folk

1

Up from Slavery

On June 17, 1889, attorney Fredrick McGhee strode into the old State Capitol in St. Paul with a single and simple task to perform. His companion, a little-known lawyer named Horace Stone, directed him to the office of the clerk of the state supreme court. There McGhee signed a paper or two, took an oath, and, with that, his main work of the day was done. Though nothing of this nature had ever before occurred in the state of Minnesota, the press and public took little notice. Of St. Paul's four dailies, just one printed news of the event, and only the keenest readers would have seen it. The notice appeared on page 7 of the *St. Paul Pioneer Press* in tiny type. It read:

> Frederick L. McGhee, a colored attorney of Illinois, was admitted yesterday on a certificate from the supreme court of that state to practice in all the courts of Minnesota. Mr. McGhee ... is the first colored lawyer who has been admitted to practice by the supreme court of this state.

This was just the first of Fred McGhee's many firsts, in law and later in politics. It would not be long before the editors of the *Pioneer Press* and of all the other metropolitan dailies became accustomed to printing McGhee's name often and in much larger type.[1]

Until that summer of 1889, Fred McGhee had been a rising young attorney in Chicago, well situated for a successful and lucrative career, with outstanding prospects for promi-

Fredrick McGhee.
Illustration by Graphic Illustrating Co.,
St. Paul, from The Appeal, *June 22, 1889.*

3

nence in black society and politics. Chicago had a black population of over 10,000, including a substantial middle class and professional corps of teachers, ministers, physicians, dentists, and lawyers. McGhee had begun his career in 1885 as a protégé of Chicago's greatest black lawyer, Edward H. Morris, had run for minor public office, and had earned a top position in black society. He gave it all up to come to St. Paul.[2]

It seems at first glance an odd decision. St. Paul and Minneapolis were booming at this time, but the combined metropolis of nearly 300,000 people included fewer than 3,000 African Americans, and their numbers were barely on the climb. The black middle class was tiny, and except for a handful of ministers, a mortician, and a newspaper editor, it included no professionals at all. By moving to Minnesota Fred McGhee had chosen to walk the color line in a most conspicuous and vulnerable way. As the first of his race to practice so public a profession, he could not avoid being seen as a representative of his people, in their eyes and to the community at large. But black Minnesotans could not provide him enough paid work to get along. To make a living he would have to attract white clients and prove himself in the all-white world of Minnesota courts. McGhee had put himself in the position of having to succeed as a "race" man while at the same time persuading clients, judges, and jurors to look past race.

All of his adult life Fredrick McGhee seemed compelled to reject the broad and easy path in favor of the narrow and thorny. At a time when nearly all black voters and leaders were loyal Republicans, he left the party of Lincoln to join the Democrats. When the vast majority of African Americans were Protestant, he joined the Church of Rome. When nearly all followed the lead of the revered Booker T. Washington, McGhee joined the camp of Washington's rival, W. E. B. Du Bois. And when he could have enjoyed wealth, prestige, possibly even power among Chicago's growing African-American masses, he chose instead to move to the nation's coldest and whitest metropolis.

Fred McGhee had to do things his own way. In matters important to him, he preferred to be uncomfortably alone, and faithful to his own beliefs, rather than popular. His stubbornness cost him dearly. Had he remained a Protestant Republican Washington loyalist he would have had an easier life: more praise, more friends, more money. But it was precisely this principled and inconvenient stubbornness that made him so effective an advocate, a civil rights pioneer, and the greatest African-American public figure that Minnesota has so far produced.

Fred McGhee's difficult life began in the humblest circumstances that the United States then had to offer: slave quarters in Mississippi. He was born October 28, 1861, near Prairie Station, Monroe County, Mississippi, the son of Abraham and Sarah McGhee and the lawful property of John A. Walker, one of the wealthiest land and slave owners of the state.[3]

We know nothing of the McGhees' life in slavery, except perhaps the day it ended. The Civil War came to northeastern Mississippi in February 1864. Union forces had taken Memphis, just 100 miles north, in June 1862, and Vicksburg, to the west, in July 1863. In early 1864 General William Tecumseh Sherman proposed coordinated Union advances from Vicksburg east and from Memphis south, the two forces to unite at Meridian and march to Selma, Alabama. A successful campaign would take control of northern Mississippi and cut the vital Memphis to Mobile rail line. That line passed through the John A. Walker farm at Prairie Station.

General William Sooy Smith led the Union raid from Memphis, wrecking the rail line and destroying Confederate assets as he lumbered south. In his book *The Civil War,* Shelby Foote describes the scene along the railroad:

> From Okolona to West Point, a distance of about thirty miles, [Smith's] troopers spent more time ripping up track and setting fires than they did in the saddle. "During two days," a brigade commander later wrote, "the sky was red with the flames of burning corn and cotton."
>
> The sky was red with more flames than these: for the blue horsemen ... did not neglect to scorch the holdings of secessionists in their path. What was more, a Federal colonel added, slaves on the plantations roundabout, "driven wild with the infection, set torch to mansionhouses, stables, cotton gins and quarters [and] came en masse to join our column," leaving only fire and absolute destruction behind them.

This must have been how emancipation first appeared to the McGhees and the other Walker slaves—rumors, agitation, a glowing red sky, and then, suddenly, blue-coated soldiers. But neither slaves nor soldiers destroyed the Walker farm. Smith's men camped there peaceably on February 21, 1864, then moved further south toward Meridian.

Had General Smith been a more effective commander, the McGhee family might have remained in Mississippi, thus denying Fred McGhee his destiny. But Smith missed his rendezvous with Sherman at Meridian, leaving him exposed to Confederate General Nathan Bedford Forrest, whose fearsome cavalry terrorized Union armies. Forrest whipped Smith in a brief battle at West Point, and the Union army scuttled north again through Prairie Station on its flight to safety in Memphis. "All along this portion of the march negroes came flocking to our lines ... by the hundreds and thousands," Smith reported later.

A week after reaching Memphis he wrote that "about 3,000 able-bodied negroes had taken refuge with us." Had Smith not been defeated, his army would
have kept going south and east, deeper into the Confederacy, but his defeat and
retreat opened the road north to freedom for thousands of Mississippi slaves,
Abraham and Sarah McGhee and their children almost certainly among them.[4]

The McGhees eventually made their way across Tennessee to Knoxville—a
sensible destination for them. Abraham McGhee had lived near there as a
young man before being sold into Mississippi. He may have visited the city
from time to time, for he was owned then by the white McGhees, one of
Knoxville's founding families. Moreover, throughout the Civil War east Tennessee had retained strong pro-Union feeling, and when the war ended many
people interested in helping the former slaves gathered there. Jobs were made
available to freemen. Schools for black children were established. Thus
Knoxville offered familiarity, the possibility of work, and the prospect of education for the McGhee children. By 1869 Abraham McGhee had found work in
the city as a blacksmith, and there the family settled.[5]

Young Fredrick's parents secured him the beginnings of an education by
enrolling him in one of the freemen's schools opened in Knoxville by the
United Presbyterian Church. But that was all they could do. Abraham McGhee
died around 1870 and Sarah within the next three years, leaving Fredrick in
the care, presumably, of his older brothers, Barclay, age twenty-two or twenty-
three, and Matthew, nineteen or twenty. Whoever took charge of Fredrick after
his parents' deaths took the next crucial step in the young man's education by
enrolling him in Knoxville College.[6]

Moving from a freemen's school to Knoxville College marked no change of
educational path for McGhee. The United Presbyterian Church had established educational missions for former slaves in Mississippi, Louisiana, and
Tennessee as early as 1864, employing mainly white teachers from the North.
In 1872 the church's General Assembly voted to end the mission system in
favor of establishing a single training school for black teachers. In 1874 the
church moved its McKee School from Nashville to Knoxville and renamed it
Knoxville College. Matriculating there, McGhee remained in the Presbyterian
freemen's system.

At first Knoxville was not a college in the modern sense of the word but
rather a combined primary and secondary school. No records from the earliest years have survived, so no one knows what Fred McGhee studied. But he
must have been taught well and learned well, for his two years at Knoxville
College formed the foundation for his legal education.[7]

By 1876 or 1877 his schooling had come to an end, probably for monetary reasons, and the teenaged Fred McGhee went to work; the 1880 Knoxville city directory lists him as a laborer. But by the time that directory came out, Fred McGhee had already left Knoxville forever. He did what ambitious young men from the provinces have done for centuries: he took on the challenges and opportunities of the big city. The big city for young McGhee was Chicago.[8]

It was the great boomtown of the continent. The catastrophic fire of 1871 had barely interrupted the city's growth; in fact it had cleared vast tracts of land for development. Chicago's population grew from just under 300,000 in 1870 to over 500,000 in 1880, and in the next ten years it doubled. African Americans participated in this growth in a tiny way. Between 1870 and 1880 their numbers rose from 3,700 to not quite 6,500; when the population of Chicago reached a million, ten years later, blacks numbered just over 14,000. Most of the black immigrants came from the border states of Missouri and Kentucky; only a handful were from the Confederate South. Two of these were the McGhee brothers; Barclay around 1875 and Fred in 1879. Both found work as porters.[9]

Vast, voracious, and indifferent to human suffering, Chicago devoured immigrants by the tens of thousands. Only a few thrived—the gifted, the ambitious, the persistent, and the lucky. Fred McGhee was one of the few. At age twenty-three he was president of the black community's Philosophy Literary Society, president of United Waiters Union no. 1, and in law school. In fall 1885, when he turned twenty-four, he attended the Illinois State Colored Convention as a delegate; was admitted to the Illinois bar; and went into practice with the city's "dean of colored lawyers," Edward H. Morris. He had transformed himself from a slightly educated laboring lad into a gentleman and a professional.[10]

To have done this despite all of the barriers, race and class chief among them, required not only ability and drive but something still more miraculous: imagination. Where did Fred McGhee get the idea that he could do such a thing? No memoir from his lips or pen has survived, so one can only speculate. Two people from his youth may have served as role models or inspirations.

His father, Abraham McGhee, he had been a most unusual slave. Though it was illegal in most slave states to teach slaves to read, the elder McGhee was literate. Though very few slaves were permitted to learn trades, Abraham McGhee worked as a blacksmith. He was a lay Baptist preacher, too. Within the constricted world of slave society, Fred McGhee's father belonged to the elite. And he was a risk-taker. He led his family out of Mississippi and across the state of Tennessee, out of the country and into the city when this was not

Edward Hopkins Morris. Photograph by Richard Atkinson.

a common thing to do. Even after the end of the Civil War, the overwhelming majority of former slaves stayed in the rural South; the great migration to the North and to the cities would not begin for another fifty years. Abraham had imagination, too, enough to see that at least one of his children got some schooling, something only a relative handful of freemen achieved.

So in his father, Fredrick McGhee had a model—of achievement against great odds, of wisdom in seeking opportunity, of appreciation for education, and of the imagination inherent in taking risks. He probably heard his father preach, too, and all his adult life Fred McGhee was renowned as an orator. McGhee's mother must have influenced him as well. Unfortunately, we know almost nothing about her.[11]

None of this, however, gives much of a clue to how McGhee got the idea to become a lawyer. It may have come from observing a Knoxville man named William Francis Yardley. Yardley had been born black but free in Knoxville in 1844. He attended a school for free black youth, then taught school briefly before reading law with a white attorney and getting his license to practice in 1872. The same year he was elected a Knoxville alderman, and in 1876 won a seat as a judge in the Knox County courts. That September, Yardley announced himself a candidate for the Republican nomination for governor. He did not get that nomination; undeterred, he ran as an independent.

The young Fredrick McGhee, fifteen years old in fall 1876, must have watched Yardley with interest. Yardley had become a lawyer and gone into politics; within a decade McGhee would do the same. In his campaign Yardley stressed issues of class as much as those of race, criticizing laws and tax policies that hit the poor man hard. McGhee would pursue a class analysis, too, twenty and thirty years later. When Yardley ran as an independent, he did so against the opposition of the political class of his own race, staunch Republicans. McGhee took a similar contrary course a decade and a half later. Yardley lost, of course, and badly, but the heights to which Yardley aspired must have provided inspiration for the young McGhee.[12]

In 1885 McGhee completed law school and was admitted to practice in the courts of Illinois that November. He then joined the law practice of Edward H. Morris, a man with a large, varied, and lucrative practice. In 1886 he married the sixteen-year-old Mattie Crane, a musically talented and socially graceful young woman from Louisville. He joined the Autumn Social Club, a black society group that despite its name put on year-round gala events—balls, picnics, and the like. In 1888 he became its president, placing him in the top ranks of Chicago's African-American society. By the late 1880s, then, McGhee had a family, a career with good prospects, and a place in society: everything needed, in short, for an ambitious attorney to enjoy a fine life and excellent career in Chicago.[13]

But four hundred miles to the northwest events were unfolding and conversations taking place that would lead Fred McGhee to his next destination and his true destiny. St. Paul in the late 1880s had a small black community, about 1,500 in a city of nearly 130,000. About 1,300 more African Americans lived in the slightly larger sister city (164,000) of Minneapolis. These black communities were growing, but they were anxious to grow faster. A key to local pride, growth, and self-sufficiency would be the development of a black professional class. At this time neither of the Twin Cities had a black physician, dentist, teacher, or attorney. They did, however, have an ambitious and forward-looking newspaper editor named John Quincy Adams, who would play the key role in bringing Fred McGhee and St. Paul together.[14]

The son of a free black Kentucky preacher, Adams had graduated from Oberlin College in Ohio, taught public school in Louisville, and held public office in Louisville and Arkansas. He and his brother, Cyrus Field Adams, had founded and edited the *Louisville Bulletin.* As that paper was failing in 1886, Adams was lured to St. Paul to take the job of associate editor of the city's first black weekly, *The Western Appeal.* It was failing, too, but within two years Adams had purchased it, brought it out of debt, and made it a going business. In 1888 he changed the name to *The Appeal* and, not satisfied with the local market, set his sights on expansion to Chicago, where *The Conservator* had had the African-American market to itself since 1876.[15]

Adams engaged his brother Cyrus to run the Chicago operations and published his first Chicago edition on February 25, 1888. Four months later *The Appeal* claimed to have passed *The Conservator* in circulation. John Adams's Chicago venture brought him into contact with

John Q. Adams, about 1892.

Fred McGhee. He had learned as early as January 1888 that McGhee had become restless and was looking to move, perhaps to Omaha. Adams may have perceived then the possibility of improving McGhee's choice of destination. It is likely that when Adams came to Chicago in February to oversee *The Appeal's* debut, he had another purpose, too: to evaluate Fred McGhee's abilities and intentions and, if things looked right, persuade him to reconsider Omaha in favor of St. Paul. If the two had not met before, they met now. McGhee had just become president of the Autumn Social Club, and the club made Adams its guest of honor at the annual banquet and masquerade, held February 25. Joining Adams at the head table that evening were Edward H. Morris and Fredrick McGhee.

Adams returned to Chicago for an extended visit in March 1888. He and McGhee must have met again and talked serious business. Though McGhee did not alter his resolve to leave Chicago, there was no more talk of Omaha. On June 9 this item appeared in *The Appeal*'s St. Paul edition:

> Mr. F. L. McGhee, of Chicago, was in the city last Saturday and gave *The Appeal* a pleasant call. He contemplates taking up his residence in our city in the near future and devoting himself to his profession, the practice of law.

Then nothing happened for a year; McGhee's name disappeared from *The Appeal* except in connection with the Autumn Social Club, never in connection with St. Paul.[16]

It was without public anticipation or buildup, then, that Fred McGhee appeared in St. Paul on June 17, 1889, for his visit to the offices of the state supreme court. So far as the evidence reveals, most black readers in the Twin Cities were surprised to see on the front page of *The Appeal*'s June 22 edition an ink drawing of Fred McGhee, a brief biography, and this announcement:

> *The Appeal* takes great pleasure to-day in presenting to its patrons the portrait of Frederick [sic] L. McGhee, and a short sketch of his life. He has the distinction of being the first Colored man admitted to practice at the bar of the Supreme Court of Minnesota.

Clearly Adams was the chief agent of all this, but another's hand was at work as well; that of Edward H. Morris. For within a month another black lawyer came to Minnesota from Chicago, to establish a practice in Minneapolis—Morris's brother, William.[17]

The town that greeted Fred and Mattie McGhee shrieked with adolescent zest and confusion. It was a river town in the throes of transformation to a railroad hub. Hundreds of steamboats still docked at the levees every year, but now legions of passengers and millions of tons of freight steamed into and out of the city each year by rail. Thousands of passengers, Germans and Scandinavians mostly, got off the trains and stayed. Between 1870 and 1890 the population grew from 20,000 to 130,000. Many people lived in hovels, tenements, and shacks. Most streets were unpaved, whole neighborhoods treeless. Wood, coal, and tobacco smoke filled the air; mud, horse dung, and traffic filled the streets; the screech of trains, the horns of riverboats, and polyglot voices filled one's ears. The St. Paul of 1889 was noisier, smellier, draftier, poorer, uglier, muddier, grittier, and busier than it is today—more irregular, more disorderly, more desperate, and more energetic. It had lots of people on the make and many more on the margins. There was plenty of drinking and whoring and stealing and gambling. St. Paul was, in short, a very good place for a young lawyer specializing in criminal law.

2

Making Headlines

Fred McGhee began his legal career in Minnesota under pressure. He had to learn his way around the courts of St. Paul and Minneapolis. He had to decipher their procedures, customs, and unwritten rules, while at the same time proving himself to attorneys, reporters, witnesses, judges, jurors, and jailers, who by experience associated dark skin with defendant rather than defender. A defense attorney is by profession "uppity"; his duty is to challenge the system and the people who have accused his client of crime. McGhee could not have known how Minnesotans would react to a black man, a southern black man with a Chicago sheen, engaging in the confrontational business of cross-examining witnesses, disputing the police version of events, and contradicting prosecutors. He had to find the places where his race interfered with advocacy and where it might help. And he had to do all of this under the scrutiny of two distinct but equally vital constituencies: the overwhelmingly white legal system and a black community eager for a champion.

An article in the July 13, 1889, edition of *The Appeal* carried the headline, "Lawyer McGhee's First Case." A black railroad car porter named William Stafford had the misfortune of living next to a brothel operated by a white woman, Alice Finerty. In the wee hours of Tuesday, July 10, a white man named Edward Warner came looking for companionship but misstepped by one house, entering Stafford's instead of Finerty's. Stafford took vehement offense and cut Warner badly in the face and scalp. Warner got two sets of stitches while Stafford ended up in jail charged with assault and battery and disorderly conduct.

Justice marched double-time in those days. Charged on Tuesday, Stafford went to trial on Wednesday, with Fred McGhee defending. McGhee got an acquittal on the assault charge, while Stafford was convicted of disorderly conduct and fined $20. According to *The Appeal*, "Mr. McGhee handled the case with such ability as to receive many compliments from the members of the bar present."[1]

The Stafford case took place in a societal vein that McGhee would mine for the next few years, an underworld of sex and occasional violence where black

13

and white came together at night. In early September two black women, Hattie Minton and Ella Aker, were charged for the third time with prostitution, for which the customary sentence was a fine of $100 plus thirty days or more in confinement. With McGhee defending, the judge fined them just $10 each and they stayed out of jail. Six weeks later police arrested a young white woman named Jennie Hendrickson on suspicion of prostitution. The *Pioneer Press* reported that she had been detained "for appearing in the street in the company of another woman," doubtless a known prostitute. *The Appeal* had it that she had been arrested "for being on the street with a Colored man." Judge Burr of the municipal court committed her for ninety days to the House of the Good Shepherd, a residence for orphans and wayward girls and women.

Courthouse, Fourth and Wabasha, St. Paul, about 1887,
where McGhee tried his first Minnesota case, and many thereafter.

McGhee got the case—his first with a white client—after Hendrickson was already put away. He sought to free her by a writ of *habeas corpus*, which demands the release of a prisoner unlawfully held. This was a popular device with lawyers at the time, apparently because it was quick and because there were frequent technical errors in municipal court proceedings. McGhee argued that his client could not be detained because she had not been accused of a crime. The city attorney responded that what had been done to Jennie Hendrickson "conformed to the uniform custom" of municipal court. The judge agreed with McGhee and set the woman free.[2]

The case, though in most respects ordinary, had civil rights implications. Custom had taken Jennie Hendrickson's liberty based on suspicion or association. African Americans had often felt the sting of such "uniform custom" in their dealings with police and courts. McGhee did what civil rights lawyers often aim to do—strike at pernicious custom by insisting on the rule of law. McGhee's early cases demonstrated the power of the presence of a competent advocate: defendants get better results even when found guilty.

During his first years in St. Paul, Fred McGhee relied on defendants from the sex trade for his living. In the early 1890s he brought petition after petition to the district court on behalf of prostitutes and brothel-keepers to get them free and, presumably, back into commerce. Someone in the sex business was paying his fees.

While probably blinking at the nature of some of these cases, St. Paul's African Americans watched McGhee's work with appreciation. The Reverend J. M. Henderson went to the courthouse one day in fall 1889 to see McGhee in action:

> Mr. McGhee arose, for a moment all was silence and suspense, never before had a Colored lawyer plead before that court. Deliberately and with an air of complete confidence in the justice of his cause, the young attorney began his argument. For half an hour he held the jury and audience spellbound . . .

Henderson urged black St. Paulites to watch McGhee at work, not only for his performance, but also to see "the respect with which our lawyer is treated." He concluded: "It is a great thing, and something to be proud of."[3]

But these cases were small potatoes. McGhee hit the front pages in March 1890 when word came that rapist Lewis Carter had been released from prison. The case had come to McGhee in July 1889 when an aged black woman, like him from Mississippi, had appeared in his office. She had just returned from visiting her son, Lewis Carter, at the state prison in Stillwater. The warden there had heard of McGhee and suggested that Mrs. Carter pay him a call.

Lewis Carter had told his mother he was innocent and she believed him. Fred McGhee told a reporter later, "She told me to go over to the prison and have a talk with him, and if I believed him innocent, she desired me to do what I could to secure his pardons." He interviewed Carter, reviewed his trial transcript and, "believing that a gross injustice had been done . . . concluded to do whatever could be done for him."[4]

The case had begun in 1885. Carter was then a twenty-one-year-old soldier serving at Fort Snelling. The fort stands atop a bluff overlooking the joining of the Minnesota and Mississippi rivers, roughly six miles from the downtowns of both St. Paul and Minneapolis. It was built in the 1820s to protect and encourage the fur trade. By the 1880s it had long since lost any compelling military mission. The fort operated in a relaxed mode, with civilians permitted to come and go unchallenged.

On the afternoon of April 17, 1885, young German immigrant Maria Kapplinger passed through the fort on her way to visit her fiancé at a nearby farm. As she walked past a barracks, Privates Lewis Carter and James Carr engaged Fraulein Kapplinger in conversation. According to her version of events, Carter suddenly produced a knife, forced her to the ground, raped her, and stole money from her purse. She ran to the farm for help, then returned to the fort to make a complaint. Carter and Carr stopped at their barracks before taking off on foot toward Minneapolis. A detachment of soldiers quickly found them, arrested them, and returned them to Fort Snelling, where Carter was charged with rape, robbery, and desertion.

At the court martial in early May, Kapplinger returned to the fort to tell her terrible story: an immigrant girl, barely conversant in English, accosted by two black men, threatened at knifepoint, raped, and robbed. Lewis Carter, who had no lawyer, conducted his own defense. He tried twice to cross-examine his accuser but quickly faltered and gave up. In the end, his entire defense consisted of his own statement of the events.

Carter agreed that he and Maria Kapplinger had met at the date and place alleged, but otherwise told a very different story. The young woman who appeared in the fort that day carried herself not as an immigrant ingenue but as a city sophisticate. She conversed willingly, told the men she had lived a year in Chicago, and exposed her ankles in a way that suggested she had plenty of experience of the world. Carter concluded that she had come to the fort on business, made inquiry accordingly, and settled on a price of two dollars for her services, which he paid in advance. But Kapplinger then refused to perform her part of the bargain. Carter demanded return of his money, using for

persuasion the two-inch blade of his penknife. Persuaded, Kapplinger surrendered her purse; Carter removed his two dollars and gave the purse back.
She then went on her way and he on his. He and Carr were simply on their
way to a boxing match in Minneapolis when soldiers arrested them a few
hours later.

The officers of the military court did not believe Lewis Carter. They convicted him on all counts and the commanding general sentenced him to thirty
years, to be served at the state prison in Stillwater. Carter protested his innocence and enlisted some support from the Twin Cities black community, but
to no avail. If he behaved well in prison he could hope for release in 1905.[5]

Four years into Carter's term, in 1889, two unrelated events produced a re-
versal of his fortune. The first occurred in March when Samuel P. Snider took
office as United States congressman for the district that included Minneapolis
and Fort Snelling. In some ways Snider was a typical Minnesota politician: he
had come to the state from elsewhere, gotten rich in the railroad business, then
turned to politics and served in the state legislature before election to Congress
in 1888. But Snider also had a history that would have interested Private
Carter. He came from a family of Ohio abolitionists, had volunteered for Civil
War service, been left for dead on the battlefield at Shiloh and captured; after
furlough and recovery he returned to the war as commander of a black infantry regiment. If Lewis Carter were ever to have a friend in Washington, it
was Sam Snider.[6]

The second event that worked in Carter's favor was the arrival of Fred
McGhee; soon he had the services of an ambitious advocate. No appeals of
Carter's conviction were possible, so McGhee concentrated on seeking presidential clemency from newly inaugurated Benjamin Harrison. His strategy
had three elements: attack the procedural and factual basis of Carter's conviction; appeal for mercy; and route the clemency petition through sympa-
thetic channels.

On procedure, McGhee raised a couple of good, though probably not winning, points. Carter insisted that he had asked for James Carr to be produced
as a witness at his trial but been refused. The Army denied this, but the fact remained that Carr, the only other eyewitness, did not testify. McGhee charged
also that the same officer who had taken Maria Kapplinger's complaint and organized the hunt for Carter, had then presided over the court martial *and* testified as a witness for the prosecution. "Was ever such a thing permitted before
upon the trial of any kind sanctioned by any law . . . of our land?" asked
McGhee rhetorically.

On the facts, McGhee directed President Harrison's attention to certain improbabilities in Kapplinger's version of events. She said that Carter had held an eight-inch knife against her neck as she struggled against him. It was not believable, argued McGhee, that in such a melee Carter, with just one hand free, could have achieved "connection" with the woman and that she could have avoided all injury, as in fact she had. No medical evidence of penetration had been produced at trial. Kapplinger testified that Carter robbed her, yet there was money left in her purse, which supported Carter's assertion that he had merely taken his two dollars back. The day of the crime was rainy, yet Kapplinger's clothes had not been muddied. These were all good points, but McGhee must have known they were probably insufficient: he could hardly expect the president to overturn the factual findings of the officers who saw and heard the witnesses at trial.[7]

Maria Kapplinger remained the key to the case in 1889 just as she had been in 1885, so Fred McGhee tracked her down. This took some doing, for she had married, changed her name to Maria Scholls, and moved, but find her he did. One day in late summer 1889, McGhee went to her house armed only with his own persuasive powers and a letter from Lewis Carter promising that if released he would do her no harm. As McGhee told it, he found Scholls and her husband at home and asked if they would sign a petition for Carter's pardon. She agreed that he had been punished enough, but feared that he might take some vengeance against her if freed. McGhee assured her that, to the contrary, Carter would be motivated only by gratitude. Satisfied, Maria Scholls signed a statement to President Harrison that Carter "has been subjected to sufficient imprisonment; I therefore earnestly petition your excellency for his pardon."

McGhee attached this request to the clemency petition and sent the package first to the judge advocate general in Washington, who recommended no mercy for Carter. Before the petition reached the president it made one more stop—the pivotal one—at the office of Congressman Samuel P. Snider. Snider and Harrison had a lot in common: both were Ohio natives, Republicans, and Civil War veterans. Snider recommended clemency and Harrison went along. On March 11, 1890, the president ordered that Carter's sentence be commuted to six years; with time served and good behavior, this meant immediate release. Lewis Carter left prison March 13.[8]

Lawyers love to see their triumphs reported in the newspapers—publicity is good for business—so Fred McGhee must have been delighted by the press response to Carter's sudden freedom. The *St. Paul Globe*, a Democrat paper, began with the headline, "An Army Outrage," and treated the story as one of correcting an abuse of Republican military justice. The Republican *Pioneer Press* disagreed, locating the outrage in Carter's release when there was "no possible room for doubt" that Carter was guilty and undeserving of mercy.

The *Pioneer Press* sent a reporter to interview Maria Scholls. She now recalled that McGhee (whom she identified only as "a Negro who has his office in the Union block") had come to her with a story that Carter's mother was starving in Mississippi and a promise that the soldier would do her no harm. Her husband was not at home, she did not read English, but she "thought it would be all right," and signed the paper the man gave her. "They tell me now that it was something asking the president of the United States to let him go free, which I did not mean at all. The man who came to see me has lied to the president. Can't something be done in this country to a man who lies to the president?" Asked by the diligent reporter for his reaction to this statement, the amused McGhee replied that "how many stories Mrs. Scholls will tell about this will depend only upon how many different times she is called upon to tell it."[9]

Whether Lewis Carter raped Maria Scholls, and why President Harrison set him free, can no longer be known for certain. We do know, though, that at the crucial moment Fred McGhee got from Mrs. Scholls the statement he needed, got the cooperation he needed from Congressman Snider, and got his man out of prison.

The Carter case led directly to another involving an inmate of Stillwater prison. In late summer 1891, sixty-two-year-old southern Minnesota farmer Frank Conway was two years into a five-year sentence for stealing a horse and a mare from a neighbor eighteen years before. Friends and even his original prosecutor had been trying to get him released earlier, to no avail. Now Conway's allies came to McGhee in the apparent belief that he had some special gift for obtaining executive clemency. They were not disappointed. Fred McGhee was at this time an active Republican who knew the state's Republican governor, William Merriam, from party work and various public events at which they had appeared together. If *The Appeal* is to be believed—and its source was probably McGhee himself—McGhee simply arranged a meeting with the governor at the capitol and soon the deed was done. On September 28, 1891, Merriam signed an order commuting Conway's sentence, and on October 1, he "went forth a free man to tell the farmers of Waseca that a black man can succeed where a white man fails."[10]

A few weeks later McGhee undertook the most difficult and highly publicized case of this stage of his career. Like many of his early cases, it dealt with sex, but this time with one great difference: everybody involved, except him, was white. And to make the defense attorney's situation more delicate still, the victim and key witness was a child.

The Ida Shenk case, as it came to be known, had begun in Minneapolis. Ellen Sheehan, a dressmaker and single parent, lived with her daughter Grace May Ellis on Hennepin Avenue. Grace worked at an ice cream parlor to help support the family. On the afternoon of Sunday, August 2, 1891, a family acquaintance, Ida Shenk, came to the house to say that she could get Grace a job at a candy store in St. Paul. Mrs. Sheehan agreed to let her daughter go with Shenk to look into the job. Events then began to take odd turns to which the police, the press, and prosecutors would soon give a sinister interpretation.

Shenk waited for the day's last streetcar to St. Paul and on the way to catch it met up with friends who introduced themselves to Grace as Mr. Shea and Mr. Reynolds. The three adults rode with Grace to St. Paul, took her to dinner, and never did make it to the candy store. They took her instead to a room at the Carlisle Hotel. There the men produced liquor and tried to get her to drink; she resisted so loudly that the desk clerk came to inquire. One of the men tried

A courtroom in Courthouse and City Hall, St. Paul, about 1889.
Photograph by Northwestern Photo Company.

to persuade her to go to a separate room with him, but again she resisted. In the end all four spent the night together in one room, Grace on the sofa. Ida Shenk kept Grace with her most of Monday before finally delivering her to a relative's house in West St. Paul. When Grace finally made it home to Minneapolis on Tuesday, August 4, her mother called the police.

The *Minneapolis Tribune* on August 6 carried a five-paragraph story headlined, "On a Very Ugly Charge—A Woman Named Ida Shenk Charged with Being a Procuress." St. Paul prosecutors indicted Shenk, David Watson, and William Demars—the real names of Mr. Shea and Mr. Reynolds—on the charge that they "did knowingly inveigle and entice Grace May Ellis into a certain room and building . . . for the purpose of prostitution." All three defendants hired Fred McGhee to defend them.

When the case came to trial in late October, McGhee faced an inflamed press that covered the trial with prurient glee. After the first day of testimony the *Pioneer Press* called the details of the case "too sensational for publication," while the rival *St. Paul Dispatch* offered the view that "if the girl's story is true it shows an astounding depth of depravity and a cool, devilish plan to entrap her [Grace] that is almost past belief." Public interest grew so great that the courtroom crowd overflowed into the hallways. Whole families came to witness the spectacle; the trial judge responded by excluding first children, then the public entirely. "Morbid sensation lovers," intoned the *Dispatch*, "had to view the proceedings through plate glass windows."

Grace May Ellis made a wonderful star witness for the sensation lovers to view. The *Pioneer Press* described her as "a lovely child of thirteen with wavy hair, deep blue eyes and demeanor at once modest and free from self-consciousness." The *Dispatch* reporter admired her even more:

> She is very pretty, with fair complexion and light hair. Her appearance on the stand was modest and self-possessed, and from her ready comprehension of the situation and prompt replies to all questions it was plain to all present that she is a very bright girl.
>
> She fanned herself with her handkerchief and leaned on her hand, as quite unabashed and in a quiet, musical agreeable voice she told her story.

Quietly, modestly, musically, and in every way winningly, Grace Ellis told the jury the tale of her enticement and inveigling. The three adults had taken her to the hotel room, pressed brandy on her, and then Watson "sat on the rocking chair and pulled me on his lap, and said that we should go to another room." She resisted and cried, but later, after she had gone to bed on the sofa, Watson returned "and began talking indecent." When the night clerk came to inquire about the commotion she had made, the defendants told him that "it was just a quarrel between a man and his wife and was nobody's business."

McGhee cross-examined Miss Ellis at length and in detail. She presented him a most sensitive problem. He needed to reduce the impact of her performance, but if he came on too strong he, the agent of her tormentors, risked making her a victim once again. McGhee chose to go at her not hard but long, to tire her, to press her into contradictions, and to show that she was not such an innocent after all. Afterward, the shaken *Dispatch* reporter lamented, "The examination was very searching, a most trying ordeal . . . The whole miserable story was gone over again. It shows that the child has not been carefully reared; that she had made acquaintances freely, and that she has had contact with men and women to a degree very unusual in one so young." Here the girl's ease and self-possession, commented upon earlier in the trial, played into the defense attorney's hands, for they were consistent with the worldliness exposed on cross-examination. McGhee clearly did not shrink from going right after the main witness, regardless of her winning ways.

After the conclusion of the state's case, which consisted mostly of Grace Ellis, McGhee tried to do again what he had done in Jennie Hendrickson's *habeas corpus* proceeding: cut through the desire to protect female virtue, upon which the prosecution relied, and apply the rule of law. The *Dispatch*, which seemed steadily to gain respect for McGhee as the trial went on, now published a portrait of him, the first in the white press, and reported his argument for dismissal of the charges:

> McGhee, the colored attorney for the defense . . . argued at considerable length that nothing had been introduced by the state to show that the girl had been assaulted or in any way injured, or that the intention of the defendants was wrong or unlawful. The attorney waxed eloquent as he progressed, and sat down at the close of an hour's harangue only to hear the motion denied.

Judge Otis ruled that even though nothing of a sexual nature had actually happened to Grace Ellis, the state had made an adequate case, because the only question was the defendants' intent: if they had lured the girl to the hotel with prostitution in mind, they could be convicted.

This left McGhee in a bad spot. There was no denying that something peculiar had happened between his clients and Grace Ellis. It certainly appeared that the adults had acted in concert and with unsavory intent when they took her to that hotel. Because McGhee represented all three defendants he could not play one against the other by, for example, casting all blame on Watson. So he chose the straightforward strategy that he used successfully his entire career, a direct battle for credibility between his clients and the state's witnesses.

Ida Shenk took the stand to tell quite a different story from the one Grace Ellis had told. The girl had gone to the Carlisle Hotel that night gladly and, far from resisting liquor, had requested it. She had eagerly climbed into William Demars's lap, and when the man tried to leave said, "You aren't going, are you Will? We don't like to stay alone." Watson told a similar tale. He and Demars had met Ida Shenk quite by accident that Sunday, and nothing untoward had happened. Demars agreed with his codefendants and added that when they all left the hotel Monday morning Grace had kissed him, saying, "Will, you have been a good boy, I want to kiss you."

Ramsey County Attorney C. D. O'Brien, in what the *Dispatch* called "the finest oratorical effort of his life," appealed to old-fashioned virtue and the jury's indecent imagination. The ruse of the candy store job, he said, was sufficient proof by itself that the defendants had conspired "to defile an innocent girl and turn her life into that of an outcast." He went on in this style—the accused were schemers, their method carousal, their objective atrocity—for more than an hour, and so effectively that "the defendants winced and Mrs. Shenk wept."

It is a shame that no detailed or even summary account of Fred McGhee's closing argument has survived, for it must have been marvelous. The scene had all the dramatic elements anyone could want: the young defender in his first big case, the comely central witness, the courthouse gaggle and enthusiastic press, the theme of juvenile sex in Victorian St. Paul—all this intensified by the wild card of Fred McGhee's race. We have just a few press comments, enough to get the general idea of what McGhee said. He had laid the groundwork in his cross-examination, picking away relentlessly at Grace Ellis's pose of girlish innocence. Now he attacked her directly, calling her a "nondescript child of doubtful antecedents," while his clients were hardworking people whose reputations had been wrongly tarnished. The case came down to whom one believed, her or them. McGhee spoke for two hours. "Naturally eloquent," wrote the *Dispatch* reporter, "he surpassed himself on this occasion."

The jurors got the case around 4 or 5 P.M., on the afternoon of October 27 and had no trouble at all resolving the credibility contest; they acquitted all three defendants in time to get home for bed that evening. The *Minneapolis Journal* reported the result under the headline, "The Incomprehensible Jury." *The Appeal,* by contrast, crowed:

> The winning of this case is a signal triumph for our able attorney... Afro-Americans have good cause to be proud of their sole representative at the St. Paul bar.... All the parties to the case were of the Anglo-Saxon race which makes the victory of Lawyer McGhee the more striking.

To make the victory even sweeter, it came on the eve of Fredrick McGhee's thirtieth birthday.[11]

Lawyer McGhee could not reasonably have expected more from his first thirty months in Minnesota. He had integrated the Minnesota bar and made a name for himself not just because of his race but because of his accomplishments. He had gone from the tiny type to the headlines.

3

Our Perfect Freedom

Though essential to the fulfillment of McGhee's destiny in Minnesota, his law practice was not his sole concern. If he had meant to develop only his career as a lawyer, he could have stayed in Chicago, a city that offered more business, social, and political opportunities, but McGhee had not come to St. Paul simply to make a living. The practice of law had to compete for his time with two other jealous avocations: politics and civil rights.

It is difficult to imagine a time in the United States when there were no prominent and effective national civil rights organizations. The National Association for the Advancement of Colored People (NAACP) and the Urban League, among others, are now so established that we almost take them for granted. But it took nearly fifty years—two generations—after the end of slavery for black America and its white allies to create a sound and enduring body, the first being the NAACP in 1909.

During the first quarter-century after emancipation, African Americans organized themselves in countless forms—churches, colleges, fraternal orders, political clubs, and many more—but on a national level they had looked primarily to the federal government and the Republican Party to protect civil and political rights. This worked fairly well until the end of Reconstruction in 1877 and the 1883 Supreme Court decision that declared the federal civil rights laws unconstitutional.[1]

After these events, civil rights protections fell more and more to the states and to the people generally, many of whom were not much interested in the subject. By the early 1890s a full-scale counterrevolution against black rights controlled politics in the South and had gained influence in the North as well. State after state took away the freemen's voting rights, in plain violation of the Fourteenth and Fifteenth Amendments, and enacted the apartheid laws known as Jim Crow. Still worse, lynching incidents were steeply on the rise. These episodes of mob violence displayed a kind of malignant genius. Because lynchings could brew up without warning anywhere in the southern states, and were fatal, they conveyed a clear and devastating message: no black life is safe. Lynch mobs were the death squads of their place and time and had the like effect of discouraging political activity through terror.[2]

Minnesota was largely unaffected by all of this. The state had a liberal political tradition, then as now. When the Supreme Court struck down the national civil rights law, Minnesota enacted a state version of it. Racial tolerance was made easy for the majority by the fact that African Americans were so few. They suffered limitations and indignities and sometimes organized or went to court for redress, but on the whole they felt fortunate to live where they did.[3]

Black Minnesotans, many of whom had come from the South or had family there, paid close attention to national events affecting their race. As conditions deteriorated in the late 1880s they saw and felt, the same as other black citizens, the need for a united national response to disfranchisement, Jim Crow, and the lynch mob. Fred McGhee arrived in St. Paul just as this need gave birth to the first serious effort to create a national civil rights organization, the National Afro-American League.

The League was the brainchild of the extraordinary T. Thomas Fortune. Born a slave in Florida in 1854, Fortune had moved to New York City as a young man, become a printer, then founded the *New York Freeman*, later named *The Age*. Fortune used *The Age* to rage and thunder against Jim Crow and for equal and lawful treatment of black Americans. He had a gift for polemics, so his editorials were reprinted in the black press nationwide. In May 1887 he called for the creation of a national protest and advocacy arm: "There is no dodging the issue; we have got to take hold of this problem ourselves, and make so much noise that all the world shall know the wrongs we suffer and our determination to right these wrongs." He named it the National Afro-American League. It took over two years for organizational efforts to get rolling.[4]

The call for an organizational convention went out in fall 1889. In Minnesota the first to answer that call was Fred McGhee. He held a private meeting in his office on October 25, 1889, and the next day announced a public meeting on November 5 for the purpose of creating a local chapter of the national League. *The Appeal*'s editor and publisher John Quincy Adams presided at that meeting and reported that "a large number of the progressive Colored citizens of St. Paul"

T. Thomas Fortune, about 1887.

attended. They voted to create a local affiliate—the Afro-American League of St. Paul, Minnesota no. 1—and in January 1890 voted to send Fred McGhee and John Q. Adams to Chicago as delegates to the League's first national meeting later that month.[5]

This Chicago convention marks Fredrick McGhee's first step onto the national stage. We do not know that he played any significant part in the proceedings, but after just seven months in Minnesota he was representing its black citizens. One hundred forty-one delegates, all black, came from twenty-three states; McGhee met people he would work with (and, as time went on, sometimes against) many times over the next two decades.

T. Thomas Fortune dominated the meeting. He had called it, he presided over it, and he gave the keynote speech—pure prophecy:

> As the agitation which culminated in the abolition of African slavery in this country covered a period of fifty years, so may we expect that before the rights conferred upon us by the war amendments are fully conceded, a full century will have passed away. We have undertaken no child's play. We have undertaken a serious work which will tax and exhaust the best intelligence of the race for the next century.

The delegates adopted Fortune's plan for the League's goals and means. The goals included battling against lynchings, resisting Jim Crow treatment by railroads and steamship companies, reforming prisons, and promoting migration of African Americans from the South to the North and West. Some goals ring with relevance yet today: equitable distribution of school funds, equal treatment in the courts, and consistent enforcement of the law for whites and blacks.

These goals were to be achieved by means that suited precisely Fred McGhee's talents and inclinations: "the creation of a healthy public opinion through the medium of public meetings and addresses, and by appealing to the courts of law for redress of all denial of legal and Constitutional rights." The League also abjured affiliation with any political party.[6]

The themes and patterns of this meeting stayed with McGhee the rest of his life. First in importance stood organization itself; until the day of his death and despite many failures, he never stopped organizing—the League would be just the first of six civil rights organizations he helped to found. He gave many civil rights speeches and used the courts in civil rights cases that ranged from restaurant snubs to fighting separate and unequal railroad accommodations. And though McGhee was at this time an active Republican, he always saw party affiliation as a trap for any civil rights group.

Back in Minnesota, McGhee entered party politics in summer 1890 as a delegate to the Ramsey County Republican Convention. Later he made a speech to the Colored Citizens Union endorsing the reelection of Republican Governor William Merriam, served as a committee chairman for the Afro-American Republican Club, and near election day gave a blistering, Democrat-hating talk to the Samuel P. Snider Club of Colored Republicans in Minneapolis. St. Paul Democrats, he said, courted black votes by promising patronage jobs, "but as soon as they got in power their promises were, in their judgment, kept by appointing one Colored man as a dog catcher and then arresting him and fining him for catching a Democratic dog." In late January 1891 he was selected—the first black citizen to be so honored—to serve on the state party's central committee.[7]

Like the great majority of politically aware black citizens of the time, Fred McGhee looked only to the Republican Party for the protection of African-American rights. The reasons were historical, sentimental, and practical. Nationally, the Republican Party had waged the Civil War and overseen Reconstruction. All the great heroes, martyrs, and symbols of black liberation were Republican. In Minnesota, Republicans had controlled the government since

Fredrick McGhee, about 1890.
Portrait by St. Paul's prominent African
American photographer Harry Shepherd.

statehood, hence that is where the power lay. So despite the Afro-American League's official nonpartisanship, when in late 1890 McGhee undertook a League organizing drive, he enlisted the help of Minnesota's two most prominent Republicans: Governor Merriam and Archbishop John Ireland.

McGhee and the other organizers chose Emancipation Day, January 1, 1891, the twenty-eighth anniversary of the implementation of the Emancipation Proclamation, for a rally to celebrate black progress and prospects in Minnesota and to stimulate interest in the Afro-American League. They hired the St. Paul Armory, invited the leading clergy of both races, engaged singers and a military band. Governor Merriam cancelled, and attendance was a little disappointing ("a fair representation of the most intelligent portion of the Colored citizens of St. Paul and a small sprinkling of the right sort of white ones," according to *The Appeal*) but those who came heard a remarkable pair of speeches.

McGhee led off. He began by comparing the state of black America with what it had been twenty-eight years before, when almost four million remained enslaved. Full freedom had not yet been achieved, but it was coming. And then these words: "The sun of our perfect freedom is rising in this Northwest. Education on the question is flowing from here and we are creating a sentiment, which will spread throughout the country. On this occasion words will be spoken which will mark the dawn of better times." Perfect freedom, the dawn of better times: McGhee seemed to be setting up impossible expectations for the speech to come. But this was calculated.

After a recitation of the Emancipation Proclamation, Archbishop John Ireland rose to give one of the most daring speeches ever delivered by a major Minnesota public figure. He condemned slavery, protested local incidents of race discrimination in hotels and transport, and then got to the heart of things: "Color is the merest accident. . . . I would say let all people in America be equal socially and politically."

Ireland had said words that even some black leaders were afraid to say in public: "equal socially." Political equality was one thing, especially in the North, where blacks remained a small minority. Social equality was something very different, more personal; it could mean that a black man might marry your sister or your daughter. In fact, Ireland said precisely that as well—"Let marriage be a question of taste."[8]

The speeches got attention in the local press. Two of the four St. Paul dailies covered the rally well, though only one, the *Globe*, quoted Ireland's "social equality" passage. Minneapolis papers ignored the event. Overall, the rally did not seem to have the desired effect of provoking public debate on race or of inciting greater interest in the Afro-American League. McGhee's speech had the paradoxical result of earning praise in the white press and his first and bitterest criticism in the black press. The *Globe* commented that McGhee had "acquitted himself with credit," while the *Pioneer Press* said that "Fred L. McGhee, the bright young colored attorney, whose oratory has attracted so much attention . . . made a rousing and patriotic speech."[9] But in the pages of *The Appeal* he and the Afro-American League took an impassioned skewering delivered by the assertive, articulate, and prickly W. A. Hazel.

Hazel wrote a letter to *The Appeal*, published in its January 31 edition, that began: "One of the most precious pieces of humbuggery to which a long-suffering people have been subjected to, is that monumental sham known as the National Afro-American League; and of all of its gaseous offspring the St. Paul League heads the list for bombast and vacuity."

Hazel, a well-educated and skilled stained-glass worker (trained as a draftsman, he would later become an architect) from Massachusetts, did not suffer racial affronts silently. In 1887 he had sued the Clarendon Hotel for denying him service; and, just a week after the Afro-American League rally, had been denied service at the Delicatessen Restaurant. He sued it, too. His experiences

William A. Hazel, who attacked McGhee's
"Perfect Freedom" speech and later became his ally.

belied talk of perfect freedom and social equality, and he made his views explicit: "There is not a city wherein ... civil rights will be more insolently denied than in St. Paul, nor in which the citizens submit so supinely to insult."

Hazel wrote that he knew of a half dozen recent violations of civil rights in St. Paul, but the Afro-American League had ignored them. "It wakes to life only when there is an occasion for feasting or a chance for a few individuals to emerge from their native obscurity." The organization was nothing but talk, in his view, and a detriment because it distracted people from real work. "A league which has never had a dollar in its treasury is worse than powerless, it is a delusion and a snare, and is worthy only of contempt."

Hazel's contempt extended to McGhee personally: "a Colored orator delivered himself as follows: 'The sun of our perfect freedom is rising ...' How much of this did the orator believe? How much did his auditors believe?"[10] Hazel misunderstood McGhee, who did not mean that justice was at hand. He meant rather that a force was about to come into play that would begin a powerful push for justice. McGhee did not make it explicit then, but the force he had in mind was the American Roman Catholic Church.

The rest of Hazel's rant against the Afro-American League had a great deal of merit. The League had never really gotten off the ground after the Chicago organizing convention. It had no permanent organizational structure, no fundraising apparatus, no corps of organizers; hence it had no system for recruiting members and giving them something to do. Everything depended on the uncoordinated work of its autonomous local chapters. These might, if they could, undertake local fights, but not national ones. What is more, the League existed almost entirely in the North, a long way from where most of the lynchings and Jim Crow incidents were taking place. Without money and firm national coordination, the Afro-American League simply could not effectively fight the fights it had picked. The black public seemed to understand this, and by 1891 the League was already failing.[11] Hazel was mostly right about the St. Paul chapter, too; it never had any money and never did sponsor any legal challenges to racial discrimination.

Nevertheless McGhee and others tried to keep it going. They brought Hazel into the organization and mounted another public meeting in May 1891 to boost public interest. Nothing came of it. That July, the St. Paul chapter dispatched Samuel Hardy to the League's second national convention in Knoxville, Tennessee. What happened to Hardy on his way there led both to the demise of the St. Paul chapter and to the first great disappointment and failure of McGhee's career.[12]

On July 12, Hardy bought a first-class train ticket to Knoxville. Upon reaching the Tennessee border he was forced to leave the first-class car for the Jim Crow car. Tennessee had just four months earlier passed what it called "an act to promote the comfort of passengers on railroad trains," requiring railroad companies to provide either separate or racially partitioned passenger cars. The law gave conductors the power to put off any passenger who refused to submit to separation; conductors and railroads that did not enforce the law faced fines. Laws like this one outraged the northern African-American elite. Many of them had been born in the South and had family there; they had achieved at least a tenuous prosperity and travelled a good deal. The experience of buying a regular or first class ticket in the North, then being forced to switch to the often-squalid Jim Crow car, cheated and humiliated them.

But this offense to Samuel Hardy's pocketbook and dignity had been no surprise. St. Paul Afro-American Leaguers had known of the statute since June, protested it, and McGhee had written a resolution of condemnation. So when Hardy returned from Knoxville they were ready for action. On August 25, McGhee and others organized for the purpose of challenging the Tennessee statute in court, with Mr. Hardy as plaintiff. What is curious is that they chose not to do so under the auspices of the Afro-American League. Hardy had not been the only League delegate subjected to Jim Crow treatment on his way to the meeting. The Reverend W. H. Heard had been similarly offended, and the League considered bringing a case in his name, but gave up before starting, for lack of money. In the view of League kingpin T. Thomas Fortune, for an organization without money to sue a railroad was simple "tomfoolery." Because the League had abdicated, the St. Paul group, though composed of League members, set itself apart: it called itself the Minnesota Civil Rights Committee. This step marked the effective end of the Afro-American League in Minnesota.[13]

The words of W. A. Hazel ("a league that has never had a dollar in its treasury is worse than useless") must have buzzed in Fred McGhee's ears as he took the post of Civil Rights Committee chairman—and in any case he had Hazel himself at his elbow, serving as Committee secretary. The Committee moved first to raise public interest and money for the lawsuit before taking action. No tomfoolery for them.

The Committee issued a manifesto, part of an effort to go national with this particular cause. The manifesto anticipated a sensible question: Why fight southern Jim Crow from the North—especially so distant a place as St. Paul? The Committee answered eloquently:

The most courageous and intelligent efforts on the part of the blacks, within the hostile lines, must be ineffectual and can only result in inhuman butchery ... Our brethren in the South are without hope, unless we who are free, prepare to strike a blow in their behalf.

This blow should have been struck by the Afro-American League, "that body having all of the machinery of organization necessary, and its executive officers being such men of national repute," but failing that, the Minnesotans would ("with great reluctance") take action. "The citizens of this state, feeling that the time is ripe for action, ... endeavor to stem the tide of persecution which threatens the progress and future happiness of the race."

So the call went out for money and support. McGhee, Hazel, and many others spoke at an October 16 rally in Minneapolis. Appeals were broadcast through the black press around the country. Rhetorical support came back, and some money, too. McGhee presided over another mass meeting on November 17 that purportedly raised over $200, enough at least to begin. Determined to make something happen, Fred McGhee set to work preparing the lawsuit. The pleadings were composed, typed, and signed in his office in St. Paul, then conveyed to the federal courthouse in Chattanooga. And on December 28, 1891, a deputy U. S. marshal in Tennessee served the summons and complaint in *Samuel Hardy v. East Tennessee, Georgia, and Virginia Railway Company*. McGhee's challenge to Jim Crow in his old home state had begun.[14]

The next month, January 1892, may have been the happiest of Fred McGhee's life. During the first two weeks, he and Mattie took a trip east, to New York City, and returned with a little orphan girl, two-and-a-half years old, whom they adopted and named Ruth. She would be the only child they ever had. Later in the month the Republican National Committee announced that its 1892 national convention would be held in Minneapolis. One could see wonderful civil rights potential in this event. McGhee and other local black citizens, notably John Q. Adams and William R. Morris, were active and esteemed party members. Samuel Snider, a proven friend of the black man, represented Minneapolis in Congress. Archbishop Ireland had become a booming voice for racial equality. Frederick Douglass, the most loved and admired African American of the nineteenth century, would attend. And of course the incumbent president, Civil War veteran Benjamin Harrison would be there, too. An optimistic young man could see in this meeting that the stars might align favorably for a revival of commitment to civil rights in the party of Lincoln.[15]

This moment marks the high point of Fred McGhee's early years in Minnesota. As a lawyer, he had enjoyed a string of well-publicized successes, and the press smiled upon him. He who had been an orphan had brought an orphan into his home. In civil rights he had dared to try what the Afro-American League would not—fight Jim Crow in a southern court. In politics he had served now for a year on the state Republican committee and looked forward to a substantial role in the coming national convention. The legal career and family life would remain solid, but rats lurked in the rest of the woodpile. By year's end both the civil rights case and McGhee's career in Republican politics would be ashes.

McGhee himself bears some, maybe most, of the responsibility for the failure of *Hardy v. East Tennessee, et al., Railway Co.* The Minnesota Civil Rights Committee had proclaimed in fall 1891 that the separate coach acts of Tennessee and other states "cannot stand the constitutional test." This was five years before *Plessy v. Ferguson,* so the doctrine of separate but equal had not yet been made supreme—the issue remained in doubt. McGhee and the Committee knew that the Hardy case presented constitutional issues squarely. But when McGhee drafted the Hardy complaint, he raised no constitutional issues at all. He framed the case instead as one of breach of contract and what today might be called intentional infliction of mental distress. The complaint alleged that Hardy had bought a first-class ticket in Minnesota, been ejected from the first-class coach in Tennessee and compelled to ride in an inferior coach, and that because of this treatment had "suffered great distress in body and mind and great mental agony from the contumely, insult, humiliation and indignity thus heaped upon him because of his color race and previous condition [of servitude]." He asked for $50,000 in damages. Every word of the complaint was true, but nothing in it required consideration of constitutional issues. The railroad could have defended the case and won without raising the Tennessee statute in defense; and Hardy could have won without calling the statute into question.[16]

We can only speculate about McGhee's reasons for approaching the case this way. Well before 1891 a few black citizens had won similar breach of contract cases against railroads, so there was some precedent for success, and certainly a breach of contract case is relatively simple to try and to explain to a jury. Perhaps he expected the railroad to raise the Tennessee statute in its defense, thus allowing him to challenge it in reply. Or it may be that, when McGhee had to put himself on the line as Sam Hardy's lawyer he did not judge himself able to take on both the railroad and the state of Tennessee by himself.

For their part, the railroad and its lawyers probably took a shrewd look at the case and decided that there was no need to rise to McGhee's bait. The Civil

Rights Committee had not been able to sustain the initial enthusiasm for the lawsuit, and McGhee had been forced to reveal this right away; along with the pleadings he had filed affidavits seeking a waiver of the $100 filing fee for lack of money to pay it. *The Appeal,* one of the initial boosters of the case, printed almost nothing about it after fall 1891, so it seems clear that fundraising for it had ceased. On April 2, McGhee traveled to Chattanooga, probably at his own expense, for a hearing—the only time opposing counsel ever met in the case—at which time the defendant simply put in a general oral denial to the complaint. This raised no legal issues at all but simply put McGhee to the proof of his complaint. The court set the case for trial in September. Fred McGhee now seemed to be on his own against the railroad with no resources at his command. Maybe T. Thomas Fortune was right; perhaps this was tomfoolery after all.[17]

Deterioration quickly set in on the political front, too. Shortly before the May 5 state convention leading black Republicans of the Fourth Congressional District, including William Morris, John Q. Adams, William A. Hazel, and labor leader Charles James, wrote an appeal to Minnesota Republicans statewide. "Does the republican party of the State of Minnesota owe anything to its Afro-American constituency?" they asked rhetorically. Of course they answered their own question with a "yes." The "constant party fealty" of black voters had created a debt "that has been accumulating with interest for years." The party rightly had "always recognized all nationalities . . . in the distribution of places (offices)," all, that is, except those of African descent. The coming national convention provided the perfect opportunity to cancel "a large portion" of the debt. Hundreds of black delegates would be coming from the South, "a section of the country where the belief is becoming prevalent that the party has tired of its ever faithful Negro voters." The Minnesota party could show its devotion to true principles by "bestowing upon one of its competent and worthy colored citizens the honor of representing it as one of its delegates at large." The right man for this honor was Fredrick L. McGhee, they noted. "We do not ask this . . . because of our race, yet we do urge that it will be good, practical politics and just dealing."[18]

The party declined this request. Instead it named McGhee an at-large presidential elector. This was an honor, but an honor only. As a delegate, McGhee could have appeared on the convention floor, perhaps made a speech, worked for his candidate, Maine Congressman Thomas Reed, and had some chance to participate in national party decisions. The post of elector gave him no such rights, and in the end he did not participate in the convention at all.

The 1892 Republican National Convention proved to be more than just a personal disappointment for McGhee. The civil and political rights of black citizens in the southern states no longer interested the Republican Party. The questions of lynching and voting rights played no part in the meeting. President Harrison won renomination, easily dispatching his only serious rival, James G. Blaine, and everybody went home. Though McGhee professed to be satisfied with Harrison's renomination (the president had, after all, freed Lewis Carter), all other hopes that he and others may have cherished in January had come to nothing.[19]

Politics turned local once again, and the disappointments continued. McGhee's appointment as elector had offended some Scandinavian Republicans. An editorial in the *Svenska Amerikanska Posten* called it "shoddy treatment" and a "slap in the face." While a relative handful of African-American Republicans got an elector, the Scandinavian masses were ignored. "Are our countrymen going to stand for such treatment?" the writer wondered, and then threatened. "When a political party which depends for its very existence in Minnesota upon the Scandinavians, treats them in such a manner, then it is simply our countrymen's duty to chastise the 'bullies' at the ballot box."[20]

The editorial writer made an unanswerable point: There were many, many more Scandinavian than African-American Republicans. Party leaders knew how to count, so when Minnesota Republicans held another state convention in late July, this one to prepare for the fall state and national campaigns, they set about to undo the decision. State law required each elector to pay $50 toward the cost of placing his name on the presidential ballot. McGhee did not pay his fee right away, as the law did not require it until four weeks before election day. This delay gave his enemies the opening they needed. The central committee met while McGhee was in Wisconsin trying a case, declared his elector position open, and replaced him with Professor J. S. Carlson of Northfield, a Swede. Black Republicans had played the game of ethnic politics and lost.

Neither McGhee nor his supporters accepted the party's action or explanations. They protested and the party agreed to hold a hearing on the question—though whether such a hearing ever took place is unknown. All the inside details are lost. The issue boiled over in mid-September, when black Republicans held a mass meeting and threatened to do no work for the party the rest of the election season. On September 19, McGhee himself made a "rousing speech" at another rally. Before election day the parties struck some sort of deal. On September 24, *The Appeal* reported that "the state central committee had made satisfactory assurances that the McGhee matter would be satisfactorily settled in a few days." McGhee did not get his spot as elector, but he did return to the platform, boosting the Republican ticket at party rallies.

What did McGhee get in the bargain? In the end, only promises, promises never fulfilled. The Republicans took a thumping in November. Grover Cleveland won his rematch with Benjamin Harrison; Samuel Snider lost his seat in Congress; the party lost all Ramsey County races except that for sheriff. After this, the state party may have had nothing to give McGhee, deals and promises notwithstanding. McGhee had nothing left to give, either; he never worked for the Republican Party again.[21]

The year 1892 still had one more blow to deliver. Trial of the Samuel Hardy case had been delayed from September to November, but this merely postponed what McGhee must have known was now inevitable. No plaintiff's case can survive without money for witness fees, travel expenses, secretarial work, stenographer's costs, not to mention a dollar here and there for the lawyer. But there was no money. On November 16, 1892, one year to the day after the great mass meeting in Minnesota to raise money for the case, the clerk of federal court in Chattanooga called the case for trial. The defendant was present, represented by counsel who professed to be ready for trial. For the plaintiff—no one, neither Hardy himself nor his lawyer, Fred McGhee. The judge dismissed the case.

Given the times, the place, and the issue, it likely made no difference to American civil rights history that the Hardy case ended as it did. Four years later, in *Plessy v. Ferguson,* the Supreme Court upheld Louisiana's separate coach law by a vote of 7 to 1, so Hardy and the Minnesota Civil Rights Committee likely were doomed from the outset. Still, the case represents an opportunity lost. Samuel Hardy had in one important way a better constitutional case than Homer Plessy did. Plessy's aborted train ride took place entirely within the state of Louisiana, so the Supreme Court in his case avoided the question of the constitutionality of race-based interferences in interstate travel: it ruled that travel within Louisiana was purely a state law question. But Samuel Hardy, a citizen of Minnesota, had unquestionably traveled across state lines to suffer the outrage required by the laws of Tennessee. Had McGhee and the Civil Rights Committee made the constitutional case they originally promised, and had the case gone all the way, it would have reached the Supreme Court before *Plessy* did. The result would have been the same, no doubt, but the Court would have been forced to face the constitutional issues more squarely. Years later Fred McGhee would have occasion to complain about the poor quality of civil rights litigation being practiced around the country; he may have reflected then, ruefully, on his own first experience.[22]

The Afro-American League and the Minnesota Civil Rights Committee did not achieve their goals, but to call them failures would be incorrect. In a sense, one can fail only where success is possible. The goals that T. Thomas Fortune, Fred McGhee, and their many collaborators pursued were simply not then achievable. The fights for voting rights and against Jim Crow and lynching had to be fought in the South, where the huge majority of black people lived. To rouse or rescue these people from their plight would have required the equivalent of a national slave revolt or a second Reconstruction. The northern black agitators were too few and too far away to carry this off. Their failures, too, were not necessarily final. They were trying to do what had never been done: integrate millions of newly freed slaves into the body politic of a hostile, or at best indifferent, nation. Errors and setbacks were inevitable. So long as they learned from the errors and kept on trying, they did not fail.

The disappointments and defeats of 1892 did not end Fred McGhee's participation in politics or civil rights work. On the contrary, a decade later he would be far more deeply and more prominently involved in both arenas.

4

Shelter in the Mighty Storm

We cannot know the state of Fredrick McGhee's soul when he arrived in St. Paul, but we do know that he had been raised a Baptist and received his first schooling from the United Presbyterian Church. There is no record of him attending any church during his earliest months in Minnesota, though joining one of the main black churches, centers of social and civic life, would have been the wise and politic thing to do. For African Americans, in Minnesota and around the country, Protestant Christianity was the very popular mainstream.

But Fred McGhee seems to have been temperamentally incapable of staying long in the black mainstream, in religion or politics. On February 15, 1891, after just nineteen months in St. Paul, McGhee put aside twenty-nine years of Protestantism, the religion of his parents and of his people, to join the Roman Catholic Church. He remained an active, faithful, and churchgoing Catholic the rest of his life.[1]

The road to his conversion probably began soon after McGhee arrived in Minnesota, and involved none other than the archbishop himself, John Ireland. Ireland, a potato-famine immigrant to St. Paul, was educated for the priesthood in Europe and served as a chaplain to Minnesota combat troops in the Civil War. No ivory-tower cleric, he was a man who knew oppression, death, and suffering firsthand. He was also ambitious for himself, his region, his country, and his church. After the Civil War he returned to St. Paul and rose quickly in the church hierarchy, becoming bishop in 1884 and archbishop in 1888. John Ireland had the imagination to see in the four million slaves freed by the Civil War a potential bountiful harvest of souls to be gathered to Mother Church.

The church, with its Latin and its medieval Western European trappings, was not a natural home for American blacks, but had plenty to offer them just the same. It had a long history of opposing slavery, in the Americas and elsewhere, and where it did coexist with slavery, as in Brazil, the church always recognized the full humanity of slaves. The church's universalism, which had the disadvantage of making its center seem far away (as it was, in Rome), also

had the great advantage of appealing to a sense of humanity united across national and racial lines. American Protestant denominations, most of them de-
centralized and democratic, were far more subject to the influences of local
prejudices. Many of them had collaborated in slavery and after emancipation
had gone along with Jim Crow. A white Baptist or Presbyterian congregation
could, on the grounds of its independence and the will of its members, close
its doors to blacks. No Catholic church could do the same without violating its
principles. Archbishop Ireland recognized that the church's universalism
would appeal to some African Americans, who suffered permanent minority
status and might welcome a connection with a higher, international power.[2]

In April 1888, Ireland brought to St. Paul Father Joseph Slattery of Baltimore, a veteran proselytizer among black Americans, for a six-week evangelizing stay. Just a week into Slattery's campaign, Ireland, apparently pleased
with the public response, declared that a priest would be permanently as-
signed to the nascent black congregation. Black Catholics in heavily Catholic
St. Paul at this time probably numbered in the dozens at most. Soon thereafter
the church organized the St. Peter Claver Sodality (a lay society named for a
missionary to Brazilian slaves) and installed it in a former Swedenborgian

John Ireland, about the time that
he met Fredrick McGhee.
Photograph by John M. Kuhn.

church in downtown St. Paul. Ireland turned Slattery's work over to Father J. T. Harrison, who conducted a long series of educational meetings on Roman Catholic beliefs, which were fairly well attended and drew praise from *The Appeal.* The newspaper also published Harrison's weekly articles on the subject for several months in early 1890. So it happened that Fred McGhee arrived in St. Paul at a time when the Catholic Church was actively seeking African-American converts.[3]

Starting around 1890, John Ireland made the causes of black conversions and civil rights his own. That February he issued a letter, which he required to be read from the pulpit of all churches in the archdiocese, that said in part, "I need but make a brief mention of the special obligation resting upon Catholics in America to assist in the conversion of the Negro population. This is a debt of justice as well as of charity. The American nation put upon the Negro the merciless chains of servitude. Let us make for past injuries the best possible restitution." Two months later, on April 7, he made a speech in which he told St. Paul Catholics that "as Catholics you are compelled to forget color … in all walks of life." In May he went to Washington, D. C., to deliver a major speech on the subject:

> It makes me ashamed as a man, as a citizen, as a Christian, to see the prejudice that is acted against the colored citizen of America because of his color. As to substance the colored man is equal to the white man—he has a like intellect; the same blood courses in their veins; they are both equally the children of a common Father, who is in heaven. … Every prejudice entertained, every breach of justice and charity against a fellow citizen because of his color, is a stain flung upon the banner of our liberty.

Ireland's audience included members of Congress and the cabinet, and the speech was made against a backdrop of race violence in the South and inaction by the government. Clearly, he desired to make an impression on people in power.[4]

We do not know precisely when Fred McGhee began to be drawn into Catholic company, but it happened quite soon after his arrival in St. Paul. In February 1890, he made a public appearance with two priests and two bishops, and "spoke enthusiastically of the work of the Sodality." A brief interview with McGhee on race matters, in which he comments favorably on the church as a force for race progress, appeared in Archbishop Ireland's *Northwestern Chronicle* in early April 1890. McGhee and Ireland almost certainly met no later than July 4 that year, when Ireland brought Father Augustus Tolton—the country's first ex-slave Catholic priest—to St. Paul for a grand "entertainment" designed to boost Catholic recruitment of African Americans. Tolton and Ireland both spoke at the public meeting, to an audience that included Fred McGhee; McGhee also joined Tolton and a large number of prominent white Catholics at a reception later in the day.[5]

Six months later, on January 1, 1891, McGhee and Ireland appeared together at the Emancipation Day event. McGhee was baptized into the church six weeks later, on February 15. As instruction leading to baptism can take several months, McGhee must have made his decision to convert around mid-1890, the very time that he and Ireland became acquainted and the archbishop had begun to speak so prominently about race. When McGhee spoke of the "sun of our perfect freedom rising in this Northwest," and education beginning to flow, it is clear now that he was speaking of Ireland and the church. The sun was just now rising because John Ireland and the Roman Catholic Church were going to be the engines of racial justice in America, and their work had just begun.

Race was central to McGhee's conversion. In 1900 he published an article in *Howard's American Magazine*, "What the Catholic Church Means to the Negro," that reveals his thinking. There, McGhee praised the church's principles of equality, its multi-racial gallery of saints, and its insistence during the era of slavery that the earthly status of slave in no way implied inequality before God. He compared Catholicism to the Protestant sects:

> No Catholic priest ever preached that slavery was permissible on "Bible grounds." No Catholic bishop has ever stood for the false notion of inferiority between men . . . Other Christian ministers were allowed, without protest from their superiors, to preach that the Negro had no soul, but no Catholic priest ever did.

He went on to assert that race prejudice did not exist in Catholic countries, except where Protestant influence had intervened. The only blacks who had ever ejected their colonial oppressors were the Catholic ones of Haiti. The reason that blacks fared better in Catholic countries was, he wrote elsewhere, "that the Catholic religion teaches and requires one common brotherhood." McGhee concluded the article by asserting: "To the Negro, the Catholic Church means a shelter in the mighty storm, a fountain of water in a great oasis, a sufficient army and navy of defense, a light shining in the darkness."[6]

He did not claim that the Catholic Church offered a truer path to salvation than any other church: the benefits he described were earthly. Fred McGhee was a race man; that is, one who devoted all the time and energy he could spare to the protection and advancement of his race. His entry into the church of Rome did not imply a rejection of African-American Protestantism, but rather the joining of a powerful ally in the race struggle. McGhee's conversion was heartfelt, sincere, and in this sense ironic: he joined the nonracial church for racial reasons.

And he began pursuing a racial agenda almost immediately. Four weeks after McGhee's conversion a man named John Rudd visited St. Paul, and the two must have met. Rudd's uncle, Daniel Rudd, published the *Catholic Tribune*, a national monthly written by and for black Catholic laity. The Rudds, Daniel especially, had advocated and organized the Negro Catholic Congresses, annual gatherings of black Catholic laymen from around the country. Its first national meeting had taken place in January 1889; Nicholas Gaillard had represented St. Paul. The second was in Cincinnati in July 1890, with Samuel Hardy of St. Paul in attendance. Rudd and McGhee probably discussed the movement during Rudd's visit, for when the third Congress convened in Philadelphia in January 1892, Fred McGhee attended as the delegate from St. Peter Claver in St. Paul.[7]

The Congresses were not at first a movement but rather a series of gatherings of like-minded people, to meet, support, and encourage one another. Such gatherings naturally inspired the participants to think about greater vision and purpose. Hence by the time McGhee joined, the Negro Catholic Congresses were searching for sustaining objectives. McGhee arrived full of vim and purpose; he had just begun the Samuel Hardy case and would soon adopt a child from New York. Perhaps for this reason he played a surprising role in the Congress for a newcomer.

According to the official record of the Congress, published by Daniel Rudd, Fred McGhee made a remarkably assertive debut. He told the assembled delegates that while the elegant speeches and beautifully written papers of the two previous conventions had been very fine, "no practical or tangible result has been accomplished." The time for effective action had arrived. "The present generation of Colored Catholics must leave to those that come after, an organization by which they can secure such rights and privileges as they are entitled to." He proposed, in other words, that the Congress transform itself into a permanent national civil rights organization.

McGhee then described how this should be done. His plan consisted of organizing the many black Catholic lay societies under the umbrella of a "permanent organization of Colored Catholics . . . . the organization would be run by an Executive Council, which would collect dues from the subordinate organizations." We can see here perhaps a reaction to the formlessness of the

Afro-American League, which did not collect dues and was in no effective sense "run" by any central authority. McGhee's proposal that the organization work to secure African-American "rights and privileges," was consistent with his "sun of our perfect freedom" speech of one year before—the Catholic Church was to lead the way in civil rights.

The other delegates were not ready to go so far. McGhee's proposal was referred to a "Committee on Union Organization" to study this and other proposals and make recommendations. The Committee, which included McGhee and Father Augustus Tolton, came back the next day with a less ambitious proposal, the creation of St. Peter Claver's Benevolent Loan Association, a fund "for benevolent purposes ... out of which loans shall be made for the building of Catholic churches and furnishing education facilities among the colored people." The Congress as a whole endorsed the proposal. The plan fell far short of McGhee's original vision—the civil rights component was gone—but the creation of any permanent, national organization of black Catholics, one with specific and tangible goals, was a significant accomplishment.

At the close of the Congress, McGhee, Tolton, Daniel Rudd, and eight others were selected to form the Executive Committee of National Organization to put the plan into effect. They met the following day, created (at least on paper) the St. Peter Claver's Benevolent Loan Association, and then proceeded to give it a more ambitious charter than the Congress seemed to have authorized. Its first official object was "the organization of colored Catholic societies throughout the United States ... into one great body." This looks a lot like McGhee's proposal for "a permanent organization among Colored Catholics." The association's second object was the creation of a building fund for churches and schools "to elevate the colored race by educating it in spiritual things as well as morally and in business affairs." It may be that McGhee, in the smaller forum of a committee of like-minded men, pulled it and the Association in his direction on that final day of business.

In practice the language of organization did not much matter because the Congress lacked the means to achieve either goal. Father Tolton had expressed the problem well at the Philadelphia meeting: "A few resolutions are all very well, but the most useful is greenbacks." Organizing the black lay societies across the country into one; extracting contributions; then investing, lending, and accounting for the money would require professional organizers, administrators, and accountants. This kind of work could not be done on a volunteer basis. The necessary greenbacks, however, were not in hand, and the church itself did not provide them. It is probable that the Benevolent Loan Association never took on more reality than words on paper; another well-meaning false start.[8]

The fourth Negro Catholic Congress was held in Chicago in September 1893, alongside the World's Columbian Exposition, otherwise known as the Chicago World's Fair. It attracted a good crowd of delegates and guests, including Archbishop Ireland. McGhee, Daniel Rudd, and five others drafted the Congress's Address to the Nation. This address took a slightly more challenging tone toward the church itself than had been the case in the past. While acknowledging that the church had long labored "to break down the walls of race prejudice," it had not entirely succeeded even within its own ranks. The address then quoted John Ireland's observation that some Catholics had "departed from the teaching of the Church in the treatment of the Colored Catholics and yielded to popular prejudice." It was the duty, then, of the organization to bring "such deviations from Catholic law" to the attention of every member of the hierarchy.

The statement is carefully phrased, especially in using Ireland's words to carry the strongest criticism, but it surprised and stung. The Congress president, James Spencer, refused to sign it. The *St. Joseph's Advocate*, a great editorial supporter of the Congress movement published by the missionary order that employed, among others, Father Slattery, called this passage, "true and mildly worded, yet ill-advised, written under a misconception of clerical liberty, and little calculated to gain its end or even promote it." The *Advocate* had it right. McGhee and his colleagues had miscalculated the church's tolerance for this degree of questioning on race. One can identify the promulgation of this Address as the beginning of the end of the Negro Catholic Congresses, for without support from church hierarchy they could not survive.

The participants of course did not know then how far they had transgressed, and so they continued to work. They shaped the Benevolent Loan Association into St. Peter Claver's Catholic Union, of which McGhee was elected secretary. It was to be based in Washington, D. C., and have as its purpose the promotion of churches, schools, and orphanages for African Americans, with the proviso that these institutions were not to be permanently all-black; they would evolve into integrated ones open to all "on equal and common grounds." This represented a step back in scope of ambition from its unborn predecessor.

Participants in the fourth Negro Catholic Congress showed a good deal more confidence in themselves, if not necessarily a shrewder sense of what they could get away with. They had moved past the stage of simply praising the church, to asking it to examine its own practices. We see the delegates wrestling, too, with the idea of creating separate black Catholic institutions. For a church that proclaimed its own universality and the brotherhood of all peoples, setting up separate black parishes, schools, and orphanages gave at least the appearance of inconsistency. This criticism had been raised in St. Paul with the creation of the St. Peter Claver parish. Its first priest, Father Harrison, tried to answer it by arguing that it was perfectly natural for black Catholics to do what German, Irish, and Polish Catholics did: set up their own parishes based on affinity but not exclusivity. Another argument, implied in the statement of purpose of St. Peter Claver's Catholic Union, was that the black institutions would be transitional; they would for a time meet the needs of a particular population—for evangelizing and for social services, plus its need to assert its own organizing capabilities—until it had reached a maturity and status comparable to everyone else. Then, presumably, separateness would become irrelevant and melt away.[9]

The Negro Catholic Congresses did not survive to continue questioning the church or participate in the debate over separate institutions. Conditions for American blacks grew steadily worse throughout the 1890s; the pace of lynching increased, reaching to an average of three people murdered per week, Jim Crow laws and customs advanced, the lily-white Democrats reclaimed the presidency (in 1893) and the Republican Party abandoned any semblance of a civil rights agenda. It was as if a shudder of revulsion against all things African American had seized the country. The Roman Catholic Church in the United States was not immune to social trends. Priests and prelates may not have read the election returns, but they could feel the shudder as well as anyone; some were swayed by the public mood. By the mid-1890s even Archbishop Ireland, beset by financial problems, criticism, and depression, had withdrawn from the civil rights fight.[10]

The fifth and last Catholic Congress—officially the first Congress of the St. Peter Claver Catholic Union—met in Baltimore in October 1894. Speakers bravely called for the church to fight racism and help smash labor unions (called "an anti-Christ, a devil who works against the colored people of this land") and for the government to limit immigration, presumably to help blacks in the labor market in this depression era.

Fred McGhee remained a prominent Congress leader at the Baltimore meeting. He and fellow delegate William Lofton proposed that the union establish a combined university and industrial school for young black Americans near Washington, D.C., and that it buy 250 acres of land to do so. The proposal was sent to a committee. McGhee made the keynote speech to close the convention, but what he said has not been preserved. He was also elected for another two-year term as union secretary. But all of this meant nothing, for the union never met again, nor did any black Catholic conference for the next twenty years. McGhee and Lofton tried to revive the movement six years later, in 1900, but failed. What they wrote then to Father Slattery suggests some of what went wrong. "We are not forgetful of some mistakes of the last meeting, yet a good cause should not be allowed to die because of a few mistakes, and hotheads, neither should all be held responsible for the shortcomings of others."

But it was not mistakes and hotheads that brought down the Negro Catholic Congresses. Father David Spalding, the historian of the Congress movement, points to two factors: increasing conservatism within the Catholic Church, mirroring the anti-black swing of American public opinion; and dissension and exhaustion within the movement itself. There had been eighty-five delegates to the first Congress in 1888; by 1894 the number had fallen to thirty-eight. The Congress founder, Daniel Rudd, had withdrawn from leadership. In 1895 the assertive Frederick Douglass died; later the same year Booker T. Washington became the anointed leader of black America with his famous "Atlanta Compromise" speech, which was interpreted as acceptance of second-class and subservient status. In this atmosphere there was no place for a black Catholic movement that made demands. The times, not mistakes and hotheads, killed the Congress.[11]

Whatever Fred McGhee may have felt about the demise of yet another of his civil rights organizations, nothing shook his devotion to Roman Catholicism. He retained the zeal of the convert, and, like many converts, his zeal was fueled in part by distaste for what he had left behind. In June 1901, more than ten years after his conversion, McGhee published a letter to the editor of the *Cleveland Gazette*, a black weekly, stating his views:

"[W]hy is it," he asked rhetorically, "that America has allowed the germs of our enforced enslavement to remain so long after emancipation?" His answer: The [white] Protestants:

> They have control of the entire government; of our national and state institutions; surely in the civil departments of the government they can do away with all caste and place the Negro on the basis of common equality. But they do not do so, and their sins of omission are sanctioned by their religious leaders.
> Again, I repeat, Protestants rule in the United States. They make the government and they can unmake it. They can right wrong. They permit it

to exist. In the face of all the wrongs we suffer, the Protestant preacher and bishop are ever silent.

In the Roman Catholic Church, by contrast, he had written a year before that the black feels himself fully the equal of the white. "The Catholic Church means to the Negro the continual holding out of hope, the encouragement of ambition."

At the time of his conversion McGhee had been virtually promised that his new church would take the lead in fighting race discrimination in the United States. Within the space of five years Archbishop Ireland had gone silent on the subject and the church had ceased to lead. This seemed to have had no im-

First all-Negro choir of St. Peter Claver church, St. Paul, about 1901-2.
Top row: Joseph Harris, Birdie King, Allen French;
middle row: Adda Tobie, Eva Harris, Hattie Shepard, Charles Miller;
front row: Mary Pitts, Emma Porter (organist), Claude Jackson (director),
Mattie McGhee, and Reverend J. T. Andrzejewski.

pact on Fred McGhee's devotion. His initial attraction to the Roman Catholic Church may have been political, but over the years it became personal. The 1901 letter quoted above is his last known utterance mixing religion with politics. After this, so far as we know, McGhee kept his religious work quiet and close to home. He did a great deal of unheralded parish work at his St. Peter Claver Church in St. Paul. He served on committees, made speeches, presided over fundraising events, escorted children on holiday outings; Mattie McGhee sang in the church choir, and she and Fred became godparents to many parish children.

The Roman Catholic Church in the United States never became the engine of black emancipation that Fred McGhee had hoped: "the sun of our perfect freedom" certainly did not shine in his lifetime. McGhee had to accept progress on a much smaller scale. Archbishop Ireland remained interested in and a regular visitor to St. Peter Claver. He brought into the priesthood and trained in St. Paul a young black attorney named Stephen Theobald. In 1910, Theobald was named the parish priest of St. Peter Claver and would be McGhee's priest for the rest of his life. Theobald went on to become a national civil rights leader himself, and took a prominent role in the revival of the black Catholic movement in the 1920s—following up on work done by his parishioner, Fred McGhee, thirty years before.[12]

5

Trials and Tribulations

While civil rights activity fell into a lull both locally and nationally during the mid-1890s, Fred McGhee concentrated on his law practice. He moved away from his early reliance on the prostitution industry and took on a higher class of criminals—professional thieves and thugs. He got clients the way criminal lawyers always have: by reputation, referral, court appointment, and by hanging around the courthouse. He also got them by being black. Blacks in St. Paul were arrested far out of proportion to their share of the population, and McGhee's race gave him a competitive advantage. So far as the surviving record reveals, most of his clients were African American.

Most of his cases were ordinary, a succession of assaults and larcenies enlivened by colorful characters and the absorbing and engaging craft of fast-paced trial advocacy. The case files and press accounts from this decade offer a glimpse of a criminal justice system rougher and less punctilious yet more accessible than the one we know today.

A typical municipal court (or "police court") case was like that of a young man named George Minea. On April 14, 1895, he got into an argument with a patrolman and "slugged the policeman so hard that it took him several minutes to rise." Arrested on the spot, he demanded a jury trial and got it five days later. McGhee gave him a vigorous defense, including a long grilling of witnesses, "several irritating tilts" with the prosecutor, an insinuation that the policeman had been drunk, and a "resounding plea" for Minea's liberty. They got it all done in a day; by 6 P.M. the jury had found Minea guilty and gone home.[1]

McGhee did better for John Costello, who faced a prison term for a bar fight. The charge was assault with a dangerous weapon; in this case an iron spittoon that Costello had used to split Henry O'Connor's ear, but the verdict came in not guilty. Felony theft cases, of which McGhee handled many, often involved what now seem absurdly modest values. He got acquittals for Henry West and Florence Young, accused of stealing a $7 "astrakhan collarette," but lost a second go-round for West a few weeks later, when a jury found him

guilty of stealing a suit and two neckties worth $26. West got a stint at the
St. Cloud Reformatory for his crime.[2]

Cases like these would almost never go to a jury trial today. In McGhee's
day the system was, in its way, exemplary: no delays (misdemeanor cases went
to trial within a week, felony cases inside five months), few plea bargains, and,
if the defendant so desired, a full-fledged jury trial with competent counsel.
Here were the Constitution and the common law in action. This was how Fred
McGhee spent his days.

Not all his cases were criminal. On behalf of Lucy Coleman, McGhee sued
St. Paul police officer James Ross for $1,500 for malicious arrest and personal
injury. Coleman claimed that Ross had arrested her without cause and
roughed her up. Ross said that Coleman had been drunk and obstreperous on
the street but that he had handled her gently. Though Ross was white and
Coleman black, McGhee did not raise race as an issue. The jury believed Ross
and gave Coleman nothing. Race of course remained important to McGhee.

Fredrick McGhee, from The Appeal, *July 24, 1909,
but almost certainly taken by Harry Shepherd in 1890.*

He represented "colored" mail carrier Joseph Allen in a long-running divorce and child custody case whose facts were so "revolting" that the daily papers declined to print them. He lost this case, too.[3]

The year 1894 brought McGhee back to the front pages, with his first two murder trials. On December 15, 1893, Henry Johnson shot Henry Rollins in a dispute over a water pitcher. Johnson ran, Rollins died. Johnson was caught and charged with second-degree murder, for which the penalty was life in prison. Johnson engaged Fred McGhee to defend him. In his first murder case, in which both victim and defendant were African American and the jurors all white, McGhee revealed how far he was willing to go to use race on behalf of a client. In defending Johnson, he played on race prejudice in a way that people would find shocking today, and he would do it again.

In his opening statement, March 13, 1894, Prosecutor Pierce Butler laid out a straightforward case of a rising quarrel culminating in murderous violence. Race played no part in his remarks. McGhee raised the issue. Rollins, he told the jury in his opening, was a bad black man and handy with a razor. He regretted having to do so, but it was his duty "to lay before the jury the dregs and absolute lewdness of mankind as found in the Negro."

McGhee had a plausible self-defense case without using race. Portraying the victim as not just a bad man but, worse, a bad black man, was calculated to dehumanize him in the minds of the jury. The implied suggestion, that Rollins's life wasn't worth much, or even that he needed killing, must have been all the more powerful coming from an educated, respectable black citizen. The chief prosecution witness was Rollins's wife, and this played into McGhee's hands, too. He knew her and knew she had a criminal record (apparently he had once represented her), so in cross-examination he accused her of being a thief and a prostitute.

Prosecutor Butler tried to respond in his closing argument by imploring the jury to reject the suggestion that somehow race should diminish guilt. Colored people, he said, have the same rights before the courts as other citizens, and their lives equal value. What's more, the "best blood of our Northern states" had been shed to secure these rights, and the only way to make good citizens of the freemen was to hold them to equal accountability before the law. Butler seemed worried, and he had reason to be, for the clear trend in criminal cases of this era showed that juries were quite willing to acquit on the basis of self defense when the victim was black.

McGhee knew this, and in his closing argument he lobbed another race bomb into the case. Responding to Mr. Butler's plea for justice, he asked the jurors to recall the recent Kate Davis case. He did not get further—the judge immediately ruled this line of argument improper—but he probably did not need to, as the case had made a big splash. Kate Davis, who ran a rooming house, had shot Samuel Blackstone as he climbed the rooming house stairs looking for his employer, J. J. Miesen. After her arrest and at trial, Davis claimed that she had shot Blackstone in self-defense when he tried to assault her. That Blackstone was a working family man and unarmed, that he denied the assault in his dying declaration, and that Miesen confirmed Blackstone's account made no difference to the jury; they acquitted Davis. She was white, Blackstone black.

By mentioning Davis, McGhee sent this message to the jury: White people routinely discount black lives in other cases—why should this one be any different? He immediately apologized after the judge intervened, and went on with the more conventional portions of his closing. It is impossible to know whether McGhee's race-conscious strategy worked, but the jury did convict Johnson of manslaughter rather than murder (whereupon he smiled and shook his lawyer's hand). The court sentenced him to eight years in prison; with good behavior, he would be free again before the century's end.[4]

McGhee's second murder trial, his unsuccessful defense of Philip Rice for a holdup killing, is noteworthy for just this: never before in Minnesota history had a black man defended a white man in a murder case, yet no one (in the press, anyway) seemed to notice. Fred McGhee had become so well established as a lawyer that his race had ceased to be interesting. In trial advocacy, McGhee little by little revealed himself capable of doing anything he could get away with. He bullied, he obstructed, he belittled, he objected *ad nauseam*, he appealed to God, and he appealed to prejudice. Adina Gibbs, the daughter of John Q. Adams, later remembered of McGhee's courtroom demeanor:

He was a man that would perform when he had cases in court. He just performed. He would weep ... just cry when he needed to, you know,

Henry Johnson, inmate #3897, after his commitment to the Minnesota State Prison at Stillwater.

to impress the jury. Or he would go through performances and roar and howl and all that sort of thing to impress the jury.

Inside the courtroom, Fred McGhee felt free, but away from the courtroom the race attitudes of the time made it hard for any African American to feel secure and at ease.[5]

Even Minnesota was not immune from the intensifying race hatred that afflicted the country at that time. On April 13, 1895, a black porter named Henry "Whisky" Brown was seen loitering around the home of nine-year-old Maggie O'Toole in the city's Mount Airy neighborhood. Later that day the girl's mother noticed her daughter running, with Brown in pursuit. She called for the help of her son and son-in-law, who soon found Brown and Maggie in the back of a vacant house in a "compromising position." Brown ran off, a crowd gathered, and, according to the press, "some hotheaded spectators talked freely of lynching Brown." This time there was mainly talk, and the action went no further than finding rope. The police found Brown and took him to safety.[6]

Houston Osborn was not so lucky. Just before dawn on June 2, 1895, he slipped into a bedroom of a house on Iglehart Street near Lexington Avenue, an area then on the western edge of the city. The Kachel sisters were sleeping in that room, and one of them, Frieda, awoke to find Osborn's dark hand over her mouth. Her screams awakened her sisters and her brother, Anton, sleeping in the house next door. Osborn escaped, with Anton Kachel in pursuit. As he ran, Kachel enlisted help from dairymen at work nearby. The chase went on for a mile and a half to the west, across open country, until Kachel at last tackled Osborn and brought him down. By the time he and his helpers had returned Osborn to the scene of the crime, a crowd had gathered. According to one press report, the suggestion, "get a rope," came from a woman. Anton Kachel brought a 30-foot length of clothesline, and as Osborn pleaded, "My God! Don't lynch me!" he was led to a cottonwood tree behind the Kachel house. Osborn's tormentors tied one end of the rope around his neck and tossed the other over a bough. His feet were off the ground and his body twitching when some women persuaded the men to let him down. Osborn felt himself the most fortunate of men to be delivered into the hands of the police. Fred McGhee took charge of his defense.

So deeply had lynching entered white consciousness that even in St. Paul people seemed to know its ritual: the accusation of sexual assault of a white woman by a black man, the gathering of an angry crowd, the call for a rope and noose. The daily press did its part, too, characterizing Osborn as a "brute," and his captors as "resolute," and their actions "a burst of righteous wrath." The *Globe* in particular treated the story as an entertaining adventure, a "thrilling and remarkable" experience for all. And then, once Osborn was behind bars, the case all but disappeared from the newspapers—there were no editorials deploring vigilante justice—as though nothing had been revealed and there were no conclusions to be drawn.

Osborn was charged with burglary (breaking and entering for the purpose of committing a felony) and attempted sexual assault. With McGhee at his side he quietly pled guilty to burglary and received a sentence of ten years in prison. Rope or no rope, Houston Osborn was doomed; he died in prison of tuberculosis less than two years later. Anton Kachel, for his part in leading the lynch mob, never faced criminal charges.[7]

We do not know how St. Paul's black community reacted to the Osborn case because all issues of its weekly newspaper, *The Appeal*, for this period have been lost. The incident must have served, however, as a dramatic reminder that laws were not always evenly enforced. Minnesota had had a civil rights law since 1885. In spring 1897, Twin Cities black leadership proposed an amendment to that law, to make it more effective. Only one prominent figure publicly opposed the amendment, and he did so loudly: Fredrick McGhee.

The 1885 statute provided that all citizens "of every race and color" were entitled to equal access to "inns, public conveyances on land and water, theaters and places of public amusement, restaurants and barbershops, subject only to the conditions and limitations established by law." It was nearly identical to the federal civil rights act declared unconstitutional by the Supreme Court in 1883. The law imposed substantial criminal penalties for those convicted of violating it: fines between $100 and $500 plus jail terms of at least thirty days with a maximum of one year.[8]

The two attorneys who proposed the amendments were William R. Morris, McGhee's old colleague who had come to Minneapolis shortly after McGhee, and the rising young star J. Frank Wheaton, soon to be the first black Minnesotan elected to the legislature. Their amendment would have broadened, or at least clarified, the scope of the protection by specifying what they probably considered a comprehensive list of establishments: "hotel, inn, tavern, restaurant, eating house, soda-water fountain, ice-cream parlor, public conveyance on land or water, theater, barber shop, or other place of public refreshment, amusement, instruction, accommodation, or entertainment," eliminating the phrase "subject ... to conditions and limitations established by law," and specifying that it applied alike to the owners, managers, and lessees of such places. The amendment also gave aggrieved parties specific rights to civil damages of $25 to $500, reduced the criminal penalties to $25 to $100 in fines and thirty to ninety days in jail, and made fines and jail alternatives rather than both mandatory.[9]

The Morris-Wheaton bill had three main objectives. One was to eliminate evasions by clarifying that all eating establishments, not just restaurants, were covered. The second was to encourage awarding civil damages, which the current statute did not (though neither did it prevent such awards). The third was to encourage criminal prosecution. It is unlikely that there were ever any prosecutions under the old law, in part because of the minimum penalties of $100 fine and thirty days in jail (the federal statute had made the fines $500 to $1000 and jail time thirty days to one year). These minimums probably struck prosecutors and judges as far out of line with the offense of refusing someone a meal or a hotel room or a shave on the basis of race. Reducing the penalties, especially the mandatory minimums, might encourage more criminal enforcement of the law.

Why did Fred McGhee oppose these amendments? He had cogent reasons, but there seemed to be great public confusion about what they were. On April 7, 1897, the *St. Paul Dispatch* reported that McGhee had called the law—the minimum civil damages portion specifically—"a measure for the benefit of the crap shooters and blacklegs ... the most disreputable of niggers." The article went on to quote McGhee, or purport to quote him, at length:

William R. Morris.
Photograph by Sweet Studios.

J. Frank Wheaton,
about 1899.

Such a law ... would be used to the advantage of the very worst and most disreputable class of colored men and women in the state. They would work up cases merely for the sake of bringing an action. If they could get one half of the $25, which would be about the limit for any verdict under the law, they would be enabled to live in luxury for a week or two, or play "craps" to their heart's content. It would build up a class of blackmailers who have no regard for themselves or for the welfare of the race to which they belong, be a detriment to every colored person who has an ambition to do something and result in more harm to the negro than can be estimated in mere words.

He complained also that the minimum damages amount of $25 would become in practice a standard price for discrimination, regardless of the offense, and that the $500 maximum was far too low in some cases and for some aggrieved parties—for example Mr. and Mrs. Booker T. Washington. "We are satisfied with the law just as it stands .... Now we go to the jury and they can give us what they consider we are entitled, be it nothing or thousands of dollars. We are willing to trust to the jurors for justice." [10]

John Quincy Adams read these comments in the *Dispatch*, and responded in a long editorial one week later:

Friends of Lawyer F. L. McGhee were very much surprised and chagrined .... at the position he took in regard to the proposed amendment to the existing civil rights law .... The opposition of Mr. McGhee to the bill is not so much objected to ... as the manner in which his objections were presented to the public.

Though Adams's editorial was mildly worded, Fred McGhee took vehement offense and responded in a long and angry letter published in *The Appeal's* next issue. He accused Adams of bad judgment and bad journalism for believing the *Dispatch* quotations. The words were not his but the reporter's, asserted McGhee, and Adams should have known better: "My record in defence of my people ... is sufficient guarantee that no such terms as 'Crap shooter,' 'Blacklegs,' and 'Niggers' are used by me in public speech or in print."

McGhee then recounted his objections to the proposed amendments. First, reducing the penalties symbolically devalued the gravity of the offenses. "I have yet to find the person who will explain to me what the benefit has or will accrue to my race by thus making lighter the punishment of the man who inflicts the wrong." Second, the limit on civil damages took away the plaintiff's power to seek and the jury's power to award a higher figure. He raised the case of Booker T. Washington, who on a recent visit had been given a room at the Metropolitan Hotel only on the condition (so said McGhee) that he not use the

hotel's public restaurant. For such an offense, McGhee implied, $500 in dam-
ages was far too little. "[T]he refusal of entertainment to Prof. Washington is a
deeper insult," he argued, "is more far-reaching than a refusal of one of our
own citizens. He is the embodiment of the highest type of the Afro-American
manhood, his position, his status entitles him to more than that to which the
ordinary colored citizen is accorded." This is the complaint of a plaintiff's trial
lawyer—let a jury decide what the damages truly are.

McGhee closed with remarks that show how deeply he felt the criticism in
Adams's editorial:

> In conclusion, Mr. Editor, I would add that if those friends of mine who are
> so deeply chagrined at my "interview" spend as much time and labor as I
> do in defence of their race, and saving them from shame, without financial
> recompense they would land themselves securely in the poor house before
> they went to their reward.[11]

This exchange reveals a serious rift between St. Paul's two most eminent
race leaders. McGhee and Adams had known each other for nearly ten years,
had worked together in many causes, and their offices downtown were minutes apart. Adams could easily have asked McGhee if the *Dispatch* quotes were
accurate, but did not. He chose instead to repeat them in print, expressing no
doubt that the words were McGhee's.

McGhee's long, emotional response makes clear that he felt unappreciated
by and estranged from many in his community: a leader secure in his position
and esteem rarely feels the need to defend himself at such length. This is the
first instance of such estrangement that the historical record provides, but not
the last. In his maturity, McGhee hewed to his own path all the more,
especially in politics. He would defend himself from time to time but never
apologize.

McGhee's opposition to the civil rights amendments counted for nothing,
and the bill passed quickly into law. This, however, was not the end of the
story. On September 22, 1897, not long after the new law had taken effect, an
ex-slave named Edward T. Rhone met a white acquaintance of his, Tom Shannon, on Superior Street in Minnesota's port city of Duluth. Shannon offered to
buy Rhone a drink, so the two ducked into the saloon in the Merchants Hotel
building. While Rhone stopped to chat with the hotel's black porter, Shannon
ordered and received a beer. When Rhone joined him, Shannon ordered
another for his friend and placed a nickel on the bar in payment. The bar
owner, Robert Loomis, responded, "We don't sell to colored people." Taken
aback, Rhone and Shannon left the bar without protest.

Edward Rhone got a lawyer and sued. An all-white Duluth jury awarded him the statutory minimum, $25, two months later. Loomis appealed the judgment to the Minnesota supreme court. The court heard the case in March 1898 and overturned the jury's verdict.

This may have been one of the most peculiar decisions ever rendered by Minnesota's highest court. Justice William Mitchell, one of the state's most famous judges and for whom its largest law school is named, wrote the opinion. The legislature, he reasoned, had listed with great particularity, right down to ice cream parlors and soda-water fountains, the kinds of establishments covered by the law, but had not listed saloons. Therefore, it must have meant to exclude saloons, perhaps to preserve public order. Race prejudice still exists, observed Justice Mitchell, and can result in conflict, "especially where the passions of men are inflamed by liquor," thus:

> [T]he legislature might have thought that the right to be furnished intoxicating drink would be of doubtful benefit to any class of people, and for that reason excluded saloons from the operation of the act .... [W]e would hesitate to hold that the legislature made it a crime under any circumstances for one man to refuse to furnish another with intoxicating liquor ... unless the provisions of the act so provided with reasonable clarity.

Justice Mitchell's decision did have a basis in law: there was and is a doctrine of statutory interpretation that when the legislature makes a list of things, that which is not included is taken to be excluded on purpose. But the majority's conclusion in this case struck the two dissenting justices as absurd. Justice Collins pointed out in his dissent that the law listed hotels, inns, and restaurants (he did not mention taverns, also included), all of which often serve liquor. How can they be covered by the law, and saloons not, if the idea was to keep whites and blacks from drinking liquor in the same establishment? "I am decidedly of the opinion," he wrote, "that the saloon is one of the 'other places of public resort, refreshment, accommodation or entertainment' mentioned in the law. If it is not, what place is?"[12]

This ruling, the only reported state supreme court case in the long history of the 1885 act and its later amendments, had no serious adverse consequences, except perhaps for poor Edward Rhone. The court not only took away his $25 in damages—it also ordered him to pay Loomis's court costs. For agreeing to accept a nickel beer from Tom Shannon, and for attempting to assert his rights to drink that beer in a public establishment, Edward Rhone ended up on the hook for $102.85.[13]

Minnesota's African-American leadership went back to the legislature in 1899 to fix the problem created by *Rhone v. Loomis.* McGhee, William R. Morris, and Bemidji attorney Charles Scrutchin, all former protégés of E. H. Morris of Chicago, drafted yet another set of amendments to the civil rights statute. These duly inserted the word "saloon" in the list of covered establishments and—no doubt at McGhee's insistence—eliminated the minimum civil damages provision, which he considered to be, in effect, a maximum. To get this before the legislature they had to go no further than their African-American colleague, J. Frank Wheaton, now sitting in the legislature as a member from Minneapolis. Their bill was passed into law in April 1899.[14]

While the Minnesota Supreme Court was pondering *Rhone v. Loomis,* the United States entered and won a war and scooped up an empire. The Spanish-American War briefly united white and black America in patriotic fervor. In Minnesota the races got together in a very showy way to celebrate the victory, with Fred McGhee literally at center stage.

To some extent the happiness that most Americans felt at the easy victory and at the acquisition of Cuba, Puerto Rico, and the Philippine Islands masked the fact that white America and black America looked at the conflict differently. African Americans generally made a more sophisticated analysis. Many had been following the Cuban independence movement for years. They knew that the majority of Cubans had African ancestry and that some of its greatest rebel generals, notably Antonio Maceo, whose exploits were covered well in the St. Paul daily press, were black men. America's entrance in the war offered the possibility of American blacks collaborating with African Cubans in the liberation of black people from white colonial rule. African Americans also recalled with pride the service of black soldiers in the Civil War. Smarting as they did from being told in countless ways by white America that they were unfit for positions of responsibility, many saw the war as an opportunity to prove themselves once again and perhaps reap some of the rewards of full citizenship. Not many white Americans looked at the war in these ways.

When the war began in April 1898, young black men volunteered in great numbers, but relatively few were permitted to enlist. The segregated army allowed just a handful of black regiments to form and prohibited black officers from command positions; they were chaplains, physicians, bandmasters. No black Minnesotans served in the war. The few black troops who saw action performed well; a black New York regiment got credit for saving the day in the famous attack on San Juan Hill. This news received wide coverage in the black press, but the war's quick conclusion in August 1898 limited black opportunities and cut short the debate over why black men should volunteer to risk death abroad for a government that would not protect them from lynching at home.[15]

Minnesotans black and white celebrated the war along with the rest of the country. Twin Cities African Americans staged a giant rally in April 1898, and a patriotic concert in September, once the war ended. Fred McGhee probably supported the war. While he did not attend the April rally, because it was a Republican affair, he made a speech at the September concert and another later in the month at St. Peter Claver, honoring the Fourteenth Minnesota Volunteers, a white unit that never got closer to the action than Tennessee.[16]

In November 1898, the Twin Cities black community put on what must have been one of the most spectacular demonstrations of patriotic enthusiasm ever witnessed in Minnesota. It came in the form of a stage production called *Cuba*, a four-act pastiche of tableaux vivants, speeches, songs, and dramatic scenes written and directed by Mrs. Cora Pope and performed by an all-black cast of 300. Two performances were given in Minneapolis, one in St. Paul. The audiences were integrated, and one house was estimated at 2,000 people.

The elites of both races mobilized to finance the production, though in separate, parallel organizations. Both Minneapolis and St. Paul had Honorary Patronesses (white) and Active Patronesses (black). The list of Minneapolis Honorary Patronesses (there were fifty-eight) reads like a Board of Directors of Minneapolis, Incorporated: Pillsbury, Northrup, Goodrich, Bigelow, McLeod, Steele, and Peavey. It was the same for St. Paul's seventy-one Honorary Patronesses: Hannaford, Sanborn, Monfort, Upham, Weyerhauser, Bigelow, Wheelock, and Otis. On the African-American side the forty-nine women from Minneapolis and the fifty-two from St. Paul represented a major portion of the middle-class black population of the region. One can see here a traditional division of labor: the white women raised the money, the black women did the work. Still, the collaboration was undoubtedly sincere.

The performers included eleven soloists, three quartets, two pianists, an orchestra, dozens of actors with speaking parts, and scores of extras. All events took place in a fancifully imagined Cuba. *The Appeal* preserved some details of the show for posterity. It began with a prologue where Mrs. J. V. Kemp portrayed Liberty, Mrs. W. A. Hazel performed something called an echo solo, and Mayme Weir "posed." In "Columbia's Festal Day," the players portrayed folk life on the island, "with plantation singing and dancing" and "a cake walk that was considered by many to be the hit of the piece." Another scene reenacted the battle of Santiago, featuring a black Clara Barton nursing dying soldiers, a nurse singing "Home Sweet Home" to a wounded man and leaving "few dry eyes in the house," the capture of a Cuban spy, and the surrender of the Spanish forces. In the last act, "all countries welcome Cuba to the sisterhood of nations."

Fred McGhee played a leading part. "The most pretentious and dramatic scene was that in which F. L. McGhee, the well known and eloquent attorney, as Gen. Maceo, recounted the wrongs of his country and called upon his followers to avenge them," assessed *The Appeal*. The *Pioneer Press* called his performance "decidedly dramatic." Before the final act McGhee also made an optimistic and patriotic speech to the effect that just as no color line was observed in the trenches before San Juan Hill, the color line was fading in Minnesota. These words reflected the glow of recent victory; it would not be long before he and many others reevaluated their feelings.[17]

The choice of Fred McGhee to play Antonio Maceo was truly inspired, for the two men's lives had many parallels. Both had been born slaves. Both were handsome and accomplished public speakers—between independence wars in Cuba, Maceo regularly travelled and spoke in the United States to raise money. Both were Catholic. When McGhee portrayed Maceo on stage lamenting the wrongs done to the Cuban people by their Spanish oppressors, both he and the African Americans in the audience must have had very much in mind the similar wrongs done to McGhee's people by the rulers of the United States.[18]

Cuba was a great victory for Twin Cities African Americans. It gave them the chance to publicly demonstrate their ability to organize and orchestrate such an event, all serving a cause that drew everyone together. So many people participated—cast, crew, and organizers must have numbered at least 400—that it was truly a community event, touching most black families in the region. The show won plenty of praise, but had no lasting effect on race relations in Minnesota; things soon returned to the customary state of uneasy toleration and informal segregation.

One scene in the show, however, landed Fred McGhee in the midst of controversy again. He ended up defending not an accused criminal or a political position but, of all things, a dance featured in the Columbia's Festal Day sequence of *Cuba*, a dance known as "the cakewalk." The cakewalk had its origins in the slave plantations of the South, where some slave owners gave cakes as prizes for the best slave dancers at special social occasions. Slaves then developed these dances into parodies of their masters' own dances and costumes. After slavery's end the cakewalk made its way into black theaters and music halls in the North, beginning with *The Creole Show* in New York in 1889.

In her book *Black Dance in the United States,* Lynne Emery describes the dance as:

> originally a kind of shuffling movement which evolved into a smooth walking step with the body held erect. The backward sway was added, and as the dance became more of a satire on the dance of white plantation owners, the movement became a prancing strut. The inclusion of women [in the stage shows] made possible all sorts of improvisations in the Walk, and the original was soon changed into a grotesque dance.

Grotesque or not, the cakewalk quickly became enormously popular and made stars of some performers, such as Bert Williams and George Walker. It spread throughout black America, reaching St. Paul theaters in April 1892 ("first time here of a real cakewalk" promised W. W. Downy's *New Orleans Creoles*).[19]

Whites enjoyed the cakewalk, too, first as spectators, then as imitators. In his book, *In Our Times,* Mark Sullivan called it "the first appearance of negro movement in ball-room dancing." White dancers made it a parody of black dance; performers "imitated a colored man strutting in a prize contest, the distinguishing features being the head held high, chin up, elbows out, shoulders thrown back, and, especially prominent, an exaggerated frontal protuberance."[20]

The cakewalk became such a society fad in New York City that even the Vanderbilts took to it, prompting Williams and Walker, the black cakewalking duo, to issue William K. Vanderbilt a public challenge. Claiming facetiously that "the attention of the public has been distracted from us on account of the tremendous hit you have made," they challenged Vanderbilt to a cakewalking contest, "which will decide which of us shall deserve the title of champion cake-walker of the world." And just as the dance had come to St. Paul as a stage phenomenon through the black music halls, it came too as a society fad several years later, reaching Summit Avenue by 1898. The cakewalk's progress was made even stranger by the fact that some black people became aware of it first, or at least most prominently, as a white society amusement, which they then borrowed from them.[21]

What bothered some people about the cakewalk, at least when performed to white audiences, was the exaggerated strutting and prancing, movements which played directly into the stereotype of black men as shiftless caperers. The black *Odd Fellows Journal* editorialized, "The cake walk of today is usually the occasion of a few empty headed colored people to cut monkey shines for the delectation of a class of white people who have no use for the negro except as clowns." Just before it first appeared in St. Paul in 1892 *The Appeal* called it "disgusting to all refined Afro-Americans."[22] This is precisely how J. C. Reid of Minneapolis saw it.

Mr. Reid had seen and enjoyed *Cuba*, in which his wife performed. In a long letter to *The Appeal* he praised everything about it except the cakewalk, which he saw as dangerous to his race. Black people lived under the constant scrutiny of the white majority; this required them, out of pure self-preservation, to maintain a far higher standard of conduct and propriety than whites did. The deeds of black soldiers in Cuba and the marvelous portrayals by black performers in *Cuba* helped the race by winning praise from white America. But antics like the cakewalk undid the good. "There is no need for outlining the moral, social, and intellectual value the [white] public places upon the cake walker," wrote Reid. "While it enjoys it, its innermost thoughts are; 'all coons are alike.'"[23]

An extraordinary article from the *St. Paul Globe* seemed to confirm Reid's analysis. Entitled "Hotfoot Was King," it told the story of a cakewalk competition at a club called Cunnningham's featuring "Hotfoot" (otherwise known as, Alec Williams), Dude Charlie, Bogus Bill, Indian Lizzie, Minneapolis Filly, and others. It described how the men flash their "razzahs" (razors), everybody drinks to excess, and much of the story has dialect such as this:

> "Doan' talk," cried a tall, lanky darkey ... "I'm jest a slippin' and a slidin'. Be flyin' dreckly. Ole woman needs de cake, chillun stahvin' an' de ole man a walkin'. I'm a comin' faster'n judgment day. Um ah cone beef an' cabbitch," and he strode past the entire outfit was if they were standing still.... "Dat's Hotfut, dat's Hotfut," cried a good looking young wench.... "My, I jest love dat Mistah Hotfut."

J. C. Reid did not want the respectable black community of St. Paul and Minneapolis associated, in the minds of respectable white folks, with the Hotfoots of the world.

Reid's letter brought to the surface a debate that must have been roiling for quite some time, in St. Paul and around the country. Now the debate drew in the McGhee family. One week after the publication of Reid's letter, Mattie McGhee responded with a letter of her own. She was well aware, she wrote, that the cakewalk "has its associations." But she had first heard of the dance in connection with the Vanderbilts of New York, and in St. Paul it had come into prominence "when Miss Abbie Warner, daughter of the head of a well known business firm in St. Paul, gave a cakewalk at her residence on Summit avenue." It was only then that the colored people of St. Paul concluded that they could cakewalk, too. The cakewalk, she concluded, "is a modest and refined dance ... indulged in by some of the most refined and cultured people of the Northwest, and who are a credit to the race to which they belong."[24]

That such a letter could issue from the McGhee home is astounding. The McGhees were straitlaced, to be sure, but Fred McGhee spent his days defending participants in St. Paul's black demimonde. It is not improbable, in fact, that he had represented Hotfoot himself. He had probably never been to Cunningham's, but he must have had a good idea what took place there. Maybe both he and Mattie just preferred not to think about it.

The debate continued, as witnessed by the fact that two weeks later both Mattie and Fred published letters in *The Appeal*. Mattie complained that Reid's letter had "called forth such an outburst of personal attacks," and asked that the discussion now be kept within "proper limitations." Fred followed up to suggest the forum; he challenged Reid to a public debate, before nine judges, with Reid to select five.[25]

The McGhees had tossed down the gauntlet, and J. C. Reid picked it up. The forensic clash took place February 6, 1899, as a benefit for Bethesda Baptist Church of Minneapolis. Unfortunately, no account of this debate has survived, but the outcome was predictable. Mr. Reid had put himself in the position of attacking something that was fun, something defended by one of the most skilled defense attorneys in the region. The judges awarded the victory to McGhee: vindication for the cakewalk.[26]

With that, the cakewalk controversy ended, at least in the Twin Cities. The McGhees persisted in their belief that it was an innocent art. We know this because on May 2, 1899, Fred McGhee served as dance director for the St. Peter Claver's May Party, where one of the featured events was "a very pleasing 'cake walk' by the little children."[27] Among adults and music hall performers the cakewalk duly passed from fashion.

The entire cakewalk ruckus was full of irony. The dance began as slaves' mocking imitation of their owners. After Emancipation free African Americans made it into their own popular art form, which whites then took up, in part as a slumming jibe of blacks. When even white society adopted the cakewalk, some black people followed their lead, in sincere imitation or in mockery of white attempts to appropriate black forms. In the end it was not clear who was mocking whom. If Mattie McGhee's letter reflects her husband's feelings, these ironies did not interest or concern them; they declined to find peril to their race in a fad. Fred McGhee, for one, had much more serious business on his mind.

6

Law Enforcement

Fredrick McGhee's rise to national leadership in the civil rights movement began in summer 1898. In some ways this was a bad time for civil rights organizing. First, the entire nation was distracted by the Spanish-American War. Second, in 1895 the country had anointed Booker T. Washington the single spokesman for and leader of African Americans, and Washington favored a low-profile, nonpolitical, bootstraps approach to black progress. Civil rights organizing, by its nature political and confrontational, did not fit comfortably with the Washington way. Still, black civil and political rights had deteriorated disastrously throughout the 1890s, so as the decade progressed, many black citizens felt ever stronger the need to organize once again. Fred McGhee was one of these.[1]

In June 1898, McGhee and the other prominent black men of St. Paul met to create yet another civil rights organization. McGhee made a speech and was elected to a committee of eleven formed to draft a constitution for the new association. In July the group christened itself the American Law Enforcement League and elected Minneapolis restaurateur Jasper Gibbs its president. The name, American Law Enforcement League, reflected one of black America's repeated demands of both federal and local government: enforce the law against white criminals as well as black, enforce constitutional protections for black citizens, as well as white. The League's officers and directors comprised the local heavy-hitters: William A. Hazel, William R. Morris, J. Frank Wheaton, John Quincy Adams, and Fred McGhee.[2]

On September 15, 1898, the League published its manifesto in the form of an open letter, typical of the "calls" and "Addresses to the Nation" that civil rights organizations of the time made upon announcing or concluding a meeting or convention—eloquent in the statement of the need for action, vague in describing the action to be taken. It began with a patriotic statement ("the flag under which we sail stands for more than any other flag that floats over a civilized people"), then described the contradiction: a great nation allows millions of its citizens to be abused. "Think of the ten millions loyal hearted, patriotic people, being outraged, humiliated, scorned, hanged, burned alive ... under this very flag of which we so proudly boast." Their cries are ignored "by a people who claim that they lead the vanguard of modern civilization."

The call then addressed what its writers saw as the nation's great law enforcement issue—lynching. It observed that the frequent reports of black men in the South raping white women were having precisely the desired effect, "uniting the North and South in sentiment unfavorable to us." Though black Minnesotans lived "practically free" of the outrages suffered in the South, they

Booker T. Washington (seated) and private secretary, Emmett J. Scott, at Tuskegee Institute, 1906.

could not simply watch their southern brethren suffer. They had a plain duty to act: "We must make the flag of these United States mean as much to the Afro-American in the sunshine of his cabin, with gourd vines growing over his door, as it does to Rockefeller and Vanderbilt."

They brought forth, therefore, the American Law Enforcement League of Minnesota. Reflecting the political weakness of black America, its anti-lynching program made no specific demand on Congress, but rather placed the responsibilities first on themselves: "We should endeavor to learn the facts concerning these reported [sexual assaults by black men]. If they be true, to see that the guilty parties be properly dealt with," but if false, the malicious accusers should "suffer the consequences of their own sins." Here again their demands were vague and their goal immeasurable: "Let us prove to the world that we are opposed to crime, no matter who the offender might be."

The rest of their program was even more ambitious: abolish the Jim Crow railroad car, restore black suffrage to Mississippi, and ensure that "the 14th and 15th Amendments be enforced both in letter and spirit." The signers recognized the scope of their undertaking and the difficulty of managing it so far from the centers of power, but professed to be undaunted. "We have counted the cost, time, labor, and expense," they wrote, and "we are willing to make the sacrifice." Their statement echoed the Minnesota Civil Rights Committee of 1891. The new organization seemed to say, "If national race leadership will not act, then we, few and isolated though we are, will try." For the American Law Enforcement League to achieve their goals would have required a mobilization of national will and use of federal power not seen since the Civil War, an undertaking so vast that no sacrifice, no cost of time, labor, or expense, could have brought it about.[3]

Nevertheless, the national leadership had felt the same imperatives. Early in the year T. Thomas Fortune had dusted off the old, failed Afro-American League and called for its revival. The same week that the Law Enforcement League published its call to action, thirty delegates, led by Fortune and Alexander Walters, the African Methodist Episcopal (AME) church bishop, gathered in Rochester, New York, to form the National Afro-American Council (NAAC). This effort received wide praise in the national black press. When the Council met again in late December in Washington, D.C., over ninety delegates came, representing the best of northern African-American leadership. John Quincy Adams and Fred McGhee represented Minnesota.[4]

The new organization bore a striking resemblance to the Afro-American League, because that is essentially what it was. It had much the same leadership, starting with T. Thomas Fortune, the same basic goals, and the same weaknesses—not enough soldiers, not enough money, not enough clout, too few allies. Still, the cause was too vital and too pressing to permit further hesitation. The prevailing feeling was that the battle must be joined in whatever way possible.

The NAAC's call to action reflected the times; it was full of compromises with the Booker T. Washington forces and with the current political realities. It dealt with six main issues: suffrage, lynching, separate coach laws, prison conditions, public education, and black migration.

On suffrage in the South, where the controlling Democrats had through laws and intimidation effectively eliminated black voting, the Council accepted the "Bookerite" position that education and property qualifications for voting were acceptable if applied alike to all. The Council went beyond Washington in asking that the congressional delegations from Mississippi, South Carolina, and Louisiana be reduced because of black disfranchisement, as authorized by the Fourteenth Amendment.

On lynching, the NAAC did not condemn Congress and the president for their inaction, nor did it call for any federal action at all. It tamely regretted the president's (at this time, Republican William McKinley) silence and "indulge[d] the hope that he will use his good offices to settle this matter to the satisfaction of all concerned." There was no chance that this would happen.

Regarding the separate railroad car issue, the Council tacitly recognized the effect of *Plessy v. Ferguson:* there was no point in raising a constitutional argument against Jim Crow. The address called instead for court challenges based on contract and common law. A generation earlier a Republican Congress had banned discrimination in public accommodations; now after thirty years of faithful Republican voting and steady erosion of black civil rights, America's black leaders asked the Republican Congress for nothing at all.

The Address called the treatment of black prisoners in the South "one of the most glaring scandals in the administration of justice in the republic." Men, women, and children were held together in convict camps and many thousands were held in prison peonage. But again the Council did not call for federal action. Instead it lamented that other regions had made reforms, "why can't the South? . . . We appeal to its inclination."

In education the Council asked for more expenditure in the South on schooling in general and for elimination of racially separate school systems. It favored industrial education for blacks—Booker T. Washington's position— but higher education, too.

On the issue of black migration out of the South, the Council, consisting as it did primarily of northerners, dissented from Washington's stay-in-the-South position. It urged blacks to spread throughout the United States and its new territories of Cuba, Puerto Rico, and the Philippines "in order to reduce the congested population of the Southern states [and] simplify the race problem."

In the face of the terror being inflicted on African Americans in the South and elsewhere, this address seems woefully pallid, milder even than that of the American Law Enforcement League. Even the little it asks for probably explored the most optimistic limits of the achievable. Given the political weakness of its subscribers, it probably went about as far as it could go.[5]

In one sense, the most important thing about the Council at this moment was that it came to exist at all. Creating an organization united behind a set of goals was, after all, the necessary first step.

The delegates went back to their various home towns and cities to spread the NAAC gospel, encourage local action, and prepare to meet again in August. McGhee chose to do his organizing work through the Law Enforcement League. It was not unusual for local affiliates to be independent organizations. John Q. Adams did his part by printing the NAAC's Address to the Nation every week for the next seven months.

The Law Enforcement League held two rallies in early 1899, the second on February 24, in honor of Frederick Douglass, and did the thing in high style. The organizers rented the chambers of the state House of Representatives and decorated it with portraits of Douglass, Lincoln, John Brown, and abolitionists Wendell Phillips and Charles Sumner, all framed in evergreens. The St. James AME choir and two soloists sang, and then the speakers took over: Jasper Gibbs, William R. Morris, Mrs. W. A. Hazel; Governor John Lind, a Democrat, entered to great applause and made "a very acceptable speech of considerable length." Fred McGhee, perhaps the only other Democrat in the room, closed the proceedings with his talk on "Douglass as a Statesman" in "his usual, masterful, eloquent style."[6]

Mr. William Hazel had criticized the Afro-American League in 1891 for putting on showy meetings, but not much else. Six weeks after the pomp in the capitol the Law Enforcement League attempted something altogether different. Trying, apparently, to effect an alliance between local black leadership and white aristocrats, League President Jasper Gibbs arranged a private meeting between former Senator William D. Washburn, milling magnate F. H. Peavey, real estate dealer Percy Jones, and former postmaster W. D. Hale, all representing the monied interests of Minneapolis; and J. Q. Adams, William R.

Morris, Gibbs himself, and Fred McGhee. The meeting took place in Gibbs's fine south Minneapolis home.

The gathering very much impressed John Q. Adams. "The society and friendship of these men are desired and sought for by the entire community and we may congratulate ourselves and feel proud to entertain and be entertained by them, while many of their own race are denied such privileges." Jasper Gibbs himself had catered the banquet, and offered a menu "in keeping with the distinguished character of the guests":

> Blue Points on half shell, radishes, Olives; Chicken Buillon en tasses, Prussian Pretzels; Fillet of Sole, Holland sauce aux Pomme natural, Salted peanuts, Sliced cucumbers, Appolinaris; Fruit Frappee; Tenderloin de Beuf larded aux Champignons, white potatoes; Pineapple Ice; Larded Quails on fancy toast, Dressing of assorted nuts, Jersey sweets; Strawberries and Cream, Vanilla cookies; Neapolitan Cream a la General Harrison, Petite four; Assorted fruits; Chocolate, coffee, Admiral Farraguts.

After the meal—two and a half hours in the eating—the guests adjourned to Gibbs's reception room, "where amid the fumes of fragrant havanas" discussions continued. "Especially prominent was the subject of the league," which all of the guests promised to support. Adams predicted that "much good will ultimately come" of the meeting. "The same number of men cannot be found anywhere, representing [a]like their spirit of fairness and desire for the upbuilding and advancement of the Afro-American along material lines."

It is safe to say that no similar gathering had ever before been held in Minnesota, and perhaps very few since: black men of modest means invite wealthy white power brokers into one of their homes for a superb banquet and cigars, and to talk serious business in an atmosphere of bonhomie. It is probable that none of the guests had ever before entered a black man's home, much less to share Havanas and Neapolitan Cream a la General Harrison. One must credit Jasper Gibbs for a stroke of imagination and political theater. If blacks could not get into the Minneapolis Club to divide up the world with Senator Washburn, they would recreate the club on their turf and invite him.[7]

Booker T. Washington had had a great deal of success cultivating white business and philanthropic support, in part through his ability to court rich men. Why could this strategy not work in rich, progressive Minnesota? It was worth trying, and may have worked that evening, but it did not take. So far as anyone now knows, Washburn, Jones, Peavey, and Hale did not become champions of African-American civil or economic rights. For its part, the Law Enforcement League seems not to have found a way to follow up on this successful evening, and never became an effective civil rights organization. It stuck around for a few more years as a local unit of the NAAC.

The National Afro-American Council, by contrast, enjoyed a relatively vigorous 1899. When the Council met in Chicago in August, Minnesota sent three delegates—McGhee and its first two women participants, Mrs. J. B. Kemp and Mayme Weir (both veterans of the *Cuba* show). Historians have dismissed the 1899 meeting as unimportant because some top leaders—among them Washington—did not attend, and because so much energy was devoted to wrangling about Washington. But attendance was good, around 120, the level of energy high, and the Council benefitted from the presence of many women.

Fred McGhee's rising esteem within the organization is shown by his selection as one of the fourteen delegates chosen to draft the new Address to the Nation. This one demonstrated a far more assertive spirit than the last.

> The country is drifting into anarchy. Day by day the lawless and barbarous spirit of the mob becomes more defiant. The lynch law is a national sin, and national sins are punished by national calamities.... Our government is known in international law as ... a sovereign power, and it cannot escape the responsibility of affording protection to all persons within its borders on the plea that the outrage was committed in a part of the Union and the rest of the Union is powerless to act.... We have abiding confidence in the ability of the government to act in every instance, and we call upon those in authority to exercise their power under the constitution for the protection of the life and property of everybody within the jurisdiction of the United States.

Black readers of the time would have recognized how well written and how assertive these passages are. Calling lynch law a national sin contradicted the general white response that these murders were isolated local phenomena of no concern to the national authorities, and the ominous reference to "punished by national calamities" recalls Lincoln's Second Inaugural Address. The citing of international law and sovereign power was sardonic. Five Italians had recently been lynched near New Orleans, touching off a major international incident that brewed for several months until the United States paid Italy a hefty indemnity. Black Americans took offense when the national government took expensive action on behalf of foreign nationals but professed itself powerless to protect native citizens in the South on account of state sovereignty. In this context the phrase, "We have abiding confidence in the ability of the government to act" rings with sarcasm; and the succeeding call to exercise federal power "under the constitution" tweaks the Supreme Court for its decisions limiting federal power to enforce the 14th and 15th Amendments and the McKinley administration for its acquiescence in lynching and disfranchisement.

The Address then cleverly proceeded to ask the federal government for some limited and specific measures: equal access to the armed forces; a commission to assess the living conditions of the black population; fair African-American representation among people hired for the 1900 national census; and a black commissioner to be sent to the upcoming Paris World's Fair. These requests were clever because they fell easily within the power of the president alone, or the Republican president and his Republican Congress, to grant. There could be no states' rights evasions.

The Council made one more specific request with far-reaching implications. In March 1898, a white mob had stormed the house of Frazier Baker, the black postmaster of Lake City, South Carolina; Baker and his young daughter were murdered. President McKinley's administration at first declined to pursue and prosecute the killers, preferring to leave the matter to local authorities, which would mean an unsolved crime. Northern black citizens, most of them faithful Republicans, were deeply offended. Postmaster Baker was not just another lynching victim. Criminal law enforcement was a state and local matter, and the federal government could make a good constitutional argument that it had no power to intervene. But Baker was a federal appointee, and it was clear that he had been killed precisely for that reason—Lake City whites could not tolerate the existence of a black public official. If the party of Lincoln would take no steps to protect its own black political appointees, what hope could there be for ordinary citizens of African heritage?

Fred McGhee had presided over a protest meeting regarding the Baker case in spring 1898. Now he had a hand in trying to put the president and Congress on the spot. The Address to the Nation demanded that the government "bring the assassins of Postmaster Baker to justice" and that Congress "so amend the revised statutes of the United States as to place beyond quibble the authority of the general government to act at once in the case of lynching." Eventually the government indicted several for the crime, but convicted none.[8]

The rhetorical transformation of the NAAC from December to August is here complete. In December 1898 it had lamely asked the president to "use his good offices" to resolve the lynching "matter." Eight months later the Council demanded an unambiguous, statutory reassertion of federal power in the old Confederacy, specifically to protect African-American lives. The demand is similar to, though much sharper than, the Law Enforcement League's request that the Civil War amendments "be enforced in letter and in spirit." Such exercise of government power in the South would have provoked tremendous resistance—passive, active, armed, and determined. To many whites, had they paid attention to the address, this language would have been nothing less than a call to reinstitute Reconstruction.

The administration of course did not rise to this bait. It did not need to, especially so long as the demands did not come from Booker T. Washington. It was much easier and more politic to ignore the Afro-American Council than to heed it.

This Council meeting proved to be pivotal for Fred McGhee. Besides serving on the Committee of Address, he was elected to the Council's executive committee and to the office of Assistant Corresponding Secretary. These offices sound grander than they were. In the handing out of offices, the Council revealed one of its weaknesses, topheaviness. At the Chicago meeting the number of vice-presidents was expanded to nine; seven bureaus were created; and the executive committee swelled to 102. Just about everybody who showed up left with an office and a title or two. Still, McGhee had now officially entered the ranks of national leadership, and his NAAC colleagues included Bishop Walters, T. Thomas Fortune, and Ida B. Wells Barnett. What's more, the position of Assistant Corresponding Secretary placed an ambitious young man (McGhee would soon turn thirty-eight) in the center of the Council's internal communications. As we shall see, McGhee rose quickly within the organization.

More important even than any of this, however, and more fateful, were the personal relations created. For it was at this meeting that Fred McGhee met the man who would become his greatest friend and ally in the civil rights struggles to come—a young college professor from Atlanta named William Edward Burghardt Du Bois—but their long friendship and combined efforts would not begin just yet.[9]

For now McGhee was devoted to the Council and its local affiliate, the Law Enforcement League (LEL). In December 1899 he travelled to Washington, D.C., for the Council's executive committee meeting. No account of that gathering has survived. In January 1900 he presided over an LEL meeting in St. Paul. A week later the League's executive committee met at William R. Morris's office in Minneapolis to figure out how to raise money to mount a court challenge to a Louisiana disfranchisement law. To this idea Fred McGhee, recalling his failure in Tennessee eight years before, might have thought, here we go again, but apparently he went along. The committee decided to raise money by producing a play, *A Social Glass,* starring Fredrick McGhee.

St. Peter Claver's Choral Association had initially mounted the show just a month earlier. In both performances, McGhee played a character against type—not a lawyer but Charles Thornley, a rich heir and irresponsible tippler. The convoluted and melodramatic plot involved illicit affections, jealousy, and alcohol, all of which led to murder; harmony is restored and Thornley returned to sobriety through the ministrations of a temperance worker. *The Appeal,* which praised everything about the show, called it "without question the best production so far presented by the AFRO-AMERICAN talent of the Twin Cities." Fred McGhee was "good in his lines, and one would have thought the Counselor had some experience in tippling. It is difficult to understand how a total abstainer could mimic so thoroughly a man crazed by drink as he did." McGhee had plenty of vicarious experience with this sort of thing: sex and drink leading to violence played a large role in his law practice. The production probably raised little or no money for the civil rights cause.[10]

The League held a more important event on January 17, when it entertained Mr. Booker T. Washington himself. Washington had booked a speech at Carleton College in Northfield, Minnesota; McGhee persuaded him to stop in St. Paul and also organized a public event under the auspices of the Law Enforcement League. He brought together the black elite—Jasper Gibbs, John Q. Adams, William R. Morris, the physician Val Do Turner, and others—plus some white St. Paul leaders, including Mayor Kiefer, Judge Grier Orr, and attorney Thomas P. Kane. One may see here an attempt to build on the Law Enforcement League's luxury banquet of the previous April. Booker T. Washington was the man both white and black America loved, the perfect figure to draw white and black elites together to talk politely about race and related matters.

The very staging of the event might have provoked a productive conversation on race. McGhee had initially booked it at the Metropolitan Hotel, the same place that had refused Washington access to its dining room during his 1896 visit. This time the hotel accepted the booking, then reneged at the last minute, forcing its relocation to the Commercial Club. McGhee must have at least entertained the thought of bringing a high-profile civil rights lawsuit, but this was not Washington's style.

The luncheon was a great success in any case. Washington made a standard speech stressing educational and material progress for black Americans, with special emphasis on vocational education and economic self-help. Genuine political and material equality between the races would have to wait. It was a positive, nonthreatening message, with no mention of the "social equality" that Archbishop Ireland had advocated eight years before. White politicians and business leaders could support Washington because he symbolized a solution to the "Negro problem" that took place without conflict and somewhere off in the hazy future. With a kindly helping hand or two, it was assumed that the African American would someday grow up and take his separate but roughly equal place in American society.[11]

History has not been kind to Booker T. Washington. He is often portrayed as a sellout, one who mistakenly or perhaps cynically identified his own aggrandizement with that of his race. He had a share of contemporary critics who saw him that way. But there is no doubt that at this time and for many years more he enjoyed tremendous popularity among African Americans, including the majority of intellectuals and political activists. His publicly conciliatory approach, though it failed in the long run, made a great deal of sense at the time. Smart race men like Fred McGhee and John Q. Adams, while supporting more radical positions, also admired and supported Washington, with good reason. Laboring in the hostile South, he had built an educational institution, Tuskegee Institute, run entirely by and for black people, which also had wonderful support from white philanthropy. Yes, electoral politics and lawsuits were ways to fight for civil rights, but for the past twenty years these had yielded only defeat upon defeat. Washington offered an alternate, perhaps parallel, path to progress, one where powerful white men said *yes* instead of *no*. McGhee and Washington would eventually part ways (in large part because of events that took place in St. Paul), and history would conclude (at least for now) that McGhee took the better road. But for the time being the two marched together.[12]

They would meet again in Indianapolis in August, when the NAAC held its next convention. McGhee's profile in the organization continued to rise. He served with Council president Alexander Walters on the committee in charge of organizing the meeting and on the press committee with leading black journalists, including Harry Smith of the *Cleveland Gazette* and E. E. Cooper of the *Washington Bee*, and secured himself two speaking places on the convention program, including a prominent one in the opening session.

This meeting proved to be a serious and ambitious one, and attendance may have reached 200. The roster of speakers was impressive. W. E. B. Du Bois, who was at the time pioneering sociological investigations into black living conditions, spoke on "The Negro as Producer and Consumer." Professor Kelly Miller of Howard University, a teacher, scholar, and superb writer, lectured on "Education Under Negro Instructors." The courageous anti-lynching investigator and crusader Ida B. Wells Barnett spoke on "The Evils of Lynching," followed by a discussion led by T. Thomas Fortune. Delegates also heard reports from the Council's bureaus on legislation (one of McGhee's appearances), literature, education, reform, and emigration. The Council leadership clearly was determined to make the organization a serious, weighty, and long-lasting engine of black advancement.[13]

This prospect did not necessarily please Booker T. Washington, who always maintained a certain distance from the Council; it was too large and multifaceted for him to control, at least for long, and its membership included some of his loud critics. It was not in his interest to foster the growth of a black organization that might in time come to oppose him; he likely believed it was not in the race's interest, either. He would try to control the Council from within through allies, spies, and persuasion. He would also undermine it by creating a rival for its members' time and attention. In summer 1900, shortly before the Indianapolis convention, he called a meeting in Boston to organize the National Negro Business League. Creation of such a group made sense—black businessmen could certainly benefit from the support and advice of their peers—and it was perfectly consistent with Washington's bootstraps approach. But participants were likely also to be Council members and unlikely to be able to afford to attend two meetings the same summer hundreds of miles apart. The *Chicago Conservator,* edited by Ida B. Wells Barnett's husband, Ferdinand, analyzed it this way. "[I]nstead of going to Indianapolis and helping Prof. DuBois and the Council" Washington had called an opposition meeting. "It looks like Mr. Washington is determined to help no movement he does not inaugurate."[14]

Something peculiar happened to the Council in St. Paul after the Indianapolis convention: it disappeared from the news. Though John Quincy Adams, *The Appeal*'s editor and publisher, had participated as a delegate, he printed only two tiny notices of the Indianapolis gathering, very little about the Philadelphia meeting a year later, and almost nothing in between. Adams gave no reason in print for his sudden about-face from enthusiastic support of the NAAC to silence; he may have been pressured into silence by Washington. *The Appeal* did not cover the Council again until Washington took effective control of it in St. Paul in 1902.[15]

Fred McGhee continued his Council work, though it did not make the news. In early February he went on a speaking tour, beginning in Chicago, to raise money for a Council-sponsored challenge to the Louisiana disfranchising law. He did not attend the Philadelphia convention, but was elected head of the NAAC's legislative bureau just the same.[16]

The huge topic of the Philadelphia session seems to have been lynching. This scourge had never afflicted Minnesota, but in October 1901, a potential lynching victim turned up in St. Paul, and presented Fred McGhee with a unique professional challenge and opportunity. In November 1900 black Harry Summers buried an ax in the head of a white man as he entered a brothel near Bolivar, southwest Tennessee. Summers somehow escaped, and disappeared. Tennessee authorities charged him with murder and set out to track him down. Summers made his way to St. Paul, where he lived under an assumed name. St. Paul police identified him through a photograph circulated by Tennessee officials and on October 1, 1901, arrested him as a fugitive. On October 4, a municipal court judge ordered him held without bail pending his extradition to Tennessee. The next day McGhee took the case.

St. Paul's African Americans took a particular interest in the case because they feared that if Summers were returned to Tennessee, he would face a rope and flames rather than a judge and jury. *The Appeal* described the black citizens as "wrought up" to a fever pitch at this prospect. They held a meeting on October 4 to raise money "to save the poor unfortunate and almost simple-minded man from death at the hands of the mob." A committee, including Mattie McGhee, Dr. Val Do Turner, and Samuel Hardy, formed to petition the governor to deny extradition.

Fred McGhee led the citizens' delegation that met with Republican Governor Samuel Van Sant on October 10. They were so many that they filled the governor's office and reception room and spilled into the hall. McGhee tried for two hours to work his powers of persuasion on Van Sant. He had sent an emissary to Hardeman County, Tennessee, to get firsthand reports of the climate Summers would face if returned, but he told the governor that the local black folks would sign no affidavits out of fear of reprisal. Consequently, the best he could do was produce several affidavits from St. Paul residents familiar with conditions in the area attesting to the general state of lawlessness toward black people. Sheriff Sammons of Hardeman County, who had come to take Summers back, assured Governor Van Sant that passions there had subsided and Summers faced no danger from the public. No one, he asserted, had ever been lynched in his county.

The governor took the case under advisement and issued a statement the next day at noon. "The chief ground urged against this action is the general allegation made on behalf of the prisoner that he will not secure a fair trial ... and fears are expressed that he will be lynched ... If I did not believe that the said Henry Summers would receive a fair trial ... I would have no hesitancy in refusing to honor this requisition." But he found Sheriff Sammons's assurances persuasive and Tennessee's extradition request in order. Under the circumstances, he really had no choice but to order the extradition, which he did.

McGhee had anticipated this decision. The next day he filed a *habeas corpus* petition in Ramsey County District Court demanding Summers's release on various grounds of technical defects in the arrest and extradition proceedings. According to one report, McGhee arrived with an order delaying extradition just 30 minutes before departure of the train carrying Summers back to Tennessee. The district court denied the petition, and McGhee appealed immediately to the state supreme court. Neither the white nor the black press took notice, but when Fredrick McGhee rose to address the panel of justices on November 27, 1901, he became the first African-American attorney to argue a case to the Minnesota supreme court. He quickly became the first to lose a case there; the court rejected his appeal and Summers was returned to Tennessee, where he was not lynched but tried, convicted of second-degree murder, and sentenced to eight years in prison. What became of him after that, no one knows.[17]

The Summers mobilization and defense, the Law Enforcement League, and the NAAC all arose from the same powerful and essentially conservative, red, white, and blue faith among African Americans in the principles of the United States Constitution. They believed in the rule of law. Fred McGhee, not alone but more conspicuously and more effectively than any other Minnesotan of his time, worked to make the rule of law a reality for black Americans.

7

All Else Is the Sea

Before examining the exciting events of 1902, it is necessary to pause and consider the aspect of Fred McGhee's life and career that more than anything else sets him apart from his contemporaries: his conversion and loyalty to the Democratic Party. Frederick Douglass once wrote, "The Republican party is the ship; all else is the sea," and so it was for political African Americans in those days. The party had supported the war that ended slavery, a war in which many of its leaders, including Presidents Grant, Hayes, Garfield, and Harrison, had risked their lives. The party had pushed through the Civil War amendments to the Constitution and waged Reconstruction—not long enough or forcefully enough, we can say today, but this was less clear at the time. The Republican Party offered the only place for politically interested black Americans to participate, get close to power, and have an opportunity for patronage.

Putting aside the rhetoric of the "party of Lincoln" and approaching the matter pragmatically, the Republicans were the people with the national swag to spread. From 1860 onward, for the next forty-eight years, they maintained almost continuous majorities in Congress and won every presidential election but two. Northern black Americans had looked around and seen that white party workers who labored loyally and delivered votes often got rewarded with patronage jobs. Black Republicans applied the lesson with some success—a clerkship here, a customs collector's position there, professional positions in the Washington, D.C. public schools. The great Frederick Douglass himself led the way, with appointments as the D.C. register of deeds and then minister to Haiti. The party was not generous, far from it, but for a people just one step out of slavery, these jobs were tremendously important. They gave appropriate employment to at least a few men of education and ability and showed everyone that African Americans could do the job, including the job of government, as well as or better than anyone else.

Fred McGhee had, when still a Republican, experienced some of the benefits of party connections. When Lewis Carter's mother wanted her son freed from prison, Republican Congressman Sam Snider had a word with Republican President Benjamin Harrison, and the deed was done. When horse thief Frank Conway's friends hired McGhee to get him out of prison, McGhee went straight to the office of Republican Governor William Merriam, and soon Conway walked free. The Minnesota branch of the party had at first welcomed McGhee; at age twenty-nine and having resided less than two years in the state, he had been named to the party's central committee, a considerable and significant honor.

The national Democratic Party reacted to black enfranchisement by going lily white, basing itself in the South, and there destroying the black franchise with relentless ingenuity, energy, and cruelty. Where the party had strength in the North, such as among immigrant and ethnic groups, it could have used some black votes to swing districts and states, but to pursue them conspicuously would have risked the white southern votes upon which it relied. Moreover, some of the party's leaders, exemplified by South Carolina governor, then Senator, "Pitchfork" Ben Tillman, were monsters of white supremacy and proud of it. Democrat sheriffs and governors across the South winked at lynchings. The party had blood on its hands, and the whole country knew that the Democratic Party stood for "keeping the niggers down."

So why did Fred McGhee leave the party of Lincoln for the party of Tillman? It all goes back to the presidential election of 1892. When the Minnesota Republican Party's central committee removed him from its roster of presidential electors, McGhee protested, boycotted, and fumed, but ultimately "pocketed" (to use a term of the time) the insult and returned to the campaign platform, ostensibly reconciled. The wound, however, had gone deep. When the party betrayed McGhee for a second time in spring 1893 he left it and never looked back, except in anger.

With the help of McGhee and other African-American voters, St. Paul Republicans had won a stunning victory in the city elections of May 1892, taking the mayor's office and majorities in city council and city assembly. This gave them the power to appoint a new city attorney and three assistants in March 1893. The state party had purchased McGhee's loyalty in the 1892 fall campaign by promising him one these jobs, probably the third assistantship. Though McGhee was overqualified—it was a misdemeanor prosecution position, and he had had lots of felony experience—the job would have been a plum. It paid a comfortable salary of $1,200 a year, offered steady trial work, and promised wonderful political connections. The black community would lose its defender, but gain a prominent and presumably rising public official. On March 11, 1893, the city council appointed Leon T. Chamberlain city attorney.

Chamberlain knew McGhee from party work, and the two had shared a campaign speaking-platform in the spring. On March 15, Chamberlain announced his choice: the job, once promised to McGhee, went to Walter Chapin.

Though Chapin was certainly qualified—he was an active Republican and had held the job before—McGhee's race probably cost him the position. The promises made to him had been state party business months ago, and Leon Chamberlain now had other concerns, local and practical ones. A writer to the *St. Paul Globe* stated that he had it on good authority that Chamberlain decided against McGhee "because the Irish people would never forgive him if he appointed a colored lawyer to prosecute them in the police courts."[1]

Chamberlain may have based his decision on the simple politics of arithmetic—more Irish voters in St. Paul than African-American ones—but Fred McGhee took it personally. He did not just leave the Republican Party; he embraced the Democrats with the zeal of a convert, and detested the Republicans the rest of his life. He next appears in Minnesota politics in spring 1894, when he made speech after speech in rallies all over the city urging the defeat of the party he had helped elect just two years before.

McGhee must have understood the profound implications of his act. The people who had brought him to Minnesota and with whom he most closely worked on race issues were Republicans. Being an active Democrat meant permanent political (though not personal) estrangement from local and national African-American leadership, which for all of his life remained overwhelmingly and steadfastly Republican. Friends and allies who had so much invested in McGhee's career, men like John Quincy Adams, must have been devastated to find Minnesota's black leadership now politically divided.

During McGhee's twenty-three years in Minnesota, Republicans controlled state government; from the moment of his conversion forward, when he went to the capitol to speak to the governor (with one exception—Democrat John Lind's single two-year term) or legislators, he no longer went as a man who could make them a speech or deliver them votes. Party events, for business and pleasure, were now closed to him. To some extent the Democratic dominance in St. Paul politics compensated—McGhee did receive some local favors—but on the whole, the practical negatives outweighed the positives.

The Democrat Grover Cleveland won the 1892 presidential election, but his performance could not have encouraged many blacks to follow McGhee's lead. He did nothing to resist the lynchings, disfranchisement, and Jim Crow legislation that his party imposed on the South. He probably could not have stopped it, but in any even he did not try.[2]

As Cleveland's term approached its end, in 1896, an irresistible westerly wind carried a very different sort of politician to the head of the party—the thirty-six-year-old Nebraskan William Jennings Bryan. Bryan's power base lay not in the South but in the West and Midwest, among farmers and the silver interests; that is, people who favored the inflationary policy of free coinage of silver and opposed the Republican policies of high tariffs and tight money. Bryan really had nothing to say about civil rights or the "Negro question." Had he advocated African-American interests, he could not have been nominated. But he was interested in economic justice, and this was something that black Americans could understand; high tariffs and tight money hurt black consumers and businessmen in the North and the millions of black farmers in the South.[3]

On the evening of October 10, 1896, William Jennings Bryan, now the Democratic nominee for president (against William McKinley, a Republican Civil War veteran), made a campaign stop in St. Paul. A large crowd filled the St. Paul Auditorium, awaiting Bryan's arrival. A little after 8 P.M., Fred McGhee

William Jennings Bryan (center), with Governor John A. Johnson (left),
and Frank Day, in Minnesota, 1908. Photograph by George E. Luxton.

walked onto the speaker's platform. According to the *St. Paul Globe,* a Democratic paper, "his appearance was greeted with cries of 'McGhee, McGhee, Speech, Speech.'" McGhee obliged, and compared the 1896 election to the Civil War; the war had been fought over the slavery of black man to white; the election dealt with the slavery of labor to capital.

> "But the bloody shirt is dead," exclaimed Mr. McGhee, "and I stand upon it. And now from one end of the country to another the common people are waiting to hear the gospel of the new dispensation preached by that great tribune of the people, William Jennings Bryan!" (Prolonged cheering.)
>
> "Remember that we, the people, made this country before capital ever breathed in it. (Applause.) It was the common people who laid the foundation for capital and it is too late now to tell the people that the foundation of a house is no part of the house.
>
> "Who is it that claims that America can't do what she wants to do? It wouldn't be wise for me to discuss the financial situation, since it is said that the common people don't know anything about it and therefore can't talk about it. And if the white people don't know anything about it, how can a poor darkey like me be expected to understand it?" (Laughter and applause.)

The *Pioneer Press* gave a similar account of the speech: "He emphasized his opinion that this was a struggle between the common people and the moneyed classes. He insisted that the people were making a fight to determine whether this was really a government by the people." A victory of Bryan and the silver forces might mean trouble for and from the East Coast financiers and European governments, but the United States was strong enough to stand the challenge. "We have made this country and we can make it over again, if we want to." [4]

This speech reveals a lot about Fred McGhee. If the *Globe* account is correct, ordinary Democrats knew McGhee by sight and knew of his oratory, hence the cries of "Speech, Speech," when he appeared. The phrase "bloody shirt" refers literally to a Union soldier's tunic stained with Union blood; symbolically it refers to the damage done the nation by the Southern insurrection. By saying, "the bloody shirt is dead," McGhee meant that the Civil War was behind the people, and that it was time to put aside blame and sectionalism and move on to the current issues. For a black man born a slave, freed by Union soldiers, and devoted to fighting Jim Crow in the former Confederacy, this is an extraordinary statement. In many ways the Civil War was not over because gains supposedly won, such as the end of slavery and full citizenship for freedmen, were being lost through peonage, disfranchisement, and the national government's indifference to both. But for this audience at least, and for this candidate, McGhee made economic issues paramount. The great battle now became a class battle, between the common people—including, McGhee's presence and complexion implied, black people—and the forces of capital.

One can see a glimmer of how McGhee could overlook the many sins of the Democratic Party. The majority of African Americans were poor farmers and farm laborers, similar to Bryan's constituency in the West, Midwest, and South. Northern blacks were mainly urban and poor, laborers like Bryan's northern urban ethnic constituency. If these constituencies could unite across racial and sectional lines, they could achieve economic improvement for all. Then perhaps race differences would not mean so much.

William McKinley, running on a platform of high tariffs and the gold standard, defeated Bryan in 1896. Civil rights played no part in the campaign, and the huge majority of black voters voted Republican. McKinley did no more for black Americans than Cleveland had done, but during his administration the economy prospered and the nation won a profitable war. As the 1900 election approached, the national mood was much happier than four years before. The Democrats nevertheless looked to send Bryan back into battle against McKinley using the same issues that had failed him the last time.

Minnesota Democrats selected Fred McGhee as an alternate delegate to the national convention in Kansas City, probably the first such honor given a black man in the state, and similar to the honor conferred and then rescinded by the Republican Party eight years earlier. When McGhee headed south in early July, he had not one but two political conventions to attend; just before the Democratic convention opened, the National Negro Democratic League met in Kansas City. McGhee did not merely participate—he tried to take over. He tried, at least, to unseat the League's founder and president, George Taylor of Oskaloosa, Iowa, by running against him for League president. He mounted a "stirring contest," but failed. At the close of the meeting, however, McGhee "spoke at considerable length and urged that a committee of twenty-five be selected to prepare an address setting forth the reasons why the Afro-Americans should no longer blindly follow the Republican party." The League adopted the suggestion, creating a committee of fourteen with McGhee as its chairman.[5]

The Address, published two weeks later, listed McGhee's name first among its signatories, and probably represents his political thinking at the time. If so, this is the best record extant of Fred McGhee's political beliefs. The Address argues effectively why black voters should reject the Republican Party; less effectively why they should vote Democrat. One of the arguments was that the

Republican Party did not reciprocate black loyalty. While black voters had remained steadfast, McGhee stated that the party leadership "has engaged in ex-
erting every effort to forget, forgive, and shake hands across the bloody
chasm." Though no Republican presidential candidate since Grant could have
been elected without black votes in crucial East and Midwest states, "the Republican party has given no fitting recognition for the Negroes in these states."

Four years earlier Fred McGhee had proclaimed to his Democratic listeners in St. Paul that the "bloody shirt" was dead; that is, that the Civil War's sectional rift should be healed. Here a document issued at his insistence and over
his signature condemns the Republicans for shaking hands "across the bloody
chasm." So, were we able to ask him: "When is it permissible to reconcile
politically with the southern whites?" The answer seems to be, "Not under
Republican leadership, because Republicans do it hypocritically and give nothing in return. Republicans have proven themselves beyond redemption. Under
Bryan-led Democracy, by contrast, there is hope of uniting poor whites and
poor blacks against the forces of capital."[6]

His second point was, *President McKinley has denied equal treatment to
Negroes in the military.* In the Spanish-American War, blacks had not been permitted to serve as command officers, even in all-black units; and black troops
had been treated terribly in their training and staging camps in the South. This
criticism was unquestionably accurate, and it indicates how African American
war euphoria had to some extent given way to a clearer analysis.

McGhee wrote, *Theodore Roosevelt has slandered the race.* Vice-presidential
candidate Roosevelt became a national hero fighting the Spanish at San Juan
Hill in Cuba. At first he had praised the black soldiers (Tenth Cavalry and 24th
Infantry) who had fought at the Rough Riders' side. Later, though, he enraged
many black citizens with comments, widely reprinted in the black press, about
blacks in battle. They are, he said, "peculiarly dependent upon their white
officers." Whereas white soldiers had shown no weakness in combat, when the
shooting started, "the colored infantry men began to get a little uneasy and
drift to the rear." So Roosevelt said he pursued them, pistol drawn, and ordered them back to the front, upon pain of instant execution. "This was the
end of the trouble, for the 'smoked yankees' ... flashed their white teeth at one
another as they broke into their broad grins, and I had no more trouble with
them ... "

One reason black citizens supported the war was because of the opportunities it might have provided to prove their patriotism and abilities. Then the
country's greatest war hero told the world that black soldiers would grin and

fight well only when a white officer had a gun to their backs; a deep and pa-
tronizing insult. This, again, McGhee said, is how Republicans repaid black
sacrifice.

Negroes should not support imperialism. With victory over Spain, the United
States had become an imperial power, ruling dark-skinned people in Cuba,
Puerto Rico, and the Philippines. The subjugation of any people is "criminal
aggression," and a violation of the principles of Washington, Jefferson, and
Lincoln. "[I]f we are prepared to support an administration that is engaged in
suppressing liberty and freedom in our so-called possessions, why not be consistent and cease to complain of the same thing being done in any part of our
own land?"

The Address might have gone further: the United States was now employing black soldiers to suppress independence movements of black and brown-
skinned people after a war conducted ostensibly to free those people from
Spanish imperialism. This criticism reflected Fred McGhee's personal opinion,
as we shall see. William Jennings Bryan also opposed these imperialist ventures, which gave blacks a positive reason to vote for him.

The gold standard hurts black Americans. "The Negro is not an investor of
capital. Those who insist that gold alone shall be the money of the land give
no employment to the Negro, though employing thousands of laborers."

This portion of the Address conflated the gold standard with industrial
concentration and the choking of small ventures by the large. It did not mention the bad effect of the gold standard, which meant tight money, even defla-
tion, on black farmers. This poorly written section seems to stand for the
proposition that Republicans favor big business, which does nothing to help
blacks though it could readily do so; and this was true.

Indeed, all of the criticisms of the Republican Party were just. But when it
came to offering reasons to vote Democrat, the Address was less persuasive.
Detaching the black vote from its heretofore solid loyalty to the Republicans
would increase its value by putting it in play—somehow, some way, this would
prove beneficial.

"Democrats are not the natural enemies of the Negro," assured the writers—not the most compelling of statements. Since the Republican-led national
government has abandoned civil rights, protection can come only from the
states where black rights are most in peril, in the South. And the South is controlled by Democrats. "It is, therefore, to use the words of Prof. Booker T.
Washington, 'The plain duty of the Negro to make friends with the southern
white man.'" Blacks can ensure protection of their life and property, and ex-

ercise of their constitutional rights "only upon the terms agreeable to and acceptable to the southern white men." The only man capable of welding this "bond of friendship" between the races is "that great commoner of the plain people, the tribune of the rights of man against money, William Jennings Bryan." The invocation of Washington has a nice irony to it: Washington was a staunch Republican.

The Address here has an illusionless, almost despairing realism to it: The masses of our people live in the South, where the national government will not protect them. So long as we remain Republicans, we are the southern white man's political enemy; and since we cannot defeat him, we must therefore embrace him. It looks forward to a long-term payoff at best.[7]

It is difficult to change a generation-long voting tradition with arguments such as these—something more compelling is usually required. Fred McGhee, it seems, chose to try a gigantic rhetorical feat: to transform in the mind of the black voter the image of the Democratic Party from that of the oppressor to that of the liberator.

In October 1900 McGhee published an article in *Howard's American Magazine*, a national black monthly, on the subject of American imperialism in the Philippines:

> We were freed by a people not of our race; a people who largely regarded us as their inferiors, and now our first generation of freedmen are called upon to decide which party we will serve; the one whose declared determination is to give liberty to an oppressed people, a race also classed among the inferior races, to give them a government of their own, free from outside interference and control, or the party which has determined to pursue the policy it has been pursuing for the past years, compelling the people by force of superior resources, army and navy, to submit to foreign control and be the subjects of a people of whom they are not a part and to accept a government in which they have no voice.

Fredrick McGhee in his office, from St. Paul Globe, *October 19, 1902.*

Also in October McGhee blasted black Americans' faith in the Republican Party. He noted that the national party owed its electoral dominance to black voters, yet not only neglected them but had positively collaborated in black disfranchisement in the South. It was "engaged in the business of oppressing mankind," he said, and blacks who supported the party joined in the crime. "The Negro who votes for McKinley becomes a party to the rape upon the Filipino .... He forgets his right to demand the benefits of the Constitution for himself. He directly contributes to the nullification of the war amendments to the federal Constitution." Imperialism abroad is inseparable from racism at home, he argued. "The fruit of expansion may look tempting to the eye," he warned, "but it is rotten in the middle, and the Negro who eats it, eats it to his own destruction."

In this formulation the Democrats were the party of "liberty to an oppressed people," while the Republicans by force compelled a brown-skinned race to submit to a government in which they had no voice. In foreign relations, at least, the Republicans at that time had become the party of enslavement and the Democrats the party of emancipation. The rightful heir to the legacy of Lincoln was not McKinley but William Jennings Bryan.[8]

Earlier that same month, Fred McGhee had made precisely that symbolic identification, Bryan with Lincoln, in a campaign rally in St. Paul, and he paid a heavy price for it. Bryan made a quick campaign stop in St. Paul on the evening of October 1. While the crowd waited for him, Thomas Kane, Democratic candidate for county attorney, made a speech attacking U.S. policy in the Philippines, and then, as Bryan entered the hall, McGhee came to the podium with a gift for the great man, a multivolume biography of Lincoln. "I present these books to you," he said, "in the name of the colored people of St. Paul, of the state, of the reunited North and South, upon which the Negro places his seal and benediction." The *St. Paul Globe* reported also that McGhee proclaimed that "the principles of Lincoln were today exemplified by Col. Bryan."

Bryan never made race a big part of his campaigns, but he did seek black votes in 1900, and he was ready on this occasion. "The Negro has fully repaid the present leaders of the Republican Party for all they have ever done for him. The colored people have conferred upon the Republican Party presidencies and received janitorships in return." The he went on to economic issues:

> The colored man knows that he is the victim of every vicious policy for which the Republican Party stands. More of the colored race are engaged in the production of cotton, and they have received no benefit from a protective tariff but were the victims of it when they spent the proceeds of their crops. The colored man is not, as a rule, a money lender and the holder of investments, and he has no profits in the gold standard. And a colored man

shares with others in the evils of monopoly, for when the trust stalks through the land and lays upon all a destroying hand, and even the blood of Lincoln, sprinkled upon the door posts of the colored cottage would not exempt him from the trust action. The colored man finds no profit, no advantage from the policy which the Republican Party stands for.

This passage could have been written by the National Negro Democrats—economics as a race issue. It was a way to court black votes without promising any positive federal action on civil rights.[9]

Fred McGhee's moment with Bryan provoked three days of bitter denunciations in St. Paul's leading paper, the *Pioneer Press*. The following day it editorialized under the caption, "Mr. Bryan Gets a Present." The editorial correctly pointed out that Bryan's hopes for election rested first on carrying the South, and the southern voters (virtually all white) would hardly support Bryan if they believed he would interfere with black disfranchisement.

In view of these facts it was pathetic to the last degree to see a representative of the race thus proscribed and oppressed by Mr. Bryan's party come forward at the Bryan meeting last night and present the presidential candidate of the Democratic party with—what do you suppose? Of all the things in the world—with a life of Lincoln, the great emancipator of the Negro race. And he did this not to rebuke the Democratic candidate, who had never uttered a word of sympathy for these downtrodden countrymen of his own color in the Southern States—but, with a stupid unconsciousness of the blasting irony of the act, in dead earnest, as a tribute of admiring homage to the leader of the oppressors of his race.[10]

The next day the *Pioneer Press* returned to the attack with another editorial, this one entitled "Comfort for McGhee." The article claimed that in Bryan's speech he had admitted that the country suffered from racial prejudice, and therefore it would be a grave error to admit into the nation yet another brown people, the Filipinos. The *Pioneer Press* reasoned that by this comment Bryan revealed that he deemed all dark-skinned people incapable of self-government.

Mr. McGhee is to be congratulated on his new Lincoln, on his new liberator, the chief candidate of the party which holds and proposed to hold the Negro in the chains of a perpetual political serfdom, and from whom not a single word could be extorted indicative of the slightest disposition with this execrable program of his party.

The paper finished up on October 5, pointing out that Bryan's remark about black Republicans being rewarded with janitorships was disingenuous in the extreme. "When did Mr. Bryan's party ever elect a Negro senator or representative?"[11]

Everything the *Pioneer Press* wrote about the Democratic Party was true; that Fred McGhee suffered from a "stupid unconsciousness of the blasting irony" of comparing Bryan to Lincoln, however, is unlikely. Lincoln, after all, had freed McGhee's family from slavery, and he had to have known that Bryan could never be a hero to black people the way Lincoln had been. Still, McGhee's praise of Bryan must have made his friends and comrades wince and wonder how he could embrace as a champion of the race the head of the party of Tillman. *The Appeal* made no comment on the incident; although John Quincy Adams was an unwavering Republican, he rarely criticized McGhee in print. If Fred McGhee ever answered his critics, his responses have not come to light.

In any event the attempt to portray William Jennings Bryan as a second Lincoln failed. He did poorly among black voters and lost to McKinley by an even greater margin than he had four years before.[12]

A year after the election Bryan revealed an astonishing, or perhaps willful, ignorance about the state of race relations in America. Theodore Roosevelt had become president upon the assassination of William McKinley in September 1901. One of the early acts of his presidency had been to invite Booker T. Washington to dine at the White House. The event brought Roosevelt praise and good feeling from black America but also generated plenty of criticism; many whites felt it unwise and a step toward the dreaded "social equality."

The dinner provoked Bryan to make a long statement on the "Negro question" in his paper, *The Commoner.* "The action of President Roosevelt in inviting Prof. Booker T. Washington to dine at the White House," he began, "was unfortunate, to say the least. It will give depth and acrimony to a race feeling already strained to the uppermost." From there he went on to say that blacks in the South had not been denied any of their constitutional rights. He counseled black leaders not to seek social equality; it would be unwise at best, dangerous at worst. Unthinkable, really: "[N]o man or party has advocated social equality between the white man or the black man." This must have come as a surprise to Fred McGhee, who had shared a platform with John Ireland ten years earlier when the archbishop called for precisely that.[13]

Nothing ever shook McGhee's loyalty to Bryan, but Theodore Roosevelt impressed him enough that in 1904 McGhee privately—but not publicly—supported his reelection. The Democratic candidate that year, New York Judge

Alton Parker (probably the least-remembered major party candidate of the century) had nothing to say on civil rights issues and so gave black Democrats nothing with which to work. Booker T. Washington saw the opportunity to draw McGhee back into Republican clutches; in August 1904 he wrote urging him to endorse Roosevelt and campaign for him.

McGhee replied in a long letter full of doubt and hesitation. "I am very anxious for the re-election of Mr. Roosevelt," he admitted, but making a public endorsement was not so simple.

First, he reasoned, it was unnecessary: Roosevelt was likely to win and certain to carry the black vote, in Minnesota and elsewhere, overwhelmingly. Were this not the case, however, "I would not hesitate to tender my services to the Republican National Committee."

Second, to support publicly the Republican *national* candidate would betray his *local* party and sunder connections and relationships built up over the course of years.

> I must also consider my own interest. . . . The Democratic party show me every consideration that I have asked for—more than any Negro now enjoys at the hands of the Republican party of this state or will for many a year to come. . . . For ten years I have worked and been associated with the Democratic party. Could I at all influence the Negro vote in other parts of the country, they would be justified in charging me with desertion when every influence was needed most. . . . I have made many attachments and alliances, and I can less afford now to break off and form new ones than I could then [ten years ago.]

Finally, he must have felt that however bad the national Democratic Party might have been in some respects, it was vital to African-American interests to maintain a presence in it. "I say, though it smacks of conceit, that one of the great drawbacks in reaching Democratic leaders and affecting good in the party is that there are but few men of respect and standing among its Negro constituents. Should those few drop away now? I fear it must need be harmful to the race."

This letter clarifies three aspects of McGhee's Democracy. His support for the national party was closely tied to his devotion to William Jennings Bryan. With Bryan out of the picture, McGhee wavered. But he made a clear distinction between the national party and the local. "The Democratic party as a whole seems committed against the race," he acknowledged, but his local allegiances were too strong to be overcome. What finally tipped the balance was the need to preserve an African-American voice in the party, perhaps especially during those those hard times, "to strengthen and encourage that right ele-ment in the party to stand out against the other." What's more, he said, he did not expect the Republican Party to follow Roosevelt's lead in race issues.[14]

Though McGhee agonized and wavered in 1904, he made the only choice consistent with his principles and values. He supported the principle, pro-claimed but rarely honored by the Afro-American League and the NAAC, of black political independence. Keeping this principle alive required black men of ability and honor in both parties. This principle had a pragmatic element, too. St. Paul was a Democratic town, then as now. For black St. Paulites to vote solidly Republican would make them a minority within a minority, and in this pre-civil service age shut them out of government jobs. With McGhee leading local black Democrats, some, including his brother-in-law, father-in-law, and fellow Catholics O. C. Hall and James Loomis, got patronage work. And Fred McGhee valued loyalty highly. The Republicans had betrayed him, while St. Paul Democrats "show me every consideration I could ask for." McGhee re-paid loyalty with loyalty.

It was personal, too: being a St. Paul Democrat brought McGhee joy. When he was still a Republican in the spring 1892 elections, the city party sent him out on just one campaign appearance. In his first campaign as a Democrat he made more than a dozen speeches, all over the city, to large and enthusiastic crowds. Newspaper accounts from this era reveal a gleeful, boisterous local politics inconceivable today. For three weeks before municipal elections the major parties held rallies in every ward, every night (except Sunday). Four, six, eight speakers would blast their evil adversaries to the delight of hooting mul-titudes. McGhee reveled in the tumult and energy of these events, and made more than 100 such speeches over the years. He specialized in caustic wit, scor-ing Republican candidates and officials for corruption and incompetence. Within months after turning Democrat, Democrat voters regularly hailed him on the campaign platform and demanded that he speak. Fred McGhee was the first black Minnesotan to be spontaneously recognized and hailed in public, and probably the last until major league professional sports came to the Twin Cities in the 1960s. For a man who loved to orate, the adulation must have been powerful. What's more, Democrats usually won elections as judges, court clerks, and prosecutors. For a man who made his living in the courthouse, it was better to have political friends there than enemies.

The only news we have of McGhee's participation in the 1904 national campaign was his signature to the National Negro Democrats' Address to the Nation. His name appears first after the list of the organization's officers,

suggesting that he remained an important player. The Address, only a frag-
ment of which has survived, has a halfhearted ring to it, reflecting no doubt
the national party's lack of interest in black votes. It urges African Americans
to vote Democrat for two reasons, neither of them likely to persuade the
undecided—to demonstrate to whites that black voters are thoughtful and
patriotic, and in the interest of the common good. It counseled them of "the
necessity of tempering the harsh and inequitable sentiment against the
Negro ... by establishing beyond quibble that back of the Negro vote is a
sturdy patriotism and pains-taking thought. Such impression can not be
made by maintaining insane political solidity in support of any party." Blacks
should vote for the people's party, he said, because "when the Negro becomes
the advocate of the rights of all men, all men will be appreciative of the
Negro's manhood rights." Not surprisingly, black Americans overwhelmingly
rejected the Democratic Party in 1904.[15]

Roosevelt continued the customary Republican practice of appointing
a certain number of black party loyalists to patronage positions; beyond that,
he mainly left race alone. Roosevelt was brave and progressive in many areas,
but not this one. Many black Americans felt betrayed by his handling of
the Brownsville affair. On August 13, 1906, black soldiers stationed near
Brownsville, Texas, got involved in a melee that ended with a riotous shoot-up
of the town and the death of a white bartender. The army did a quiet investigation and submitted its report to the president. Roosevelt made a disciplinary
decision, but withheld it until after the 1906 elections, when black votes were
valuable in some northern states and districts. The following day, as he travelled to Panama, the decision became public: 167 black soldiers, many of them
Spanish-American War veterans, were dismissed from the army with forfeiture
of pension. The soldiers would have no day in court and no appeal. None of
their white officers was disciplined. African Americans, especially loyal Republicans, took deep offense.[16]

For some, such as W. E. B. Du Bois, this was the last straw. The president
and the party had revealed their true natures: black Americans would be used
for their votes and whatever other services they might provide, but be sacrificed whenever politically convenient. Fred McGhee had been saying this for
over a decade, so he probably enjoyed feeling a little less lonely during the
1908 presidential campaign, when he once again supported William Jennings
Bryan. Du Bois came out publicly for Bryan as well: "It is high noon, brethren,
the clock has struck twelve. What are we going to do? I have made up my
mind. You can do as you please—you are free, sane, and twenty-one. If between

the two parties who stand on identically the same platform you can prefer the party who perpetrated Brownsville, well and good! But I shall vote for Bryan." At this time, McGhee and Du Bois were close friends and comrades in civil rights work.[17]

McGhee campaigned and spoke for Bryan in 1908, but we have no details. It did not help. Bryan received almost precisely the same number of votes he had gotten in 1896 and 1900, with the same losing result.[18]

As the 1912 presidential election approached, McGhee made clear that his 1904 moment of weakness—when he considered supporting a Republican— had been a passing thing. On July 10, 1912, the *Pioneer Press* printed a short editorial complaining that Republicans in Alabama, almost all of whom were black, were being given delegate representation at the Republican National Convention far out of proportion to their production of actual votes. They had in the last elections given the party just 19,290 votes in the entire state, compared to 21,390 in Ramsey County alone; yet Alabama received 12 delegate positions, Ramsey County just two.[19]

McGhee wrote in reply two days later. He did not dispute the unfairness, but rather asked readers to consider where the fault lay. It was not with the black Republicans of Alabama.

> Why is it that there is no Republican party in the South? ... Is it because the people are indifferent and won't vote, or because by reason of grandfather clauses, educational tests and other make shifts put into the hands of registrars by which Negroes ... are denied the right to vote? ...
>
> Is there no power in the country to re-enfranchise these Negroes? Yes, there is, but those who have the power have stubbornly refused to exercise it and now these self same men who have stood by, saw the ballot taken from the negro, refuse to raise a finger to restore it.

He recalled the 1884 Republican National Convention, held in Chicago, when, as he remembered it, the party had made a fateful decision: to give up trying to build a black voting base in the South. "[T]hus ended the old order of doing things and thus began the new, that has been a sham, an injustice and a disgrace to both my race and the Republican party."[20]

And thus, in nearly the last letter McGhee ever published, he returned to the fundamental and unchanging reason why he had left the Republican Party and refused to return: It had the obligation and the power to enforce African-American civil rights, but it refused to do so. It had betrayed the race.

8

Crossing the Rubicon

The city of St. Paul has never hosted a more distinguished and accomplished assembly of citizens than it did in summer 1902, when Booker T. Washington, W. E. B. Du Bois, Ida B. Wells Barnett, T. Thomas Fortune, and a host of others came to the fifth annual National Afro-American Council meeting. It proved to be a grand event and a watershed in the life of the Council and the career of Fred McGhee.

For such a small community as the Twin Cities' African Americans, hosting such a prominent national gathering meant both opportunity and peril. The stakes in such occasions are high. The hosts want to show off their city, run everything smoothly, make sure everyone has a good time, and, if possible, achieve important substantive results as well. In short, they want everyone to go home thinking, "That St. Paul meeting was the best ever." But when they have never before arranged so large or so politically sensitive a gathering, and where resources are limited, the chances of failure—that people will recall the St. Paul meeting as not up to par—increase. The man given chief responsibility for making the meeting turn out right was Fred McGhee.

As chairman of the general committee on arrangements, McGhee was responsible for hiring meeting halls, finding housing for the guests and delegates, raising money to cover costs, persuading people to attend, and a host of related details. He also had a keen interest in the substantive program, for technical success in staging the event would be forgotten if the organization failed to meet its political goals. Wrapped up in all of this too, were McGhee's own interests: he was an ambitious man searching for his proper place in national leadership. A successful St. Paul meeting—for the city and for Fred McGhee personally—required large attendance, the most distinguished headliners possible, and a showing of unity, momentum, and purpose. These things McGhee set about to achieve.

The single most vital ingredient of a truly successful NAAC meeting would be the participation and support of Booker T. Washington. He had skipped two of the three previous ones, and the 1901 convention in Philadelphia had turned out to be a notable failure, with low attendance and very little press coverage. McGhee had no intention of letting this happen on his watch. As early as March 1902, possibly before, he corresponded with Washington, through Washington's secretary, Emmett Scott, about the terms of his participation. On March 29, he wrote to Tuskegee that insofar as the business sessions were concerned, "everything connected with that is left to your discretion and suggestion." He added a handwritten note asking Scott to be sure to get Washington to come; "our people will feel bad if we do not get him."[1]

A week later McGhee wrote again, this time to Washington directly, expressing his "deep anxiety concerning your coming to the meeting." The Council, he lamented, "has no well defined course." It needed wise counsel to devise sound policies and strategies, he wrote. "It is not a flattery when I say that we can't safely adopt that policy without your judgment and advice." McGhee feared that without Washington's restraining influence, others would push their own selfish agendas. But recognizing the great man's distaste for "wrangling," he assured Washington that "we are free to arrange our program so that you will not be placed under an embarrassment."[2]

This is a revealing letter. Two weeks earlier McGhee had written to Washington's secretary, Emmett Scott, that the Council's bureaus were not functioning, and that it was hard to get reliable information from anyone, including its president, Bishop Alexander Walters. Here he confessed to Washington that the Council had "no well defined course" and needed his guidance to set itself right. Indeed, the NAAC could not "safely" adopt any policy without the great man's counsel. The letter read like a plea: "Come and take over, and all will be arranged for your convenience." It is a letter that McGhee would come to regret.

If Washington replied to the letter, no copy has survived. When the Council published its official call for the meeting in May, Washington's name appeared nowhere in the program. But McGhee and others probably knew that he would attend—as always, on his own terms.[3]

As spring 1902 wore on, McGhee and the other organizers, including John Q. Adams, William T. Francis, and photographer Harry Shepherd, had a thousand things to do. They designed and printed stationery featuring photographs of Minnehaha Falls, St. Paul's new High Bridge, Fort Snelling, and Como Park. They hired the senate chamber of the old State Capitol for business sessions and Central Presbyterian and House of Hope Presbyterian Churches for evening entertainment and education sessions, and the University of Minnesota Armory for a banquet. They arranged lodging, mostly in private homes, for scores of guests. They organized parties, receptions, and musical programs featuring the best of local African-American talent.⁴ By the time June gave way to July it is likely that nearly every middle-class black family in the Twin Cities had contributed time, effort, or talent to the enterprise. For three days, July 9–11, St. Paul would be the political and intellectual capital of black America.

A musical program held on the evening of July 7 illustrates the extent to which the black citizens of Minnesota had resolved to show their guests a good time. It began with a piano solo written for the occasion by W. A. Weir. Next came "Hail to the Chief" by a chorus of ten with organ accompaniment, followed by an aria from Bizet's *Carmen*. Cyrus Field Adams gave a speech, "The Outlook for the Race," and then music resumed: a soprano solo, the soldiers' chorus from Gounod's *Faust* sung by a choir of 30, a piano duet from *Il Trovatore*, Handel's "Hallelujah Chorus," a violin solo and, to end, "Ave Maria" sung by two members of the St. Peter Claver Choir.⁵

The Council sessions began the morning of July 9 in the old capitol. Mayor Robert Smith (a Democrat) gave a welcoming speech, as did Governor Samuel

National Afro-American Council meeting, St. Paul. Booker T. Washington stands in the front row, hat in hand; McGhee stands two rows behind him.

Van Sant, who recounted an incident from his own Civil War service. He had been a private in the army when the order came from Lincoln that black soldiers would be used in combat. When it was read to the troops, "I stepped out and proposed three cheers. There was not a response from my regiment. A short time after that a black brigade saved that regiment from annihilation. Then there were cheers for the Negroes and they were given with a will." Many more speeches followed—this was a great speechifying age—and then there was a stirring and commotion, for suddenly the great man himself, Booker T. Washington, appeared and was escorted to a seat on the platform "amidst the applause of the Council." He held no office in the Council nor any place in the program, but everyone knew that his influence would be felt and his voice, sooner or later, heard.[6]

That afternoon Council President Bishop Alexander Walters made his keynote speech, in which he concentrated chiefly on two issues of abiding concern: black suffrage and whether black Americans in the South should stay or leave. On both, he took the Bookerite position.

Across the South, one method legislatures had used to keep blacks from voting was to require them to demonstrate a certain level of education. Blacks did not have the political strength to resist such laws, so one of the few strategies available to their leaders was to say, in effect: "All right, impose your educational qualifications, but impose them on all, white and black alike." If that were truly done, then only the better-educated and presumably more enlightened whites would do the voting, while blacks worked to educate themselves for the franchise in the not-too-distant future. Walters endorsed this approach: "I have no objection to an educational restriction upon suffrage, provided it is reasonable and reasonably enforced upon all alike, without regard to race or color."

This was an extremely slender hope, one not entirely consistent with the rest of the political part of Walters's message:

> The negro has been too indifferent to the loss of his rights by proscriptive legislation in the Southern states. He must stand shoulder to shoulder with other men of his race in defense of his constitutional privileges. If the present Congress will do nothing for the enforcement of our rights, then we should see to it that men are sent to Congress that will force that body to act in behalf of the lives and property and manhood of all classes of citizens.

It would be terribly hard for black citizens to do this so long as a majority of them remained nonvoters in the South.

Yet Walters, like Washington, urged blacks to stay on the southern farm rather than come to the cities. This position was not irrational, for cities were dangerous, unhealthy, and inhospitable to African Americans. But neither was it consistent with the assertion of political rights. Blacks could hardly stand shoulder to shoulder, demand their rights, and elect good people to Congress so long as most of them were spread across the rural South, where their bitterest enemies held all political power. Blacks got political clout only when they congregated in northern cities.[7]

Walters's speech illustrates the fundamental weakness of the NAAC. It offered no clear course of action simply because there was no effective course of action available. In the North, where political action was possible, blacks lacked what U.S. Grant had in another context called "the arithmetic," the force of numbers. In the South, where blacks had the arithmetic, they had no way to use it. This was not the Council's fault, merely its burden.

That first day's official sessions had been busy, the evening program busier still. First, more music: the Hallelujah Chorus again, a Chopin polonaise on piano, "Come Holy Spirit" sung by a quartet, and "The Rosary" sung in English, French, and German by Cyrus Field Adams. Four speeches followed. Josephine Silone Yates, president of the National Association of Women, gave the kind of optimistic and nonpolitical address that Booker Washington, had he attended, would have enjoyed. She looked to the South, the new colonial territories, even Germany and Africa (but not the U.S. North) as good places for the African American to prosper. Blacks must work to develop their own skills, self-reliance, and inventive genius, and stay away from politics. "The product of his imagination . . . will accomplish more toward molding the future of the race than any amount of favorable legislation."[8]

W. E. B. Du Bois spoke that evening, too, on "The Problem of Work." In keeping with his position as professor of sociology at Atlanta University, he took an analytical approach and made specific recommendations. In order to achieve a greater place in American life, black people needed to "understand the modern organization, and we must teach our children to work." He suggested that over the next fifty years they seek to decrease slightly the number of farmers, halve the number of domestic servants, double the number of professionals, and triple the numbers of merchants and manufacturers.[9]

Booker T. Washington would not have disagreed with any of this, but there is a hint of the differences in emphasis that would contribute to driving the two men apart. For blacks to understand "the modern organization of industry," they would need intellectuals, like Du Bois. Professional men, too, re-

quired the best of higher education. Du Bois was moving toward his formulation of the key role of the black elite, the "talented tenth," in achieving, or perhaps forcing, race progress. Du Bois was a northern intellectual and a Harvard
man. Washington, a self-made man, a southerner, and a former slave, had a
different vision: race progress arising primarily from the economic development of the southern black masses.

While the first day of the meeting had been all speeches and ceremony, the
second, July 10, was all work—work and intrigue. The morning session featured Ida B. Wells Barnett, the country's unrivaled expert on lynching, followed by a report from Harry Smith, publisher and editor of the *Cleveland
Gazette,* on anti-lynching legislation. Wells Barnett's speech got plenty of local
press attention, precisely as desired. Northern white people needed to know
the dreadful truth: 2,658 lynchings since 1885 by her count, 135 of them in
1901—two or three per week for seventeen years. The popular impression that
most lynchings arose from black men assaulting white women was simply incorrect: in 1901 allegations of sexual assault figured in less than a quarter of
the cases.[10]

Still that same morning Emmett Scott spoke on black commercial enterprises, Dr. James Henderson on "Race Mortality: Causes and Prevention," and
Isaiah Montgomery on "The Economic Status of the Negro in the South." Vital
issues all.[11]

When the delegates broke for lunch, most probably expected a dull afternoon; reports on education, ecclesiastical reform, and the role of religion in
race issues. They should not have been deceived by the official program. A
sort of palace coup had been planned and so poorly concealed that the *Pioneer Press* had that morning predicted the coming fight. Nevertheless, when
the meeting reconvened at 2 P.M. fewer than twenty delegates were present
when the plotters struck. Instead of introducing the report from the education bureau, the day's chairman, William A. Pledger, called for the report from
the nominating committee, an item officially on the agenda for the following
afternoon.

What happened next is not completely clear. The nominating committee
report recommended, among other things, that T. Thomas Fortune and Bishop
Walters swap positions, with Fortune assuming the Council presidency and
Walters chairmanship of the executive committee. It seems that the delegates
approved the report, only to find that this approval was interpreted by the
chairman to amount to election of officers. Pledger then attempted to turn the
speaker's chair and gavel over to Fortune, the new president-elect.

This move set off a ruckus in the senate chamber. Many delegates had strong feelings about Fortune, that his faults overwhelmed his talents. He drank too much, had severe and chronic money troubles, made intemperate statements, and was often pessimistic; what is more, he was known to be seeking a political appointment from President Roosevelt and to have very strong ties of personal and business loyalty to Booker T. Washington. His critics figured that with Fortune at the head of the Council its pretensions to political independence would become a joke and that he would be a disastrous and divisive leader.

Harry Shepherd, a successful St. Paul photographer and the state's sole delegate to the 1901 convention, struck the first blow that afternoon, rising to attack both the man and the process: Fortune was utterly unfit for the position, he said, because he was personally abusive. "He is driving our friends from us." Moreover, the election of officers had been illegal. "To place T. Thomas Fortune in the presidential chair of this Council by underhanded means, without allowing delegates to have a vote, means the extermination of the Council as a body."

Fannie Barrier Williams, Ida B. Wells Barnett, and W. E. B. Du Bois, all people the Council could not afford to lose, joined in the protest, too, but Fortune had the gavel and would permit discussion of one motion only—the motion to adjourn.[12]

Fred McGhee apparently did not participate in the argument, but he soon made his feelings clear. He must now have regretted his earlier pleas to Washington to, in effect, take over the Council, for his wish had been granted in an unexpected way. That evening he told a reporter for the *St. Paul Globe:*

> There is a deep feeling ... that the way the election was carried out was an outrage. .... The arbitrary ruling of the presiding officer is subject to no other construction than trickery. One thing is certain, and that is that a Council like this cannot long exist unless such actions as this of today are guarded against and made impossible in the future.

McGhee had asked Washington for his "safe and sound guidance" for the Council. What he got instead was a crude but effective takeover, which he must have known had been approved by the great man himself. Now McGhee, a man with a deep personal stake in the success of the meeting (and who had in the protested election been made the Council's financial secretary), was telling the local press that the Council's very existence had been threatened by the trickery of its leaders.[13]

With the day's official business ended, but hardly concluded, the delegates, guests, and observers moved on to the evening program. Now, at last, Booker T. Washington would speak. To those whom he had defeated, irony barked from every title in the musical program that preceded his remarks: "The Heavens Are Telling," "Lead, Kindly Light," and "Achieved Is the Glorious Work."

By the time Washington took the podium at the House of Hope Church, those present must have squirmed with anxiety and anticipation. Would he mention the election controversy? He did not. He gave what was surely a standard speech, well written and practiced, counseling faith, patience, and progress. He said that blacks had made great progress since emancipation, and that progress was continuing. He suggested that they must educate themselves, work hard, and get along with southern white neighbors. In the midst of this he added a sentence that surely shocked some of his listeners with the depth of its cynicism: "I am glad to see in this Council so many evidences of the fact that we can sink the individual preferences and differences and unite in the one direction of uplifting the race."[14]

The next morning Council delegates awoke to this headline in the *Pioneer Press*:

Election Causes A Row On The Afro-American Council
Those in Control Fix Up Slate to Retain Their Supremacy
and Rush Ticket Through When Majority of Delegates Are Absent

This was perhaps not the best atmosphere in which to sink individual differences and unite in one direction. In any event, Fred McGhee and others had no such intentions; they showed up on the morning of July 11 ready to renew the fight.[15]

McGhee led off with a lawyer's challenge to the elections, citing four technical irregularities. Amid what the *St. Paul Dispatch* called a "hot crossfire of objections" from Washington loyalists, among them McGhee's recent correspondent Emmett Scott, the chairman dismissed all of McGhee's points. This of course did not end the dispute; wrangling went on most of the rest of the morning. As adjournment neared, dissident delegate Nelson Crews asked to speak on a point of personal privilege. After thanking the Council for his election as head of the immigration bureau (one of the scraps tossed to the losers), he advised the Council to elect future officers fairly and without trickery, then referred to T. Thomas Fortune as the "alleged" Council president.

This remark set off another row. Fortune jumped to his feet and challenged Crews to meet him outside to settle their differences. Crews, having made his point about the foolishness of making so volatile a character as Fortune the Council's leader, declined the invitation. "I do not wish to question his motives nor reflect upon the gentleman in particular," he lied, but "when you throw a stone among a pack of dogs and one of them squeals, it is pretty good evidence that he is hit." A loud multiparty argument ensued, and order was restored only with difficulty. Crews then demanded that all new officers resign so that new elections could be held. Motion denied. Then both he and Ida B. Wells Barnett resigned their posts, and the morning session ended.

This was not exactly an ideal way to conclude an annual meeting, so the afternoon session must have been tense. Some reports were read, Louisville designated the meeting site for 1903, and the resignations of Crews and Wells Barnett rejected. The delegates also adopted that year's Address to the Nation, which included an endorsement of President Roosevelt. This provision contradicted the Council's policy of nonpartisanship and exemplified Booker Washington's now firm control of the organization. It also surely offended Democrat Fred McGhee. With this, the official business ended; the NAAC remained intact, but more divided than ever. One more occasion remained before the delegates dispersed—the great celebratory banquet.[16]

This banquet may have been the greatest African-American social event in Twin Cities history. Fred McGhee, John Q. Adams, and William T. Francis led the organizing committee, which spared no effort to make the final evening

William T. Francis.

memorable. They rented the University of Minnesota Armory (which still stands) and had it extravagantly decorated. The high, vaulted ceiling was hidden by miles of red and white bunting, into which sixteen electric arc lights were set "in large red balloon-like covering which caused a rosy glow to cover the scene." The decorators covered the wall with cedar panels and evergreens, then set in the center of the room a fountain that sent jets of water 16 feet into the air, and adorned the fountain with palms and flowers, "making a fairy-like scene that beggars description."

The banquet began with formal ceremonies. William T. Francis, presiding, introduced the keynote speaker, whose presence was almost certainly secured by McGhee: Archbishop John Ireland. Then came the grand march, with Fred and Mattie McGhee leading the way. They must have made a proud and handsome couple, Fred in a tuxedo and Mattie in pink silk and diamonds. "The evolutions [of the grand march] were artistic and the long lines and curves of the column filled with handsomely gowned ladies made a scene long to be remembered." Then came the buffet supper, polished off quickly so that people could clear the floor for dancing. It was a nice twist that music was performed by Kuhn's orchestra; at this dance the only white folks in the hall (except possibly the archbishop) were the musicians.

The guests numbered perhaps 200, among them T. Thomas Fortune, Emmett Scott, Cyrus Field Adams, W. E. B. Du Bois, Fannie Barrier Williams and Josephine Silone Yates. Most of the out-of-town guests came without spouses, so the dance presented the "ladies and gentlemen" of St. Paul and Minneapolis a once-in-a-lifetime chance to dance with some of the great names of their time. Booker T. Washington did not attend.

The Appeal, mindful of its female readers, printed brief descriptions of the gowns of eighty-eight of the women and girls who showed off their finest for the occasion. Twenty wore diamonds, three pearls, and two emeralds. Scholars of turn-of-the-century fashion would enjoy bringing to life descriptions such as this one of Mrs. John Q. Adams's dress: robin's egg blue organdy, court train ecru cord embroidery, valenciennes lace insertion, black velvet, diamonds, and American Beauties. The armory and its occupants that evening must have made a truly amazing sight. The evening ended with the orchestra playing "Home Sweet Home," and with that the 1902 meeting of the National Afro-American Council came to a close.[17]

Press reaction to the meeting varied dramatically. Three St. Paul dailies had covered the proceedings in detail and at length; and the various reporters seemed to catch on quickly to the Council's internal politics. At the conclusion, however, the *Pioneer Press* and *Dispatch* gave entirely different assessments. The *Pioneer Press*'s final story omitted all mention of the bitter contention that marked the meeting's end. Its only nod to the day's rancor was the observation that "the victory of the ruling faction had not been won without leaving many hard feelings." But the headline read, HARMONY SEEMINGLY REIGNS. The *Dispatch*, by contrast, headed its final story, AS SHARP AS RAZORS, referring to the words wielded in the senate chamber that Thursday. The reporter seemed to enjoy recounting the fray in detail. The *Pioneer Press*, alone among the dailies, printed the Council's Address to the Nation in full. By comparison, all three papers had printed the entire text of Booker Washington's speech and followed with editorials praising his work.[18]

The Appeal published its account of the meeting a week later, on July 19. John Q. Adams gave his readers a portrait of the occasion as it might have been, or as he would have wished it to be, all statesmanship, harmony, and progress. Not a single word acknowledging the election controversy appeared. He gave what might be characterized as the official institutional version of events: the speeches, the reports, and the outcomes, all sanitized and praised.

The black press around the country took some note of the meeting, but only in brief, suggesting that the Council's doings did not much interest most readers. The *Indianapolis Freeman* regretted that "the dignity of the convention should be upset by a wrangle over the election of the officers," and called for the Council to continue its work. The *Cleveland Gazette* called the meeting "a good one, all things considered." The *Colored American* of Washington, D.C., concluded that the convention had been "a roaring farce" whose genuine accomplishments "can best be expressed by a cipher." The *Washington Bee* scorned the NAAC men as Washington's "satellites" who "trotted and pranced just as he pulled the reins." The Address to the Nation "was nothing more than a pronouncement of his Nibs, the boss of Negro beggars." The black press agreed on only one thing—the excellent work of Fredrick McGhee. "At St. Paul, local arrangements were superb, thanks to the hustling F. L. McGhee," wrote the *Colored American*. And from the *Gazette:* "F. L. McGhee, esq., chairman, and the local committee of arrangements are certainly entitled to an exceptional amount of praise."[19]

Fred McGhee appreciated the *Colored American's* praise, but he seemed to like the criticism (of the Council) even more. After reading the editorial calling the meeting a farce, he purchased a one-year subscription to the paper, asked for several extra copies to give "to white friends of mine," and commented, "Can you tell me if you ever saw more smoke coming down the pike that we are making for the Council?"[20]

The Booker T. Washington forces thought the St. Paul meeting a great success. Washington's private secretary and right-hand man, Emmett Scott, wrote him this assessment on July 17: "It is not hard for you to understand that we completely control the Council now. . . . It was wonderful to see how completely your personality dominated everything at St. Paul."[21]

The Tuskegeeans might not have felt so pleased with themselves had they appreciated Fred McGhee's reaction to their manipulations. They stung him

as deeply as had his betrayal by the Minnesota Republican party ten years before. McGhee had put himself very much on the line in organizing the St. Paul
meeting; he had devoted countless hours to the task and no doubt invested a
good deal of hope that his work would help elevate the NAAC to greater emi-
nence and efficacy. Instead he watched the Council demeaned by trickery and
reduced to an appendage of the Tuskegee political machine and, by extension,
to the Republican Party he so despised. McGhee remained in the Council a
year or so longer, but no longer as a Washington ally. By the time of the 1903
Louisville meeting, he would become an enemy, and two years later he would
join Du Bois in the strongest challenge yet to Washington's pre-eminence.

Events of the next eleven months seemed to confirm the harshest judg-
ments of the NAAC's critics. In December 1902 Council President Fortune finally got the federal job he had sought for so long; it was only temporary, but
coming as a favor from President Roosevelt it could only serve to link Fortune
yet more closely to the Republican Party. As he prepared to take a six-month
leave from the presidency (that is, all but one month of the rest of his term),
Fortune circulated a letter to Council members and the black press, analyzing
in bleak terms the organization's problems and prospects:

> The main difficulty and drawback to the National Afro-American Council
> today is that it has no substantial basic organization. The masses of people
> do not belong to it or support it with their sympathy and money.... The
> official board of the organization really constitutes the only member-
> ship.... No organization constituted as the National Afro-American Coun-
> cil is today, as to its basic membership, can do the important work mapped
> out by its founders and expected by the people at large.[22]

William A. Hazel's attack ten years earlier on the old Afro-American
League's St. Paul chapter could have been repeated with equal justification to
the Council. Thanks to Fred McGhee and others it stayed intermittently active,
and was very good at putting on public events, such as Lincoln Day programs
and occasional protests—but in truth it had no sustaining work. It did not take
on civil rights cases or push legislation, probably because the people did not
feel they really needed it to do these things. When they needed civil rights legislation, as we have seen, they went directly to the local Republican Party and
the legislature quite effectively. When black people wanted to take civil rights
cases to court, they just got a lawyer (and not always a black lawyer) and did
it on their own.[23]

Two other factors contributed to NAAC's failure to become a truly effective
civil rights force in Minnesota. First, Minnesota had no lynchings, no separate

coach laws, no mandatory school segregation, no immediate threat around which to mobilize people. McGhee and others tried from time to time to rouse people to contribute to distant cases, such as the Sam Hardy lawsuit in Tennessee, but these causes were too far away and produced no successes, no return on investment. Second, one suspects an exhaustion factor among leaders and followers alike. The Twin Cities black community had so many organizations, permanent and ad hoc, so many claims on its time, attention, and resources, that without an acute and compelling need for the NAAC's aid and authority, the Council could not rise above other associations as particularly worthy of support.

Nevertheless, both national and local organizations kept plugging away. The national executive committee met in Washington, D.C., soon after Fortune took his leave, and issued yet another call to the nation. This one used a bit stronger language than usual, but also reaffirmed its loyalty to President Roosevelt, commending him "to the affection and confidence of our people regardless of party affiliation." The St. Paul chapter met soon after, in early February 1903, elected Fred McGhee its president, and scheduled a Frederick Douglass Day event for February 19. McGhee presided at this large gathering, held in the House of Representatives chamber of the capitol, and made a speech, as did Governor Van Sant and the Reverend Reverdy Ransom, a prominent pastor and NAAC man from Chicago. In the national organization, McGhee served as one of the Council's legal directors, searching for promising cases to test Jim Crow laws in the South.[24]

William Monroe Trotter.

In public McGhee played his familiar role of Council leader and supporter. In NAAC internal politics, however, his approach had changed forever. Before the 1902 meeting in St. Paul, he had been a loyal servant. Around mid-1903, as the Louisville convention approached, he became a conspirator. He had concluded that the Council must free itself from the domination of Booker Washington or die; he did not wish the latter, so he set about to achieve the former.

By late spring 1903, and probably earlier, McGhee was in contact with one of

Washington's bitterest critics, William Monroe Trotter of Boston. Trotter was a Council man, but had stayed away from the St. Paul meeting. He wrote afterward in his paper, *The Guardian*, that T. Thomas Fortune was Washington's puppet in the Council, "a 'me too' to whatever Washington aspires to do." McGhee wrote to Trotter on June 15 (in response to Trotter's lost letter of June 12) urging him to send as many of his followers from Boston as possible: "[w]e will need your men to help overthrow the present officers of the Council."

Just before leaving for Louisville, McGhee made a speech fairly announcing his intentions. "We negroes have become tired of the manner in which we have been made toys of for forty years. We have pursued a path of humility only to be trampled on the more." Informed African Americans would have understood the implicit references—they had been toys of the Republican Party pursuing a path of humility laid out for them by Booker T. Washington. For McGhee it had come this far—he was now conspiring with Washington's enemies to take the Council back from the man he had one year earlier begged to come to St. Paul to give his "judgment and advice." McGhee would demand that the Council reassert its political independence. The well-informed *Globe* reporter understood the situation perfectly. "[A]s it is known that Booker T. Washington will be present and that his platform is one of 'peace at any price' the struggle may be sharp." [25]

In this St. Paul speech Fred McGhee offered an entirely original vision of an African American civil rights organization. He proposed, in effect, abandoning (or at least supplementing) the traditional exhortation and protest model in favor of the exercise of voting power, along the lines of a modern political action organization. The Council should organize itself to identify electoral districts throughout the country where black voters might swing elections to one party or another, then "go to the politicians and say: 'You must give us our rights; for if you do not we will, in the coming election, take care of certain districts that we control, and the results will not be the most beneficial to you.'" Black citizens should achieve their goals not by pleading for them or invoking ideals but by pushing politicians around. McGhee's proposal required that the Council, and black voters generally, aggressively assert their independence from the Republican Party. They must reject their foolish loyalty and brandish their votes like swords. "[N]ow we are going to fortify—I do not say we shall strike, but we will at least guard against attack."

To carry out this revolutionary transformation would have required the sustained persuasion, mobilization, and discipline of African American voters to a degree never yet attempted. McGhee did not spell this out, but such an enterprise needed a permanent organization, paid professional staff, first-rate communications, and a reliable and ample supply of money to support it. Probably no one, not even Booker T. Washington, could have achieved such a thing in 1903.

It was certainly beyond McGhee, whether he knew it or not, but he pressed on just the same. Step one would be taking over the Afro-American Council. He and the Trotterites had a plan that centered around the election of Council officers. Trotter did his part, at least at first. He brought a few Bostonians plus thirty-six New Yorkers organized as the National Negro Suffrage League. They planned to merge the League into the Council, then use the thirty-six new votes to swing the election against the Washington men Fortune, William Pledger, and Alexander Walters, and replace them with independents. Washington probably knew all about it.

The plan ran into trouble right away, when the Council's executive committee decided that new delegates would have to pay $5 to join the organization and have a vote. The New Yorkers were unwilling and perhaps unable to pay. McGhee had been blindsided, and with his plan in peril of collapse, he worked frantically to save it. He lobbied through the first night in Louisville with Walters, chairman of the executive committee, to get the New Yorkers admitted in time for the next day's election, to no avail.

McGhee felt betrayed, and his anger would still boil two years later, when he wrote an open letter to Bishop Walters in the *Washington Bee:*

> You will remember how that at Louisville I labored, and with what devotion I tried to save the whole from its ruin. . . . Who can forget the pledge, the sacred pledge, guaranteed by the honor of every member of the executive Council, upon which the New York delegation came into the convention uniting their forces, merging their efforts and work into that of the Council;
>
> AND HOW UNMIXED WAS THE BAD FAITH PRACTICED WITH THIS FAITHFUL AND TRUSTFUL PEOPLE AND WHEN TREACHERY HAD RUN ITS FULL COURSE, FAITHFULLY DID I POINT OUT TO YOU AND BEGGED EVEN THEN FOR AN HONORABLE CHANCE TO SAVE IT. TO NO AVAIL.

Despite the treachery at the meeting, McGhee apparently believed he had votes enough to defeat T. Thomas Fortune, returned from his six-month political job, for reelection as Council president. He was wrong once again. When election of officers came up on the agenda the Bookerites executed the same trick they had pulled in St. Paul a year before: rather than hold a vote on each position they simply offered the majority report prepared by the nominations committee, for an up or down vote. No nominations from the floor were permitted. McGhee protested loudly and accused the Council secretary, John Q. Adams's brother Cyrus, of altering the Council's constitution. Chairman Pledger dismissed all of McGhee's objections, and Fortune and his cohorts won reelection easily.

There were more humiliations still to come. McGhee had made a formal report to the Council on its business affairs, criticizing it for financial mismanagement. The Council responded by reelecting him financial secretary, the organization's most difficult and thankless (and futile) position. Was this a slap in the face, a cynical attempt at manipulation, or a genuine effort to keep the insurgent but talented Fred McGhee in the organization? This is a question now impossible to answer.

These events seem to have unhinged the volatile William Monroe Trotter. The next morning he and his ally William Ferris arrived at the meeting hall to find an oil portrait of Booker T. Washington on the platform. Enraged at this apparent anointing of their archenemy, Ferris and Trotter raised a loud ruckus, to which the majority responded with shouts and hisses. Fred McGhee, witnessing yet another catastrophe in the making, "poured oil on troubled waters," according to one press report, and eventually a face-saving compromise was engineered. Nothing, however, could disguise the caliber of thrashing that the McGhee and Trotter faction had absorbed.

The Washington forces triumphed completely in Louisville. Washington's secretary, Emmett Scott, exulted that the Bostonians had been routed "in a delightful fashion," and Trotter himself admitted that "there never was a clearer case of being dominated to death by one man." The Council, conceived as a politically independent and nonpartisan organization, now belonged completely to President Roosevelt's friend and adviser, Booker T. Washington.[26]

The Rubicon does not flow through Louisville, but that is where Fred McGhee crossed it. After the events of that July conference, he could not stay in the Council except as an act of submission to Washington. This he would not do. Though McGhee did not resign from the Council, after Louisville he never attended another general meeting, and seems to have quietly ended his association a few months later. He had crossed to the anti-Washington side of the river. W. E. B. Du Bois came over a few months later and joined McGhee in a collaboration that would last the rest of McGhee's life.

9

The Italian Murder Case

Fredrick McGhee's political and civil rights work took a great deal of his time and rewarded him by providing outlets for his energies and ambitions, but it did nothing to help him make a living. Every hour he spent organizing meetings or on the road making speeches for William Jennings Bryan, was an hour he could not use to find clients and prepare cases. McGhee of course had calculated the financial sacrifice, but he did not give up professional ambition. Like most criminal defense attorneys, he enjoyed the challenge and the publicity a spectacular case could bring. What's more, a criminal trial, unlike organizational politics, ends with a clear result. As 1903 drew to a close—bringing a pause to nearly two straight years of NAAC wrangling—McGhee probably felt that nothing would be so refreshing to his career and his pocketbook as a nice murder.

Very late on the night of November 18, 1903, police found the body of Salvatore Battalia on the Minneapolis side of the Franklin Avenue Bridge over the Mississippi River. Battalia had a revolver in his pocket and twenty-four stab wounds in his chest. A trail of blood in the fresh snow led across the Mississippi to St. Paul. Within hours the police had learned that Battalia, an Italian immigrant, had last been seen that evening with another immigrant fruit vendor, Antonio Calderone—and Calderone could not be found.

Around 3:40 A.M., November 19, the telephone rang at the home of Dr. Val Do Turner at 419 Sherburne Avenue in the Frogtown neighborhood of St. Paul. A voice told him that a man who had been kicked by a horse would soon be in his office for treatment. Dr. Turner dressed and hurried to his downtown office, where he found a man fevered and bloody from knife wounds to the head and chest. Turner recognized the man from having treated him a couple of years earlier; he was Antonio Calderone. Turner dressed the man's wounds and arranged for him to stay for the time being in a boarding house operated by a black woman, Mrs. Charles Davis. Calderone remained there for three days, receiving just two visitors: Turner and the doctor's good friend, now Calderone's attorney, Fred McGhee.

The Minneapolis police, having followed the bloody trail (one detective testified later that he had followed it to 620 Robert Street, several miles), concentrated their search in St. Paul. The manhunt went on for three days without result, making the police progressively more frustrated and angry. Fred McGhee observed this with a certain bemusement. He intended to effect Calderone's surrender on his own terms, and seemed to enjoy the police's discomfort. On November 20, he called St. Paul police and "asked them if they had an interest in the capture of Calderone," knowing, certainly, that the call would incite a lively interest in him. Sure enough, the police put him under surveillance. The next evening he called Deputy Arthur Jones of the Hennepin County (Minneapolis) sheriff's office to say that he was coming to Minneapolis shortly to meet him on important business. The same day, November 21, St. Paul police learned that McGhee had hired a carriage and horses, and alerted Minneapolis police to watch for him.

Minneapolis Police Superintendent E. J. Conroy ordered all bridges between the cities patrolled and put his men on the alert for a hack headed for Minneapolis pulled by a roan team and driven by a man in a fur cap—details supplied by a tipster. Detective Conley, patrolling University Avenue (which runs east and west between the two downtowns), spotted a hack headed west toward Minneapolis. It did not quite fit the description, but he stopped it just the same. McGhee later described the incident this way:

> After I had ordered the carriage in which I intended to drive with Calderone to Minneapolis in some way it was learned that I had ordered two roan horses and a driver who would wear a fur cap. This description was sent out ahead of me, but the work of the sleuths was a trifle coarse. I foiled them by taking a sorrel horse and a white horse and a driver who didn't wear a cap....
>
> An amusing incident happened while we were driving to Minneapolis. Our carriage was held up by Detective Conley as we were getting into the city. I opened

Salvador Battalia,
from the Minneapolis Tribune,
November 20, 1903.

the door of the carriage. I recognized the detective and he remembered me. The detective told me that all carriages were stopped as he was looking for Calderone, and I invited him into the carriage, but he declined, saying it was all right. The officer put up his gun and our carriage passed along.

At least two other versions of this story made the rounds: One, that McGhee told Conley that he and two colored friends were on their way to Minneapolis, and that Conley declined his invitation to enter; and, two, that McGhee and Dr. Turner had Calderone hidden under a pile of blankets. The police, for their part, later claimed that they let McGhee through because they knew where he was headed.

A short time later, in any event, McGhee's hack pulled up at the Hennepin County courthouse in downtown Minneapolis, where Fred McGhee and Val Do Turner surrendered Antonio Calderone—not to the Minneapolis police but to the county sheriff.[1]

The story of how McGhee and Turner had outwitted the police filled the next day's newspapers. The *Pioneer Press* headline included this: "After Fooling the Police of Two Cities for Three Days, a Colored Doctor and a Colored Lawyer Take Calderone in a Hack to Minneapolis." Police Chief Conroy took great offense and threatened both men with prosecution. While conceding that it was proper for Dr. Turner to treat Calderone's injuries, he concluded that Turner and McGhee had gone too far. "These people think they have a perfect right to shield criminals and secrete facts. I would like to know how the public expects the police to punish crimes if members of the public are allowed to harbor and secrete criminals. We owe it to our protection to have these people punished." Conroy referred the matter to the county attorney for presentation to the grand jury then in session.

The threat did not bother McGhee; in fact he seemed to enjoy the controversy, and he used the press to tweak the police still more. When a *Pioneer Press* reporter called for his reaction, McGhee threw down the gauntlet: "If it can be proved that I committed a crime I ought to be punished. If Dr. Turner is guilty he ought to be punished." In fact, he claimed, the Minneapolis police were simply "sore" because he and Turner had so easily outfoxed them. He boasted that they could have hidden Calderone for a month and "if we had wanted to we could have gone right through the city of Minneapolis."

McGhee justified his actions to another reporter even more explicitly: "I did not surrender Calderone to the police because I knew he would be hounded to death in the sweat box and probably killed in the strenuous work of the inquisition." Dr. Turner echoed the theme in his own dealings with the press. He had merely treated Calderone until he was well enough to surrender. "In this case, even after I had discovered he was wanted by the police, if I had surrendered him then, and he had been subjected to a severe strain in the sweat box, he might have died, and then where would the ends of justice be?" In the end, neither McGhee nor Turner faced charges for harboring Calderone.[2]

They may have saved Calderone from death in the sweat box, but not from interrogation without counsel (the Supreme Court case of *Miranda v. Arizona* came 60 years later). McGhee had instructed his client to say nothing to the police, but within 48 hours the authorities procured a statement from Calderone that they called a confession, and which they immediately released to the newspapers. (Years later, Calderone would claim that the statement had been coerced.) The *Pioneer Press* printed it in full on the morning of November 24, 1903, less than three days after Calderone's surrender.

Calderone had said that he and Battalia had eaten supper together at Calderone's house on the evening of November 18, then met again later in downtown Minneapolis. Battalia came with another man whom Calderone did not know. Battalia persuaded Calderone to come to a dance; all three walked a little while, then took a streetcar. When they got off the streetcar near the Franklin Avenue Bridge, Calderone realized that the dance invitation had been a ruse of some sort. Battalia told him to walk along the rail tracks toward the bridge, and as he did Battalia suddenly struck him from behind with a knife. Calderone turned to defend himself, grabbed the knife by the blade, took it from Battalia, then stabbed him until he fell. The third man ran away. Calderone discarded the knife and walked across the bridge to St. Paul, to Dr. Turner's office.[3]

To Calderone it was self-defense; to Hennepin County prosecutors it was murder. They secured an indictment for first-degree murder on December 1, 1903. Jury selection for the trial began, amid high public interest, especially in the Italian community of Minneapolis, on January 18, 1904. Judge Brooks's small courtroom in the Hennepin County courthouse could not accommodate all who wanted to witness the spectacle.

Both sides had used the press from the beginning. McGhee had won the first round, with his scorching statements about police bumbling and "sweat box" interrogation. But law enforcers won the next round with the publication of Calderone's "confession." McGhee now set about to limit the damage by fighting about the jury. "Attorney McGhee, the colored attorney," reported one daily, "who is conducting the defense, goes at every juror and if he ascertains that he has read anything about the case, he gets rid of him without more ado."

He got rid of plenty. In the first day of jury selection he used six of his nine peremptory challenges, and only three citizens made it through to become jurors. The next day, just two were seated. During one stretch over those two days fifty-two potential jurors in succession were challenged and rejected, fifty-one of them by McGhee; the lone exception was the single black man called, accepted by McGhee but removed by the prosecution. The jury panel finally reached twelve on the fourth day. When all was done, 163 prospective jurors had been questioned and McGhee had challenged 159. Of the final twelve, eleven joined the jury over Fred McGhee's objections. Antonio Calderone, it was now clear, would receive a vigorous defense.[4]

Hennepin County Attorney Fred Boardman made his opening statement on the afternoon of January 21. He laid out the state's case briefly. The killer and his victim had been seen together that evening; Battalia found stabbed to death; Calderone's knife and bloody handkerchief found nearby; Calderone himself left a trail of blood; and Calderone's confession . . . At this moment McGhee leaped to his feet and interrupted: "Let me enter an objection right here to the use of that term 'confession' by the state's attorney, unless he is prepared to show that it was a genuine confession." Boardman replied that he was prepared to do precisely that, but McGhee had probably accomplished what he wanted—putting the jury on notice that what the state called a confession might not be an admission of guilt. Boardman finished with a theatrical touch: "He could not keep his awful secret. . . . The fearful cries of Battalia . . . haunted him in his hiding place in St. Paul . . . . And now he sits before you, trembling and frightened, scarcely able to contain himself, the memory of his cold-blooded deed haunting him night and day." The *Minneapolis Tribune* reporter noted that in fact Calderone did not tremble or seem frightened or even nervous; he maintained a demeanor of calm interest in the proceedings all day.

McGhee deferred his opening statement, so testimony began right away. The first witness placed the victim and Calderone together at 7:30 the evening of November 18, with Battalia departing first, Calderone fifteen minutes later. A deputy county surveyor brought diagrams of the murder scene and the trail of blood that led toward St. Paul. The coroner testified that Battalia's body bore twenty-four stab wounds. The fatal knife thrust had entered just under Battalia's collarbone, passed through a lung, severed the ascending aorta, and entered the heart.

The first day's entertaining events, recounted in detail in the press, excited an enormous crowd the next day. The throng grew so thick that the courthouse corridors became impassable, even for the sheriff. When he tried to clear the halls he was answered with jeers. "Well, if you will act like brutes, you will have to be treated like a drove of hogs," he answered, and with that vaulted over the shoulders of a big man near him, then walked across the heads and shoulders of the crowd the full length of the hallway. "If they won't let us through we will have to walk on them," he explained. So reported the *Minneapolis Tribune*.

The coroner returned to the stand with damaging testimony: Battalia had been found dead with a pistol in his pocket. If, as Calderone asserted, Battalia had attacked him, why would he leave the pistol in his pocket? More damaging testimony followed. A shopkeeper testified that he had sold Calderone the bloody knife found near the scene just five days before the crime. In his statement, Calderone said that his first contact with that knife came when he was struck with it moments before Battalia's death. McGhee scored something of a point on cross-examination when he pointed out that the witness had failed to identify Calderone as the knife buyer at the coroner's inquest.

Drawing by Frank Wing of the Calderone trial,
from the Minneapolis Journal, *January 22, 1904.*

Perhaps because the morning testimony had cast doubt on the theory of self-defense, someone, presumably Fred McGhee, caused Calderone to have his head shaved during the lunch break. When the jurors returned for the afternoon session, then, they saw distinctly the scars on the defendant's skull. The defense had plans, when its turn came, to demonstrate an attacker had inflicted the wounds. It was a fine bit of theater.

The two sides battled away the afternoon. The state called a detective who had examined Battalia's corpse and inventoried his property. McGhee spent a long time trying to push him into admitting that Battalia's pistol was partly removed from his pocket, suggesting that he had it at the ready for use against Calderone. The state then introduced Calderone's "confession." McGhee tried to blunt its impact by showing that it had been written with the assistance of an "interpreter" on the police payroll.[5]

While all this was going on the press and public vibrated with excitement and anticipation over the sudden appearance of the mysterious third man, a smalltime criminal named Francis Henry. He had been found and arrested in central Minnesota and shipped to Minneapolis. From jail he told the press that he had seen the whole thing: On the bridge, Calderone had suddenly seized Battalia by the arm and struck him with a knife. While Battalia pled for his life he also reached with his left hand for his revolver, but Calderone brushed the hand away and continued stabbing until Battalia fell and moved no more. He then went after Henry, but Henry escaped.

This story deeply impressed the *Tribune* reporter, who now looked at Calderone with fresh eyes. The ordinary-sized young fruit peddler (jail measurements put him at 5 feet 7 inches and 163 pounds) now appeared "a Hercules." "Muscles stand out like whip cords on his wrists and arms, and great cords of power are knotted in his back and ridged in his massive neck. His back is built with the strength of a chimpanzee . . . . In his hands, Battalia would have been but a child." Though the defense had not yet begun its case, the reporter concluded, "Antonio Calderone will in all probability be hanged."

This trial, however, still had some surprises to offer. The prosecution got a one-hour recess to confer with Henry; upon prosecutor Boardman's return to court, for reasons never revealed he rested his case without calling Henry as a witness. The jury would never hear from the only impartial witness to the crime.[6]

McGhee now gave the opening statement that he had deferred at the beginning of the trial. The essence was, "Calderone went out that night without a weapon except his hands, the other man was armed to the teeth." Battalia had attacked; Calderone killed him with Battalia's own weapon in simple self-defense, McGhee said.

McGhee's self-defense theory required proof that Battalia had attacked Calderone. So McGhee presented as his main witness that day a Dr. Gravelle from St. Paul who had examined Calderone on November 21, three days after the homicide. He found that fingers on both of Calderone's hands were badly cut and that he had a long wound extending from the center of the back of his head to the base of his neck. As he testified, Calderone sat on a low chair in front of the jury with his head shaved and hands extended to display his various scars. In Dr. Gravelle's opinion it was impossible for Calderone to have given himself the cuts on the head—leaving the jury only one possible conclusion, that Battalia had inflicted them with a knife attack from behind.

Calderone himself did not testify. In every other case of McGhee's for which we have accounts, he put his client on the stand. In this case, he must have judged the risk too great. Calderone seems to have been an angry and emotional young man (he was twenty-four); also, he may have been guilty. And as it happened, much of his "confession" was self-serving; it claimed self-defense and told a story perfectly consistent with his wounds. So McGhee already had his client's version of events on the record, without subjecting him to cross-examination. It was better to leave this alone.

He bracketed his case with the testimony of physicians. First Dr. Gravelle, then a series of minor witnesses, then, to finish, Dr. Val Do Turner, whose testimony was made more dramatic by his taking the stand carrying a mysterious valise. All in the crowded courtroom must have strained as he opened it to see what was inside. The contents turned out to be a bloody suit of clothes, the clothes Calderone had been wearing when Turner found him in his office. The clothes were rather nicer than one would have expected, and the overcoat light for snowy November weather, suggesting that Calderone thought that he was indeed going to a dance, not to commit murder. Then Turner drew the jury's attention once again to the strongest part of the defense case, Calderone's wounds, which Turner had been the first to examine. Calderone had said that he grabbed the blade of Battalia's knife; Turner found that the first three fingers of the defendant's right hand had been sliced to the bone. He found also that the knife blow to the head had gone through to bone. The clear suggestion to the jury once again was that only a vicious attack could have inflicted such a gash.

Press accounts suggest that the closing arguments favored the state. "The case is so strong that it is hardly necessary for me to say a word," began prosecutor Boardman. He attacked the gravest implausibility in the defense theory: Battalia was smaller than Calderone and carried a pistol, so it would have been senseless for him to stab him in the head when he could simply have shot the man. Boardman made clever use of the clothes Dr. Turner had brought to court. He had Calderone rise and put on the hat he had worn that evening. It entirely covered his scars, yet bore no cuts; how could Calderone's story be true if the hat was undamaged? Boardman queried.

He had his assistant counsel, a taller man than him, stand before him as he raised the murder weapon, to show how ridiculous it would be to try to attack a person in the manner described by the defense. Then he demonstrated how a person could, easily in his view, cut his own head the way Calderone's was cut. Pointing to the defendant, he told the jurors, "They want you to give the murderer the benefit of reasonable doubt. That's all right, but Calderone did not give Battalia the benefit of any doubt. The state's position is murder in the first degree." With that, he closed.

McGhee got his chance at the jury the afternoon of January 26; and interest in the case and McGhee's reputation as a speaker were so great that the biggest crowds of the trial came to listen. He pointed out the state's failure to demonstrate a plausible motive for murder. The two men were competing fruit vendors, but their bank accounts showed that Calderone was the more successful and so had no reason to kill his competitor. On the fatal night he had not acted like a man who planned murder; he was dressed for pleasure, not dirty work, argued McGhee, and after the bloody encounter had made no attempt, as a murderer would, to hide the body or the weapon. He had not tried to escape, merely sought medical treatment and then surrendered when sufficiently recovered. And then there were his wounds: they proved that Battalia had been the aggressor. "Calderone did not hold that knife, and Divine Providence left the marks on the prisoner to show who did hold it," concluded McGhee.

For all the courtroom theater and oratory that both sides had planned and performed so well, the key bit of lawyering in the case probably took place in the judge's chambers. Calderone had been indicted on a charge of first-degree murder, which carried the penalty of death. After the testimony, Judge Brooks gave the jury four options: verdicts of justifiable homicide, that is, acquittal; first-degree murder, requiring premeditation; second-degree murder, which is intentional killing without premeditation; and first-degree manslaughter, the taking of life without the intent to do so, such as in a heat of passion. With Calderone facing the rope and the evidence against him strong, the addition of the manslaughter option favored the defense: it gave the jury room to compromise.[7]

The jury got the case in the late afternoon of January 26, and deliberated until midnight without reaching a verdict. The verdict came the next day: guilty, but only of manslaughter. Calderone had apparently expected acquittal, for he shouted, "I did it in self-defense," and wept as he was led from the courtroom.

The *Minneapolis Tribune* reporter got access to the jurors immediately after the verdict, to inquire how they had made their decision. (This good reporting might have been helped by the fact that the *Tribune* had provided the jurors with a gramophone during its sequestration, for which the jurors made a statement of thanks after the trial.) The jurors had never accepted either side's theory, rejecting both premeditated murder and self-defense from the beginning of deliberations. They differed only over the degree of the homicide, finally agreeing to manslaughter as a compromise.

While Antonio Calderone shouted and wept his way to prison (Judge Brooks gave him twenty years, the maximum), Fred McGhee had reason to be pleased. An acquittal would have been better, but in fact he had achieved an excellent result for his client. The twenty-four stab wounds in Salvatore Battalia's chest made the claim of self-defense a hard sell and made a compelling case for second degree murder at a minimum. By securing the manslaughter option Fred McGhee had saved his client many years in prison, for according to the *Tribune* reporter who interviewed the jurors, "if there had been no charge involving the manslaughter theory the jury would finally have settled on murder in the second degree," for which the penalty was life in prison.[8]

The case won McGhee mountains of publicity; it appeared eighteen times on the front pages of Minneapolis and St. Paul dailies. And the coverage was overwhelmingly positive. Its tone makes clear that McGhee was well known to the reading publics of the Twin Cities as a formidable defender—*What does McGhee have up his sleeve?* was a common theme—and transfixing speaker. References to his race were few and passing.

In this case McGhee achieved something more than a good result for his client and renown for himself. He had established himself as a black professional in the mainstream—that is, as a professional first and foremost, whose ethnicity is interesting but incidental.

10

Heart and Soul I Believe

The Italian murder case did not provide the complete relief from political wrangling that Fred McGhee probably desired; he had to break off trial preparations in early January for a week of intense political activity and a trip to New York City. Both Booker T. Washington and W. E. B. Du Bois urged McGhee to come to New York during the first week of 1904 for a three-day summit meeting of the nation's African-American leadership. For the past twenty years, most African Americans had suffered a steady erosion of their political and civil rights. Their leaders, McGhee among them, had struggled to create a unified and effective response. Since 1895 many had believed that Booker T. Washington offered the best leadership and program. The sudden rise of a dissenting movement, led now by Du Bois, threatened the hopes of unity and offered instead a long period of internal strife. The ostensible purpose, then, of the New York meeting was to unite the Du Bois and Washington factions behind a single political program. Both factions wanted McGhee.

The meeting, known to historians as the Carnegie Conference or the Washington-Du Bois Conference of 1904, had been in the works for almost a year. It completed a long and peculiar sort of dance between the two great men, in which they pushed, pulled, and circled around one another, separated, embraced, and finally parted, never to dance again. Washington had since 1895 been the most popular and powerful of black leaders, and he had the ear and support of politicians and philanthropists. Du Bois had come to prominence first as an academic; drawn somewhat reluctantly into race politics, his determination, brilliance, energy, and writing talent moved him to the front ranks of African-American leadership and eventually into rivalry with Washington.

Like almost everyone else, Du Bois had at first admired and supported Washington, but this feeling progressively lessened the longer he observed Washington's policies and tactics. Du Bois was an intellectual from a northern, free family. He believed strongly in the value of higher education and political action for black Americans. As time went on he became ever more thoroughly convinced that Washington's emphasis on vocational education,

W. E. B. DuBois, 1918. Photograph by C. M. Battey.

friendship with the southern white man, and political quiescence would lead nowhere but to perpetual peonage.

Washington early recognized Du Bois as a potential rival and tried for years to manipulate and co-opt him. Events prior to the 1904 meeting illustrate the ambivalent and sometimes strange relations between the two. Du Bois was already a critic when he observed firsthand Washington's takeover of the National Afro-American Council at the 1902 meeting in St. Paul. Then in spring 1903 he published his most famous book, *The Souls of Black Folk*. That book's most controversial essay was entitled, "Of Mr. Booker T. Washington and Others." There in calm tones Du Bois evaluated Washington's place in African-American history and his contemporary role. He concluded that the great man's policies had, "without a shadow of doubt, helped [the] speedier accomplishment" of black disfranchisement, the creation of a distinct legal class of inferiority, and the withering of black higher education. He acknowledged Washington's many achievements, but argued that:

> so far as Mr. Washington apologizes for injustice, North or South, does not rightly value the privilege and duty of voting, belittles the emasculation effect of caste distinctions, and opposes the higher training of our brighter minds—so far as he, the South, or the Nation, does this—we must unceasingly and firmly oppose them.

Other critics of Washington's had been saying and writing similar things for years, but Du Bois said it better and at a time when more people were willing to listen. His book received national attention and wide circulation. *The Souls of Black Folk* raised Du Bois to the top rank of anti-Bookerites and gave new prominence and legitimacy to their position. It also made public and irreconcilable the split between the two leaders.[1]

Washington reacted shrewdly and phlegmatically. Instead of responding to Du Bois, he put him on the payroll, hiring him to lecture at Tuskegee's summer session. Du Bois took the job for the opportunity to meet with Washington and probably for the money. Du Bois stayed away from the NAAC meeting in Louisville that July, leading to this ironic scene: just days after McGhee, Trotter, and other Washington critics had been thrashed at Louisville, the greatest anti-Bookerite of all dined cordially with Washington at his home in Alabama.

Before *The Souls of Black Folk* came out, Washington had proposed to Du Bois that they organize a major conference of race leaders. Du Bois had responded in February 1903 with an ambitious plan and proposed agenda. Washington seemed to lose interest then, and Du Bois made no progress with it while at Tuskegee in July. After leaving Tuskegee he went north with plans to spend the rest of the summer with William Monroe Trotter. Just days before Du Bois arrived Trotter and others had disrupted an appearance by Fortune and Washington in Boston, resulting in fistfights and Trotter's arrest and prosecution for disturbing the peace. Trotter was sentenced to thirty days in jail. Du Bois took Trotter's side in the controversy. Washington's people then began suggesting to Du Bois's employer, Atlanta University, that Du Bois himself had been behind the so-called Boston Riot.

It must have come as quite a surprise, then, when in late October Du Bois received a letter from Washington reviving plans for the conference of race leaders. The letter included a list of proposed invitees, mostly Washington men. Du Bois responded with a list of his own. The two traded names and plans over the next several weeks.

Both Du Bois and Washington wanted McGhee to attend, though for different reasons. To make the conference work, which for him meant to appear democratic but bend to his will, Washington needed a significant number of his known critics to attend. McGhee qualified, plus he had a long history of not letting personal defeats get in the way of his loyalty to the greater civil rights cause. Washington probably also harbored hopes of one day bringing McGhee back into his fold. Du Bois invited McGhee because he knew him, trusted him, and simply needed troops. He also hoped that McGhee would help him persuade McGhee's old patron, the powerful Chicago lawyer Edward H. Morris, to come.

Washington finally set the date for January 6-8, 1904 (an inconvenient time for McGhee, less than two weeks before the Calderone trial) Du Bois and McGhee consulted about people, strategy, and tactics in December 1903. Though they may have hoped for a productive conference, they did not expect it to be so. McGhee saw even more clearly than Du Bois that the invitees were heavily pro-Washington. Both anticipated guile. Du Bois asked all of his people to bring documentation of Washington's previous machinations, and specifically requested McGhee to "bring newspaper comments about the St. Paul meeting. . . . The main issue of the meeting is Washington," Du Bois advised. "Refuse to be sidetracked." Du Bois urged his men to "keep up a good temper and insist on free speech," but also to be prepared to walk out if the Bookerites went too far.

McGhee, characteristically, resisted the idea of a dramatic break-off. He wrote Du Bois on December 31: "My best judgment is that we should not go to the extent of leaving the meeting. [It is] better to stay and contest every inch of ground." This letter makes clear that McGhee expected that he and the other Du Bois men had been invited to the conference more to be defeated than to be consulted. Still, it was better to go than not go; and so it was that on January 5, 1904, Fred McGhee boarded a Baltimore and Ohio train bound for New York City and his third confrontation in an eighteen-month period with the man he had once called "the embodiment of the highest type of Afro-American manhood."

And so it was, that on the morning of January 6, Fredrick L. McGhee gathered with Booker T. Washington, W. E. B. Du Bois, T. Thomas Fortune, Emmett Scott, Kelly Miller, Edward H. Morris, and the other guests—a very distinguished group—to listen to the titanic (but diminutive) steel magnate and philanthropist Andrew Carnegie lecture on the wisdom of Booker T. Washington and, as David Levering Lewis put it, "the chaos certain to engulf those who challenged or deserted" his leadership. It was polite, certainly, to invite the man who paid for the conference to give its opening address. Carnegie's appearance might also have carried this message from Washington to his challengers: "Here, gentlemen, is the man I have in my corner. Whom do you have in yours?"[2]

The conference went much better than Du Bois and McGhee had anticipated. There were no walkouts. As political operators, McGhee and Du Bois were no match at all for Washington, who administered his thrashing in such a subtle way that it did not become clear for months. The group in fact agreed on eight points that represented compromises by both sides:

1. Negroes should be encouraged to stay in the South, especially in areas where they held numerical majorities, BUT "under favorable circumstances" individuals may be encouraged to move north and west.
2. The right to vote is paramount and all Negro citizens should vote on precisely the same terms as white citizens. What is more, the Civil War amendments to the Constitution "should be upheld and enforced by national authority."
3. All Jim Crow laws in travel and public accommodations must be attacked in the courts. "We stand for no compromise ... respecting our civil rights, but insist on the equality of all men before the law."
4. In education, there should be vocational training "of the masses," BUT ALSO elementary schooling for every Negro child and "thorough training of leaders and teachers in the higher institutions of learning."
5. Lynching is condemned, though without calling for any state or federal action against it other than the publication of the truth about all accusations of rape.

6. Negroes should cooperate "with the fair-minded and progressive element of the Southern white people."

7. A national conference of Northern whites, Southern whites, and Afro-Americans should be held to "consider methods of solution" of the race problem.

8. The conditions of black people in the United States should be studied and the results published.

This statement tilted in the Washington direction, which appropriately reflected the balance of power in African-American leadership at the time, and on the whole constituted a very good program. From the point of view of people such as McGhee and Du Bois, the provisions emphasizing suffrage and calling for the use of "national authority" to enforce the 14th and 15th Amendments were excellent. The document also created a Committee of Safety to coordinate the work of organizations around the country in support of the program. Washington, Du Bois, McGhee, and 27 others signed the statement.[3]

The conference work pleased Fred McGhee a great deal. On January 12, 1904, he wrote Washington a long letter, which closed, "I take this liberty to extend to you a personal compliment for your conference, and beg to assure you ... that all differences are at an end, and that the support you shall now receive will be a wholly united and full faith support." Twice, then, in the early part of the year McGhee performed political missions urged by Washington. In January he met with the archbishop of Baltimore to ask for help defeating a disfranchising bill in the Maryland legislature; and in April he organized rallies and lobbied Minnesota's U.S. senators to support the confirmation of a black man, W. H. Crum, as a customs official in the port of Charleston, South Carolina. Washington's influence did not, however, induce McGhee to remain in the NAAC: it met that summer in St. Louis, without Fred McGhee for the first time since 1901, and just the second since its founding.[4]

While this was going on, Du Bois was learning how, despite the language of the New York agreement, Washington had whipped him once again. The agreement gave three people—Washington, Du Bois, and Hugh Browne—the power to name the nine other Committee members. Browne turned out to be a puppet of Washington's, so Du Bois soon found himself outnumbered and outvoted at every turn. One by one the compromises made to the Du Bois faction were reversed. When the Committee published its official program in July 1904, the commitments to higher education and to voting had vanished. Du Bois resigned from the Committee a month later, and with that the agreements forged in New York in January turned to ash.

Du Bois biographer David Levering Lewis describes this final, irrevocable break between the two leaders:

> There was no turning back now for Du Bois. . . . As [Kelly] Miller had lamented, "It was war to the knife, knife to the hilt." . . . Du Bois began to impugn the man behind the message. He was discovering a truth that Washington had known his entire, calculating life—that the force of an idea, at least in the short term, is only as good as the politics of the people advancing it. . . . To get at the Wizard's ideas, Du Bois now saw that he would have to cripple the man.[5]

For the next act of the struggle, Du Bois needed and wanted Fred McGhee. This is not to say that he needed and wanted McGhee above all others; he needed all the help he could get. But the two men had been through some battles together and had a high regard for each other that became a durable friendship—and Du Bois did not make friends easily or keep them long.

The two men probably corresponded in the fall and winter of 1904 and early 1905. The next known contact between them occurred in late February 1905 when Du Bois came to St. Paul to speak and raise money for Atlanta University. It is probable that McGhee arranged the speaking dates and that Du Bois stayed as his guest. He spoke first at House of Hope Church (site of Washington's speech at the 1902 NAAC meeting). The innocuous title of his address, "Atlanta University," probably belied, perhaps concealed, a political purpose. Atlanta University survived on the crumbs of white philanthropy that did not go to Washington's Tuskegee Institute. One weapon Washington used against Du Bois was to discourage white donors from giving to Atlanta, thus threatening his rival's base of operations and main source of livelihood. Thus every dollar that Du Bois could raise for his employer indirectly supported the struggle against Washington. So beneath all the pleasantries associated with a famous man's visit to provincial St. Paul—the soprano solos, the refreshments, the "timely and well-received remarks"—the "war to the knife" was being fought.[6]

If Du Bois were going to war against Washington, he would need an army, an organized, disciplined, reliable body of men. The only pretender to the status of a national civil rights organization, the National Afro-American Council, had long since (and in St. Paul) been taken over by the Bookerites. The most energetic leaders—Du Bois, Trotter, McGhee, and others—had left it, and the Council was on a fast track to oblivion. On the national scene, African-American men and women who believed that black citizens should be politically active and vote, and that the federal government should actively enforce the civil war amendments to the Constitution, had no organization to carry out their will. Du Bois and McGhee undoubtedly discussed this during Du Bois's visit to St. Paul. Indeed, it may be that the determination to create a new national civil rights organization was born in conversations between the two during that late winter 1905.

In early June 1905, Du Bois circulated a proposal for a meeting among a few dozen race leaders, including Fred McGhee:

> The time seems more than ripe for organized, determined and aggressive action on the part of men who believe in Negro freedom and growth. Movements are on foot threatening individual freedom and our self respect. I write to you to propose a conference during the summer for the following purposes:
>
> 1. To oppose firmly the present methods of strangling honest criticism, manipulating public opinion and centralizing political power by means of the improper and corrupt use of money and influence.
>
> 2. To organize thoroughly the intelligent and honest Negroes throughout the United States for the purpose of insisting on manhood rights, industrial opportunity and spiritual freedom.
>
> 3. To establish proper organs of news and public opinion.

Every politically aware black citizen would instantly have understood that Du Bois's language—the strangling of public opinion, corrupt use of money and influence—referred to Booker T. Washington. This letter was a call to arms to unite all anti-Bookerites under one banner.

The twenty-nine who answered the call met July 11–13, at Fort Erie, Ontario, across the border from Niagara Falls, New York. The best known among them were Du Bois, William Monroe Trotter, Boston lawyer Clement Morgan, editor Harry Smith of Cleveland, and McGhee. Did they know they were making history? Probably not, but they did have a sense of trying to create something new: a national civil rights organization that had learned from past errors, would be politically independent, and would not be controlled by T. Thomas Fortune or Booker T. Washington. By all accounts, the men went forward with a high sense of purpose and camaraderie, abetted by wonderful weather, good food, and delightful hospitality from the Erie Beach Hotel.

They produced a Declaration of Principles, setting forth their positions and recommendations on the greatest issues facing the black people. In most of this there was nothing new; the ills assailing black America were well known. But this statement had a much broader scope. It touched not only on suffrage, Jim Crow, and education, but also on labor unions, the courts, public schooling, the churches, and the military. But what made it new most of all was the vigorous, assertive language (we demand, we urge, we refuse, we repudiate, we

Twelve of the twenty-nine founding members of the Niagara Movement, 1905.
TOP ROW: *H. A. Thompson, New York; Alonzo F. Herndon, Georgia; John Hope,*
Georgia; unidentified; MIDDLE ROW: *Fredrick McGhee, Minnesota; Norris F.*
Herndon, son of Alonzo; J. Max Barber, Illinois; W. E. B. Du Bois, Georgia;
Robert Bonner, Massachusetts; BOTTOM ROW: *Henry L. Baily, Washington, D.C.;*
Clement G. Morgan, Massachusetts; W. H. H. Hart, Washington, D.C.;
and B. S. Smith, Kansas.

protest) and the emphasis on public action: " ... this class of American citizens should protest emphatically and continually against the curtailment of their political rights." The Declaration rings with energetic Du Boisian rhetoric (he and Trotter wrote it). The paragraph entitled "Oppression" is a fine example, still thrilling over ninety years later:

> We repudiate the monstrous doctrine that the oppressor should be the sole authority as to the rights of the oppressed. The Negro race in America stolen, ravished and degraded, struggling up through difficulties and oppression, needs sympathy and receives criticism; needs help and is given hindrance, needs protection and is given mob-violence, needs justice and is given charity, needs leadership and is given cowardice and apology, needs bread and is given a stone. This nation will never stand justified before God until these things are changed.

The phrase "needs leadership and is given cowardice and apology" spit directly in the face of Booker T. Washington and his many allies. There could be no mistaking the directness of the challenge to his leadership.

The men of the Niagara Movement (no women participated in the founding) paid attention not just to rhetoric but also to structure; they were all veterans of failed organizations. Du Bois was undoubtedly recalling the top-heavy organization and vague goals of the Afro-American League and NAAC when he wrote that "what now is needed for success is ... 1. Simplicity of organization. 2. Definiteness of aim." Niagara adopted a structure based on a proposal that Du Bois had made to Washington in connection with the 1904 Committee of Safety: Niagara would be based on state chapters (not independent or ad hoc organizations); state chairmen would then constitute the executive committee. This would give Niagara a more cohesive center than its predecessors had achieved.

We do not know the precise role of Fred McGhee in the Fort Erie meeting that gave birth to the Niagara Movement. If he ever spoke or wrote about it, his words have not been preserved. *The Appeal,* which printed the Declaration in full on July 29, wrote not a word about McGhee's participation. Still, it is clear that W. E. B. Du Bois considered McGhee to have been a key participant, for in his 1905 article explaining the Niagara Movement to the public, he wrote: "The honor of founding the organization belongs to F. L. McGhee, who first suggested it...." That fateful suggestion probably came when Du Bois and McGhee met in St. Paul in February 1905.[7]

Du Bois's giving McGhee first credit in the founding of Niagara was kind (Du Bois himself was the real engine) but also fitting. McGhee had qualities that people value in an advocate and an ally: persistence, resilience, and optimism despite defeat. Du Bois had these qualities, too. McGhee also had a great deal of experience in organizing—the Afro-American League, the Minnesota Civil Rights Committee, the St. Peter Claver Union, the Law Enforcement League, and the NAAC. Few leaders had more firsthand experience with trying, failing, and trying again.

What's more, McGhee had the convert's passion. Soon after returning to St. Paul in summer 1905, he read Bishop Alexander Walters's appeal to the Niagara men to abandon their separate efforts and return to the National Afro-American Council. McGhee replied to this in a long, angry letter published in August in the *Washington Bee*. There he condemned those who controlled the Council for their treachery, bad faith, and betrayal of many working selflessly for the race, and concluded:

> I believe in organizations, HEART AND SOUL I BELIEVE, BUT THE ORGAN-IZATION MUST BE FOR THE ACCOMPLISHMENT OF GOOD HELPFUL AND PROFITABLE ENDS AND MUST BE KEPT TRUE TO ITS OBJECTS.
>
> What can possibly be the gain in reviving the council over and against further strengthening and making all potent the "Niagara Movement." Until it fails of its purposes . . . what little I can contribute shall be given to that movement. What its purposes are, how high, how good, how all inspiring, its declaration of purposes, its address to the American people, speak and tell plainly. Think thou upon them as should every Negro, and choose whether you will stand for its success or against it.[8]

Fred McGhee devoted a great deal of his time and treasure to the Niagara Movement for the next three years of his life. No one except Du Bois himself gave more.

11

The Raverty Murder

While enjoying the scenery of Niagara Falls and the intensity of helping to create the Niagara Movement, Fred McGhee's thoughts surely strayed now and again toward his St. Paul home; he had waiting for him not just friends and family but, of more immediate concern, the most challenging and spectacular trial of his courtroom career.

The story began in St. Paul in early May 1905. Peter Raverty, age fifty-five, worked as a night watchman (or "special policeman") in a commercial/industrial zone just east of downtown, near the present-day Lafayette Bridge and East Seventh Street; St. Paul police officer Joseph Pugleasa patrolled roughly the same area on his beat. The two men encountered each other regularly in their work and did so several times on the rainy night of May 2 and early morning of May 3. During one of their meetings, they had stopped to talk when Dr. George Moore, who was in a hack driven by Elzeard Godbout, hailed them; Moore needed a telephone to inform a man that his wife was in labor. Raverty had a key to the office of the Johnson Lumber Company, near the corner of East Seventh and Kittson, and told Dr. Moore that he could use that telephone.

They all then drove the short distance to the Johnson office. Raverty opened the front door and went in, followed by Pugleasa and Godbout (why Dr. Moore also did not enter is not known). As Raverty lit the bare electric bulb that hung in the center of the room, two gunshots exploded from behind the wooden counter that divided the office in two. Officer Pugleasa dropped to the floor, struggled through his raincoat for his pistol, then exchanged gunfire with the figures escaping through a side window. Pugleasa chased them into the adjacent rail yard, but they escaped.

Raverty, meanwhile, staggered out of the building and told Godbout that he had been shot. Godbout loaded the watchman into his hack and, with Dr. Moore attending, hurried him to St. Joseph's Hospital, about two miles away downtown. Peter Raverty died several hours later of a single gunshot wound to the abdomen.

WATCHMAN SHOT

BY SAFE LOOTERS IN

DESPERATE FIGHT

YEGGMEN'S BLOODY WORK.

Watchman Peter E. Raverty fatally shot.
Revolver fusillade between Patrolman Pugleasa and three tramp burglars.
Place—W. W. Johnson Lumber company's office, 412 Kittson street.
Time—Three o'clock this morning.
Burglars were at work in office when policemen entered.
Burglars opened fire, surprising police.
Raverty fell at first shot with bullet wound in abdomen.
Pugleasa pursues the three men until his revolver is empty.

Three desperate burglars, surprised in their work of blowing the safe of the W. W. Johnson Lumber company, 412 Kittson street, at 3 o'clock this morning, shot and fatally wounded Peter E. Raverty, a special policeman, and fired several shots at Patrolman Joseph Pugleasa and E. Godbout, a hackman.

The robbers escaped into the railroad yards after a running fight with Patrolman Pugleasa, during which a number of shots were fired.

Raverty is in a dying condition at St. Joseph's hospital.

The discovery of the burglars engaged in opening the safe was a surprise to the officers as well as the Yeggmen, and came about through a curious circumstance.

About 2:50 o'clock Police Surgeon Moore was called to the corner of Neill and East Seventh street to attend a confinement case. Riding down in a hack he there met Patrolman Pugleasa, whose beat is in that district, and Special Officer Raverty, who is night watchman for a number of firms in the neighborhood, including the Johnson company. The couple to whom the baby was born were known to the officers. After Dr. Moore had gone up stairs, Godbout proposed that they call up by telephone the father and congratulate him. Said Raverty:

"Come over to the wood office, they have both 'phones there, and you can call him up."

The three walked down to the office of the lumber company, a block and a half away.

Raverty took out his pass key and opened the door. He entered, followed closely by Pugleasa, with Godbout bringing up the rear.

Shooting Began.

Raverty walked into the room to a high desk which spans the room at right angles. Above this desk is a small incandescent lamp, suspended from the ceiling. Raverty reached up and turned on the light. At the first flash the Yeggmen began firing. Raverty was struck in the stomach by the first shot. He fell to the floor, and Pugleasa dropped down

Joseph Pugleasa,

The policeman who put up a desperate fight against the burglars.

had run down Kittson street toward the railroad yards. At Sixth and Kittson street he came up with them. At his call to halt, the men turned again and opened fire upon him. Several shots were exchanged, one of the bullets whistling by the officer's head.

Having emptied his revolver Pugleasa gave up the chase and returned to Raverty. The hackman and officer assisted the wounded man to walk to the hack and Dr. Moore was called. Raverty showed the surgeon where he was shot and Dr. Moore realizing that the wound was a grave one took him at once to St. Joseph's hospital, where he was placed upon the operating table. The operation upon Raverty lasted three hours.

Looting the Safes.

A search of the lumber company's office showed that the burglars had been surprised in the midst of what would have

As Raverty lay dying, the St. Paul police mobilized an energetic and determined search. Chief John O'Connor guessed that the gunmen, having run into the rail yard, would try to escape by train to Chicago, so he concentrated the search along the rail lines leading southeast into neighboring Washington County. He called upon every resource at hand. He had the railroads watch their trains, summoned every available St. Paul police officer to duty, sent posses to comb the countryside, even authorized a contingent of cowboys from the South St. Paul stockyards to join the search on horseback. Tips came in by telephone; one caller reported a couple of suspicious characters looking for a train to Point Douglas on the Wisconsin border, a junction point for trains to Chicago. O'Connor ordered his men to intercept that train, then sped toward Point Douglas as fast as animal power could carry him: "Get a team of the best horses you can find and a guide that knows the shortest road to Douglas Point . . . and get there if you have to kill the horses."

At about 4 P.M. on May 3, just thirteen hours after the killing, as the police checked boxcars near Point Douglas, two men leapt from a car and began running toward the woods along the St. Croix River. The police caught James Egan right away and found on his person a .38 caliber pistol. The second man dashed into the woods, beginning a straight-from-the-movies foot chase. Spurred by fear, the fugitive raced among the trees. He got such a lead—as much as a quarter mile at one point—that he was able to pause to conceal something in a patch of tall grass, then run again. The excited policemen followed, firing ineffectually as they ran. On and on it went, a mile, two miles, three (one report had it as long as five). Finally the fugitive reached limits imposed by nature: his own exhaustion and the river's edge. There he hid behind a boulder and waited, listening to the officers' voices as they neared. They could not find him, and were about to move on when one of them turned and spotted the prey. Harry Laramie raised his hands and said the appropriate words, "I surrender." Other officers, alerted by a witness to the chase, searched the spot where Laramie had paused in flight. There they found a .44 caliber revolver. After a little bit of roughing up, Laramie and Egan were taken to jail, first in nearby Hastings, then in St. Paul.

Chief O'Connor felt sure he had the killers, though even after some heavy sweating they refused to confess. The chief himself came one day to Laramie's cell, but it proved a sterile encounter. He entered, stared at the prisoner in silence for a few minutes, then left without a word. Harry Laramie and James Egan, both transients, were charged with the murder of Peter Raverty, a capital offense.[1]

McGhee got this case by appointment. A Minnesota statute in effect at the time provided for court appointment of counsel for indigent defendants, with compensation at the rate of up to ten dollars per day "for the number of days he is actually employed in the court upon the trial"; nothing, apparently, for trial preparation. McGhee got a small portion of business this way.

After a preliminary hearing on June 5, the court ordered the two men held for trial in the fall term, which gave McGhee an unusually generous amount of time to prepare. He needed it, for he was very busy. On June 6, the trial began in another murder case of his, and four weeks later he left for Niagara Falls. After Niagara he vacationed for the rest of July, then returned to work.[2]

Trial began the second week of November, and McGhee led off just as he had in the *Calderone* trial, with a fight over the jury. Seventy-eight veniremen were brought into the courtroom for questioning; McGhee challenged seventy-six of them, sixty-seven for cause. The state challenged and removed the two prospective jurors that McGhee had approved, so when the jury was finally seated, every one of the twelve had come in over Fred McGhee's objections.

Testimony began on November 16, 1905, in the old Ramsey County courthouse (demolished in the 1930s), before Judge Grier Orr. Prosecutor Thomas P. Kane, a McGhee colleague in local Democratic Party politics and a civil rights supporter, laid out a straightforward case in his opening statement: Laramie and Egan were tramp safecrackers who had been robbing the Johnson Lumber Company office when Raverty and Pugleasa surprised them. They shot Raverty to conceal their crime. Three witnesses would place them very near the scene just hours before the murder. Others would describe their guilty flight. And most important, Officer Pugleasa would positively identify them as the killers.

Kane used his key witness first. Officer Joseph Pugleasa, an eight-year police veteran, told how he had met Peter Raverty that evening, then Dr. Moore and the driver, and gone to the lumber office to use the telephone. Upon entering the office he had said, "Pete, light the light." The light revealed two men standing behind the counter that divided the room, just three feet away from Raverty and Pugleasa. The taller man fired two shots over the counter and Pugleasa dropped to his knees behind the counter shouting, "Look out, Pete!" Two or three more shots came from behind the partition. Pugleasa returned fire and heard one of the men say, "Let's get out of here." The two covered each other with their pistols as they escaped through the south window, then ran up Sixth Street and disappeared into the train yard. Pugleasa said he pursued for a while, and then, "I ran back up Seventh street and met Raverty in the middle of the block. I called him back for not following me. He said, 'Don't abuse me. I am shot.' . . . I got the hack and sent him to the hospital and then telephoned the police station." When Pugleasa returned to the lumber office he found the light still on, a safe door detached and lying on the floor. Pugleasa positively identified Harry Laramie as the taller man who had fired first, and James Egan as the other.

This was compelling testimony—eyewitness identification by a veteran police officer. The press made no report of McGhee's cross-examination, but there is evidence that he gave Officer Pugleasa a hard time, for his version of the events had some problems. The first accounts of the crime, for which Pugleasa must have been the source, did not entirely agree with the officer's trial testimony; good defense attorneys use such discrepancies to attack the credibility of witnesses.

The initial reports were quite specific that the shooters had not been standing behind the office counter when they fired, but crouching underneath it. Here is what the *St. Paul Dispatch* reported on May 3, the day of the crime:

> When the burglars were surprised at their work they evidently crawled upon their hands and knees to the shelter of the desk. When Raverty walked to the desk to turn on the light he stood directly in front of the thin boarding and within a foot of the Yeggmen's guns. As he flashed the light the thieves saw that discovery was certain and they began firing through the boards. Three bullet holes show in the woodwork, the splinters indicating that the shots were fired from beneath the desk. . . . the police secured only a meager description of the men, as the officer saw them only during the excitement of the firing and there was not time to take accurate account of their appearance. Two of the men were short and one tall. They were dressed like ordinary tramp burglars.

Such detail could only have come from the police, and all of the other initial press reports were very similar. If the men were under the desk when they fired, and Pugleasa himself ducked behind the partition when the shots went off, the question was, how could he have gotten a good look at their faces? And if he could give only a "meager description" on May 3, how could he make a positive identification on November 16? Such were the points that Fred McGhee must have raised in his cross-examination.

Fortunately for the prosecution, the state did not have to rely entirely on Pugleasa. Prosecutor Kane next called several witnesses who corroborated parts of the officer's testimony, including his identification of the suspects. R. E. McDonald, the night yardmaster of the train yard, heard gunfire at about 3:10 that morning and saw two men resembling the defendants running from the direction of the Johnson office. Gus Pabst, a switchman, had seen them, too. Mrs. Rose Ledeger, who ran a cigar and confectionery shop nearby, said that around 12:30 the night of the murder two men had come briefly into her shop. They did not buy anything or say much, except the shorter man asked, "Are you alone?" On May 5, after the arrests, she had gone to the police station and identified Laramie and Egan as the men she had seen. Henry Poppenburger owned a saloon and boarding house near the corner of Seventh and Kittson, not fifty feet from the Johnson office. He identified the defendants as two men who had bought beer in his saloon just twelve hours before the crime.

John J. Hoffman owned a saloon at 454 East Seventh Street, just two blocks from the scene of the crime. He testified that Egan and Laramie had visited his place several times during the four or five days before the murder, including the afternoon of May 2. Counselor McGhee probably made an error in cross-examination when he asked Hoffman how he had taken such particular notice of these two customers. Hoffman replied, "When a man who comes into your place is well dressed you don't pay much attention to him, but when a man comes in poorly dressed and looking tough you remember him." Both Ledeger and Poppenburger had also testified that the men were poorly dressed and looked kind of tough (though to today's eyes the men as they appeared in their arrest photos look quite well-groomed—they could easily be policemen or newspaper reporters).

Whoever had killed Raverty had been surprised in the act of cracking the office safe. Prosecutor Kane connected Laramie and Egan to the safecracking through two witnesses. A safe and lock expert named George Garrow said that the Johnson Lumber Company safe had been blown open with nitroglycerine. And a Mr. Schulze testified that he had searched the abandoned barn where the defendants had been staying before the crime and found a bottle containing a liquid that appeared to be nitroglycerine. McGhee objected to Schulze's evidence—it is striking that Kane offered no scientific proof that the liquid in fact was nitroglycerine—but failed to keep it from the jury; objection overruled.

It was now Monday, November 20. Testimony had begun the previous Thursday and so far almost everything had gone the state's way. Near the end of the prosecution case, however, McGhee scored a point for the defense. The bullet that killed Peter Raverty was of .41 caliber, but the gun that Laramie had tried to hide as he ran from the police was a .44 caliber revolver. Kane brought to court a gun dealer named William Burkhard, who described the similarity of .41 and .44 caliber bullets; the same weight, just slightly different in length. He left it just at that, apparently to suggest that the difference in caliber was inconsequential.

This did not get past McGhee, who had focussed on the gun evidence from the outset. On cross-examination he showed Burkhard the .44 caliber revolver carried by Laramie. Burkhard said that that gun could have fired the fatal bullet, but that it could handle only one .41 caliber bullet at a time; the others, being smaller than the revolver's magazine chambers, would fall out before they could be fired. Shown the weapon taken from Egan, he said that it was a .38 caliber revolver, incapable of firing the .41 caliber bullet.

McGhee had exposed a thin spot in the state's case. Egan's gun could not have been the murder weapon, and Laramie's did not seem so likely, either. Why would he load it with bullets that did not fit? Pugleasa had testified that Laramie fired two shots in rapid succession: How could he have done so with bullets that had to be loaded one at a time?

Prosecutor Kane called two more witnesses of little consequence, then rested. He had not called to the stand the one remaining eyewitness to the crime, the hack driver Elzeard Godbout. This apparently surprised McGhee, for he immediately moved the court that the state be required to call him to the witness stand. Kane answered that "Godbout had been close to the defense of late, and the state did not desire to call him as a witness in view of this fact." McGhee also tried once again to get the nitroglycerine evidence stricken. Judge Orr denied both defense requests.

The weakness in the firearms evidence notwithstanding, County Attorney Kane had presented a persuasive case. Three disinterested witnesses had placed Egan and Laramie near the scene on the days leading up to the crime, the day of the crime, even the night of the crime, no doubt casing the joint. They had nitroglycerine, the tool of safecrackers. They had guns. They had run like guilty men. Most important, Officer Pugleasa had with his own eyes, at close range, seen them commit the crime. This was enough, more than enough, to send the two transients to the gallows.

Defense attorney McGhee, having deferred his opening statement at the beginning of trial, gave it now. He spoke for ninety minutes, laying out what was essentially a simple defense. Laramie and Egan were not safecrackers and killers but honest hobos who had not even been in St. Paul when the crime occurred. The police had seized upon them as the killers, then shaped their evidence to fit. The crime simply could not have happened the way Joseph Pugleasa said it had.

Between May and November McGhee had spent a good deal of time with his clients and, apparently, developed confidence in them. As defense testimony went forward, it became clear that he was willing to wage a straightforward battle of credibility—his hobos against the state's cop.

He began with Laramie. McGhee had him introduce himself to the jury by telling his life's story. Then thirty-three years old, he had been born in Missouri and grown up in California with his mother and stepfather, from whom he took the surname Laramie (he was born Ryan). At age twenty-eight he had left home and the settled life. He had worked on the railroad in Missouri, gone to New York City, worked as a telephone lineman in California, then hit the road again and landed in Chicago in January 1905. He had left Chicago on April 26 in search of work to the north. At Eau Claire, Wisconsin, he had run out of money and soon after that, at Knapp, was forced off the train. Homeless and broke, he had become a tramp, even had to sell some of his clothes for food money. As he cooked a meal over an open fire in a vacant lot near the Knapp train station, he had met another hobo, James Egan.

McGhee then had Laramie give a minutely detailed account of his and Egan's movements over the next week, the days leading up to and including the date of Peter Raverty's murder. From Knapp they had gone to Woodville on the 28th, Baldwin on the 29th, Roberts on the 30th, then on May 1 to Hudson, Wisconsin, Stillwater, and finally Lakeland in rural Washington County, Minnesota. Laramie salted the tale with memorable images: falling asleep atop a rail car full of oats; a detailed description of a night in an engine house, at Baldwin; sleeping in a schoolhouse at Roberts; getting three free glasses of beer at a brewery at Stillwater; fetching an awl-handle for a red-headed hobo they had met along the way; washing their underwear in a big metal can along the St. Croix River shore.

Most of this had nothing to do with the events at the Johnson lumber office on May 3. McGhee's thinking seems to have been this: The more the jury gets to know this man, the less they will believe he is a killer. Plus, the details were too particular and peculiar to have been invented. And McGhee made sure the jury knew that Laramie and Egan had had no opportunity to concoct a story together; Laramie testified that they had been jailed apart since the moment of their arrest.

At last McGhee took Laramie to the crucial time, May 2 and 3. Another tramp had told them about an abandoned barn near Lakeland, a good place to sleep. They were sleeping there the night of May 2, when Raverty was shot more than twenty miles away. The next morning, May 3, Laramie had arisen

INQUEST IN RAVERTY MURDER

Coroner Decides to Hold It Probably Next Monday—Body of Murdered Watchman Is Taken to Sleepy Eye—Police Are Getting New Evidence Against the Two Men Under Arrest.

An inquest will be held, probably Monday, on the death of Peter E. Raverty, the watchman who was shot early Wednesday morning by burglars, whom he interrupted while they were blowing open the safe in the office of the W. W. Johnson Lumber company, Kittson and East Seventh streets. A jury was sworn in yesterday and viewed the body.

The remains of Watchman Raverty were taken to Sleepy Eye last evening for burial. That was his home before he came to St. Paul, and his mother and other relatives still reside there.

James R. Eagan and Harry Laramie, the two men arrested near Hastings after the brilliantly successful and exciting man hunt by the St. Paul detectives, were questioned closely yesterday by Chief O'Connor. The police are still working hard on the case, gathering more evidence, and Chief O'Connor says that the additional information only convince him more certainly that he has captured the men that murdered the watchman. The prompt capture gives the police a fresh trail to work on and they are making the most of it.

Chief O'Connor questioned the two men yesterday as to their whereabouts for the past year, and especially for the last three weeks. They deny having been in St. Paul, but Chief O'Connor says that they have been identified by several people who saw them in St. Paul recently.

Henry Poppenberger, who runs a saloon and boarding house at East Seventh and Kittson streets, opposite the Johnson Lumber company's office, says that the men were in his place on the afternoon before the night when the saloon of Henry Connor, Third and Commercial streets, was held up, and that they closely resemble two men he saw hovering about the vicinity on the day before Raverty was killed.

The police believe that Laramie and Eagan were implicated in the Elk laundry robbery as well as in the Henry Connor saloon affair.

HARRY LARAMIE.
He gave the police a thrilling chase of several miles at Hastings.

JAMES R. EAGAN.
He was arrested as he got off the train at Hastings.

—Photograph by Shepherd.

MEN CHARGED WITH THE MURDER OF WATCHMAN RAVERTY.
The two men arrested by the police near Hastings, after a successful man hunt, which ended in an exciting chase for one of them. They are charged with being the men that were interrupted while they were blowing open the safe in the office of the Johnson Lumber company on Kittson and East Seventh streets, early Wednesday morning.

Article about Harry Laramie, James R. Eagan, and the Raverty murder case, St. Paul Pioneer Press, May 5, 1905.

early and gone in search of a frying pan to cook breakfast. After being refused at one house, he tried a second, where he interrupted a woman fixing her daughter's hair. She lent him two skillets, which he used and then returned. Later, he and Egan had gone to Afton and then grabbed a train headed south, just moving on, looking for work. Laramie had run when the police hailed him because he guessed they were railroad detectives; and then, of course, the police started shooting at him. Why did he have a revolver? He had found it in the old barn. He had not tried to conceal it during the chase; it had simply fallen from his pocket when he stumbled. He and Egan had never been to St. Paul before being taken to jail there. They had not killed Peter Raverty and knew nothing about the crime.

James Egan's testimony followed the same pattern as Laramie's, but was more brief. He was the less articulate of the two. His real name was Dick Taylor. He had been born in Illinois and from his youth forward lived a hardscrabble life, much of it working in the southern Illinois coal mines until he hit the road. From his meeting Laramie at Knapp, Wisconsin, Egan's story matched his co-defendant's closely. Prosecutor Kane failed to shake either man on cross-examination.

McGhee then presented a handful of witnesses to confirm his clients' story. The town marshal of Baldwin, Wisconsin, recalled seeing the two men in his town on the approximate dates they claimed. They had gotten his permission to sleep in the town's engine house, just as they had said. McGhee was not really concerned with where his clients had been on April 28; his real goal was to show that they spoke the truth. The next witnesses got more to the point. Frederick Johnson, a railroad foreman, testified that he had seen Laramie and three others near Lakeland around noon on May 2, the same time that Harry Poppenburger had said the men were buying beer in his St. Paul saloon. Joseph Harrison lived across the railroad tracks from the old barn at Lakeland. He told the court that on the night of May 2 he heard odd noises from the barn; he had seen men there at dawn the next day, and had spoken to Laramie (he refused him a skillet) at about 8 A.M., just five hours after the crime.

McGhee saved his best alibi witness for last. Thirteen-year-old Anna Olson told the jury that, yes, her mother had been fixing her hair on the morning of May 3 when a strange man came to the door looking to borrow a frying pan. She identified that man as Harry Laramie and fixed the time as around 8:30 or 9:00 in the morning. Fred McGhee had done his legwork and produced the perfect witness for a Minnesota jury, a Scandinavian farm girl. With her testimony McGhee had his clients placed near Lakeland from noon on May 2 to nine in the morning on May 3. Though not impossible, it would have been exceedingly difficult for them to have gone to St. Paul, committed the crimes, and returned in that space of time. And on the morning of May 3 they were acting much more like hungry hobos than killers on the lam.

For his last major witness McGhee called the only other person known to have been present at the crime, Elzeard Godbout. Despite County Attorney Kane's fears that he had been "too close" to the defense, the man did not make a superior witness—the *Pioneer Press* called his testimony "of a very uncertain character." McGhee used him for a limited purpose, to cast doubt on Pugleasa's ability to identify Raverty's killers. It had to do with light. Pugleasa had testified that the shots came right after he asked Raverty to switch on the light in the office. According to Godbout, "He no more than said it when the shooting commenced. I saw two flashes and heard three shots." He was not sure whether the light came on or not, but it seems more likely that he would have seen flashes, especially if the shooters were crouched behind the partition, in the dark rather than in a lighted room. If the light was not on, then Pugleasa's identification of the culprits would lose all credibility. As for himself, Godbout had not seen the shooters at all, though he had been standing right behind Pugleasa.

McGhee also made a show of asking the court to bring the jury to the lumber company office to see for themselves the crime scene, specifically the layout of the office, the desk, the partition, and the escape window. He believed the jurors would see the implausibility of Pugleasa's evidence, especially the unlikelihood of his getting a good look at the killers. Judge Orr denied the motion, but McGhee may have made his point.

The defense case took just two days; closing arguments began the morning of November 22. County Attorney Kane did what any lawyer would do, emphasized the strong points of his case: the policeman's eyewitness testimony, the corroboration from the saloonkeepers, the defendants' lack of respectability.

> These two men have chosen to be wanderers, leading a useless life without baggage or substance, but always with a bull dog revolver loaded to the muzzle, wandering with those of their class from ocean to ocean. The confirmed tramp will not work, but he must eat, and therefore if they will not work, they must steal or starve, and they do not starve. They are always and forever, "looking for work."
>
> If you met them on the corner and they told you where they had been, would you believe them? Yet their story stands against the testimony of five witnesses who stand unimpeached. Oh, but there may have been a mistake. But such visitors as these are not happily frequent in St. Paul. . . . The

Hoffmans, Poppenburger, Ledeger, and Pugleasa all say they saw them in St. Paul and they say they were never here. Would you not remember them after seeing them once, and if a cold-blooded murder had been committed, would that not entice the memory to its office?

Kane was forced, though, to acknowledge a weakness or two. McGhee's alibi witnesses required him to argue that Laramie and Egan, through well-timed train-hopping, had appeared in both Lakeland and St. Paul on both May 2 and 3, a rather unlikely scenario. And he effectively abandoned any claim that Laramie's revolver had been used to kill Raverty. "Is it to be considered such a strange thing that a man . . . could have changed the guns?"

Fred McGhee began his address about 2 P.M. It is a shame that no good account of this or any other of his summations has been preserved, for comments here and there in the press indicate that they were renowned for their eloquence (and length). About this particular closing the *St. Paul Dispatch* reporter commented that "McGhee in his address quoted the Bible freely, told Bible stories, drew freely from his own religious experiences, which appeared to be opulent, and often appealed to Heaven."

The accounts of this speech have left us just a few passages. Responding to Kane's deprecations of the "confirmed tramps," McGhee reminded the jurors that not every tramp was a rogue. "Thanksgiving is coming, but many a poor man will enjoy his bowl of soup in an attic. A man could on his travels meet many an honest tramp." In reference to the state's reliance on the tavern owners and Mrs. Ledeger to place the defendants near the crime scene, the tee-totalling McGhee employed his own bit of deprecation. "When was it that the saloonkeeper became the keeper of men's consciences? Save us from the saloons of lower Seventh street." He scorched Hoffman and Poppenburger: "Put a glass on the counter and ask the man, what mind has he left?" Mrs. Ledeger fared still worse. "The Ledeger store—open at 12 o'clock at night—an unusual hour for an innocent candy and cigar store—with candy in front to entice our innocent children and what behind?" (McGhee's aspersions here were not empty: Mrs. Ledeger [or Ledegar] had been charged in 1898 with keeping a disorderly house, and the police at the time commented that every plainclothes officer who entered the place had been propositioned.)

He dissected the critical issue of time on that early morning of May 3. His alibi witnesses, golden citizens all, placed Egan and Laramie at Lakeland at dawn. Only two trains had gone from St. Paul toward Lakeland before dawn that day. One left at 3 A.M., a few minutes before the killing. The second left at 5 A.M., long after the all-out search had begun. "[Police Chief] O'Connor would never have allowed that train to leave St. Paul without having it searched," he asserted, and the defendants had not been found. This left only one conclusion: they had not been there.

McGhee concentrated most of his scorn on Officer Pugleasa's version of the crime. Both the darkness of the room and its physical layout made it impossible for Pugleasa to have seen what he said he saw. He reminded the jurors of Godbout's testimony about the muzzle flashes, strong indications that the room was dark. He maintained that from where Pugleasa said he had crouched, it was impossible to see the south window through which he said the criminals had escaped. And why would the officer testify falsely? Ambition, was McGhee's answer, meaning the desire to be the key figure in bringing killers to justice. "Nero, burning his city of Rome, and Judas selling his master, were ambitious, and it is natural for a policeman to be ambitious."

Judge Orr charged the jury with a range of three possible guilty verdicts: murder in the first degree (hanging); in the second degree (life in prison); or in the third degree (up to twenty years). Laramie and Egan had not been charged with burglary, though a murder conviction would seem to require that the jury believe them to be safecrackers.

The jurors got the case about 5:20 P.M. Their first decision was to break for supper, which they did about 6 P.M. They returned at 7 P.M. and began work in earnest. Surely there can be few experiences in life more torturous than awaiting a jury's decision when one's life is on the line; Laramie and Egan at least did not have to wait long. Many must have been astonished when the jury announced at 9:15 P.M. that it had reached a verdict. All were assembled in court at 10 P.M. to hear the decision: Not guilty on all counts.

Harry Laramie stood and made a short speech to the jurors. "I thank you all from the depths of my heart. I hope that your paths in the future will be sprinkled with health and prosperity." James Egan shook each juror's hand, saying that he had been certain from the beginning that he would get a "square deal" from them. The jury foreman, printer Oswald D. Curtis, replied that no thanks were needed and that he hoped both defendants would lead such a life that they never again would be put in such a position. Another juror told Laramie that he would try to find him a job in St. Paul as a telephone lineman, but he declined. The two hobos, who had passed their last previous free night in a barn, spent that night as guests of the McGhee family at 665 University Avenue, and left the next day for Chicago.[3]

Fred McGhee had done nothing less than knock the stuffings out of what had once seemed a strong prosecution case. There had been three key battles in the trial: credibility of witnesses, alibi, and weapons. The defense had won them all. Jurors said afterwards that they had not believed Officer Pugleasa and that there had never been any sentiment among them for conviction. The *Dispatch* understated when it called the verdict "no small triumph for the colored attorney, F. L. McGhee." Though not the last, it was the greatest courtroom victory of his career.

The year 1905 showed Fred McGhee, at age forty-four, at the peak of his powers. In race politics he displayed the imagination, daring, and resolve to strike out with W. E. B. Du Bois in a new venture, one that would lead eventually to the creation of the NAACP and the defeat of the Booker T. Washington approach to race issues. The *Raverty* case showed him at his courtroom best. McGhee's strengths were his legwork and his presentation. In his trials he preferred straightforward combat, witness against witness, lawyer against lawyer; he had great confidence in his rapport with Minnesota jurors. He was a foreigner in origin, accent, and complexion, but he had the common touch.

12

Home

The practice of law and the politics of race took most of Fred McGhee's time; but he had a home and social life, too. In his youth McGhee had never enjoyed a settled home life; there was slavery, then escape at age three, resettlement in Knoxville, his father's death and then his mother's, two years of schooling, work, then relocation to Chicago at age eighteen. For steady companions he had his two older brothers, Barclay and Matthew.[1]

As an adult, however, McGhee was blessed with a stable and, so far as we know, happy domestic life, at least from his arrival in St. Paul forward. In Chicago he had met and married sixteen-year-old Mattie Crane, who, like him, was an immigrant to the city from the upper South, in her case Louisville, Kentucky. The marriage had one rough patch early on: they separated once in 1888, when Mattie moved to Galesburg, Illinois, to be joined by her mother. A few months later she returned to Chicago with her mother, and some time after that rejoined her husband, this time for the rest of his life.[2]

The McGhees added the last two enduring elements of their home life in the early 1890s. In January 1892 Mattie accompanied Fred on a trip to Philadelphia for a meeting of the Colored Catholic Congress, then to New York City, where they adopted a two-and-a-half-year-old toddler, whom they named Ruth Lamar McGhee; she would be their only child. And in February 1893 they purchased a very handsome house at 665 University Avenue, for $2,000. The location was good; on a major streetcar line, near the capitol, St. Peter Claver Church, and the black community's Rondo Avenue axis. Here the McGhees entertained many friends and guests, including Booker T. Washington at least once and W. E. B. Du Bois on several occasions; here Ruth grew to adulthood; and here Fred McGhee died.[3]

Upon coming to St. Paul, Fred and Mattie McGhee immediately entered the elite ranks of the city's small black community. Fred, at least, had been well prepared for this in Chicago, where he had served as president of the Autumn Social Club. There he learned the elaborate, by today's standards, social forms of the era: toasts, speeches, fancy dress balls, grand marches, and the like. This training served him very well for the rest of his life.

In his book *Aristocrats of Color*, the scholar and writer Willard Gatewood places McGhee among "an aristocracy of a dozen persons [who] dominated intellectual, social, and political life" in the Twin Cities black community. It was certainly true that McGhee was among the elite in all these areas, but "aristocracy" is too strong a word. Older black communities to the east and south that predated Emancipation had long-established free families, well-educated and prosperous, that fit the term "aristocracy" much better. St. Paul and Minneapolis by contrast had tiny black populations until the 1880s. The so-called aristocrats of the late nineteenth and early twentieth centuries were almost all immigrants to the area, and the social scene was much more egalitarian than elsewhere. Janitors, porters, and artisans held leadership positions, along with the handful of professionals and well-to-do. That said, Fred McGhee's friends were mostly middle class and educated: John Q. Adams (off and on), Dr. Val Do Turner, attorney William T. Francis, the labor leader Charles E. James, and W. E. B. Du Bois.[4]

The McGhee residence at 665 University Avenue, St. Paul. Fred McGhee stands at front.

What is more interesting about Fred McGhee than his local social status, is how well he seemed to fit in with both more "genuine" black aristocrats around the country and with ordinary citizens alike. Most members of the African-American privileged class came from well-established free families, had received a university education, and enjoyed relatively substantial financial means; a fair complexion didn't hurt, either. Du Bois was a Harvard man from a free family; William Monroe Trotter the same. Kelly Miller was a college professor. T. Thomas Fortune came from a humble background, but was very fair. Closer to home, William R. Morris had grown up in Ohio and graduated from Fisk University. John Q. Adams had graduated from Oberlin and, like Charles James and William T. Francis, was fair enough to pass. By comparison McGhee had a spotty education; law school, yes, but before that no university training and just two years of primary school. Financially, he never achieved more than middle-class status, and his complexion was middling. In St. Paul he was the only member of the black leadership class who had been a slave. He had much more in common with Booker T. Washington—both were self-made former slaves—than with his good friend and collaborator W. E. B. Du Bois. That he rose so quickly to social prominence in Chicago, before he had made a professional name for himself, suggests that McGhee had personal qualities, a natural grace and charm, perhaps, that overcame his exceedingly humble origins. At the same time his professional life, representing criminals and appealing to juries, kept him in close touch with the middle and lower reaches of the social order.[5]

The McGhees, Fred in particular, had a very busy social life. One center of it was St. Peter Claver Church. Fred was a leading parish layman from the day of his conversion forward. When the church incorporated in 1892, he and Archbishop Ireland were two of the incorporators. Mattie sang in the choir and participated in the women's club. Both of them helped with the frequent bazaars, teas, fundraisers, and picnics. They served as godparents to many baptized into the congregation.[6]

One curious aspect of Fred McGhee's Catholic social life was his association with the Catholic Order of Foresters. Fraternal organizations of all kinds were hugely popular in turn-of-the-century America: Masons, Elks, Odd Fellows, and countless smaller ones. In St. Paul just about all of McGhee's friends were black Masons, Elks, or Odd Fellows or members of the United Brotherhood of Friendship (UBF)—but not McGhee himself. Though he sometimes supported the Elks and the UBF in various ways, the only fraternal organization he joined and stayed with (all his life) was the almost-all-white (Owen

Howell was a member, too) Catholic Order of Foresters chapter in the nearby all-white town of White Bear Lake. Apart from this, McGhee lived in a black social world; so far as can be determined from this distance, he had no white friends—colleagues, collaborators, and admirers, yes, but not friends.[7]

Another major area of Fred McGhee's social and intellectual life was the Pilgrim Baptist Church Men's Sunday Club. Being Catholic kept McGhee away from Protestant services (and perhaps from lodge membership as well), but not all Protestant-sponsored activities. The Men's Sunday Club met often to talk about serious matters such as social issues and literature. The men did not simply show up and gab; often they prepared presentations about books, for example, for consideration and discussion, or read aloud from the works of black authors. McGhee attended regularly, gave presentations of his own—on the black-hating black novelist W. Hannibal Thomas and on the black poet and novelist Paul Laurence Dunbar, for example—and sometimes served as an officer.[8]

Party politics has a very large social component, so Fred surely satisfied a good part of his need for hanging around with the guys at the many political meetings and conventions he attended, especially once he became a Democrat. Some of these were national black Democrats' gatherings, but mostly he participated in St. Paul, Ramsey County, and Minnesota Democratic party events, probably hundreds of them—another category of activities where the great majority of his colleagues were white.[9]

Clubs of all kinds were extremely popular in this era. People created them, it seems, following a certain formula; there would be an announcement, a committee to draft a club constitution, another meeting to select officers, and so on. McGhee got in on plenty of this, too. One of the longer-lasting was the Business Men's Club, which he formed in July 1900 along with John Quincy Adams, William Morris, and a few others. The club's ostensible purpose was to promote black business enterprise, but it seemed to have trouble keeping to its agenda. In July 1901 it reorganized itself "to make business and not pleasure the main object of the club." This exhortation did not take, however, and in November the members gave up pretending that the business of the club was business and changed the name to Business Men's Social Club.[10]

In April that same year, McGhee and a group of other music lovers formed the Samuel Coleridge Taylor Club, with Fred as business manager. Named for the African-American composer, the club's purpose was the cultivation of vocal music. The club did not last, but the McGhees' interest in vocal music did. Fred was no singer; Mattie, however, not only sang in the church choir but sometimes also performed in duets and trios. The McGhees also sponsored the concert appearances in St. Paul of touring black artists such as elocutionist Henrietta Vinton Davis and singers E. Azalia Hackley, Franc Glenn, and Clarence Cameron White.[11]

Though Fred did not sing, he did like to perform on stage occasionally, all in benefits: *The Last Loaf,* in 1894 and again in 1895; as General Antonio Maceo in the *Cuba* extravaganza of 1898; and as an alcoholic businessman in *A Social Glass,* in 1899. Mattie had a role in that play, too, as a town gossip, and in the 1895 presentation of *The Last Loaf.* She also directed children's plays for St. Peter Claver. On at least one occasion McGhee performed dramatic readings from the works of Paul Laurence Dunbar. Both McGhees performed in a minstrel show produced by the Ladies Home Catholic Club. The McGhees, in short, participated actively in the arts, as patrons and performers.[12]

It was not the stage, but the platform, where Fred McGhee's talents truly shone. The number of his speaking engagements, of which we have record of only a fraction, was staggering. He gave major speeches, of course, on political and race issues, such as the "Summer of Our Perfect Freedom" speech in 1890 with Archbishop Ireland, and in his campaign work for William Jennings Bryan. He regularly gave addresses for Lincoln Day, Frederick Douglass Day, and Charles Sumner Day celebrations, which in his time were staples of black civic life. On one occasion, in 1909, he travelled all the way to Spokane,

Mattie McGhee.
Photograph by Harry Shepherd.

Ruth McGhee,
Fred's adopted daughter.

Washington, in response to an invitation to make a speech for Lincoln Day there. He travelled around the country recruiting and raising money for the Afro-American Council and later the Niagara Movement. He was in constant demand in the Twin Cities to speak at benefits, fundraisers, and club meetings. He participated in debates and mock trials, on one occasion acting as defense attorney for Carrie Nation, accused of smashing saloons; other times he judged mock trials and oratory contests. During his first full calendar year in Minnesota, 1890, McGhee made eleven speaking appearances (that we know of), attended his local Republican district convention (where he made a short speech), organized a reception for visiting dignitaries from the National Education Association, and met Ida B. Wells, Hallie Q. Brown, and Father Augustus Tolton. That year set the pattern for the rest of his life. The total of his unpaid public appearances probably exceeded 500.[13]

Occasions such as Lincoln, Sumner, and Emancipation Days celebrated Afro-American history. This is a popular subject today, bookstores and libraries offer many fine works, but in McGhee's time finding even a handful of books on the subject would have been difficult. Still, McGhee knew his history remarkably well. In 1894 he made a speech honoring John Blair, the St. Paul railroad porter who had saved many lives in the horrific Hinckley, Minnesota, fire. Though Blair's deeds had been heroic, McGhee found them in a way unsurprising. "When saw you," he asked his audience, "the occasion when a Negro was called upon to perform duty but that he did not perform his whole duty— never." Indeed, our nation's history so demonstrated. "The first blood spilt for the liberty of the Country was a Black man's. The blood that produced the liberty of the slaves was the black blood of the land; and so it is not to be marveled at that on a disastrous occasion like this that a Negro is to be found performing his duty and doing his duty well." McGhee anticipated the revelations of scholars and historians of the mid-twentieth century forward: "[R]emember you this, that history is never made up until every part is in the record, and when it is fully made up there will be written upon the top line the names of the Black men of the world."[14]

McGhee did a great deal of charity work. Most of it came in the form of speaking or presiding at fundraising events. Bethesda Baptist Church of Minneapolis, especially, seemed to rely on him. For a period in the first decade of the twentieth century, both McGhees took an active interest in orphan care, probably because their daughter, Ruth, and Fred had been orphans themselves. In late 1902 and early 1903 Fred and Mattie led a drive in the black community to raise money to furnish the reception room at the Jean Martin

Brown receiving home, a shelter for infants then being built by the Children's Home Society. They raised about $600. Later in that decade, Fred made speaking appearances and did some advocacy work on behalf of the Crispus Attucks Home, a combined orphanage and home for the elderly for Minnesotans of African descent. There is reason to believe, too, that Fred performed many acts of private charity, through St. Peter Claver Church, for which no records remain.[15]

He was gone from home a great deal, which brings two other aspects of the McGhee's family life into focus. One was Mattie's vital role at home, as homemaker, family anchor, hostess, and mother to daughter Ruth. There can be no doubt that Fred was a loving father, but as is so often the case with busy and ambitious men, frequently an absent one. He relied on Mattie to rear Ruth and to provide the support services that a prominent man requires—family obligations under control, the house ready for social events, the hostess and companion charming and prepared.

The second aspect of family life that McGhee's many absences highlight is money. McGhee's only source of income was his solo practice of law. While it is not possible to calculate McGhee's income, the record does permit a few conclusions. He must have been good at extracting cash from clients' pockets, especially in the early years. In the early and mid-1890s, for example, he mostly represented the impecunious, prostitutes and other smalltime criminals. Yet he took many cases to trial, few of them as appointed counsel. Unless he was working for free, which is unlikely, people must have been paying him.

How much would have been enough to support him and his family comfortably? An 1894 list of St. Paul public employees' salaries gives a sense of it. The mayor made $2,500 per year; the chief of police and chief fire engineer earned more, $3,500; police lieutenants and detectives, the mayor's secretary, and the third assistant city attorney, all made $1,200; the city librarian, $1,000; health inspectors $900. For McGhee to keep economic pace with, say, an assistant prosecutor, he would need to take in about $5 per day, every day. When criminal courts were in session, at least, this was probably feasible. It is not hard to imagine, for example, McGhee getting a tip from his friend, jailer James Loomis, about a potential police court client, meeting the client at arraignment on a Tuesday, arranging a $5 or $10 fee, and trying the case on Wednesday.

However McGhee did it, he must have done it pretty well: he owned a lovely house; by his late forties took rather long vacations; and of course travelled a great deal. These absences came at a financial sacrifice, for when a solo practitioner is not in the office or in court, he is not making any money.

His skin color also probably limited Fred McGhee's earnings. So far as the available record reveals, McGhee never had a well-to-do white client (though the family of his 1906 client, Henry Sussman, did have some means.) The careers of successful criminal defense attorneys often follow a pattern: start by trying lots of cases for ordinary criminals, often as court-appointed counsel; get a big break or two in high profile cases; with experience and reputation now established, get paying clients and start to make some real money. In a world without racial categories, this should have happened for a lawyer of McGhee's demonstrated and well-publicized ability; but it did not. Even at the end of his life he was taking court-appointed and penny-ante cases. In 1907 he went to court over an unpaid fee of $25, and lost. The next year McGhee sued to recover $20, deposited in court as the fruit of an alleged crime, from his client, probably a prostitute. The result was not reported. In 1911 he took a case to trial in which the entire amount in controversy was $15.50. Even with a generous adjustment for inflation, these matters must have been worth his time only if he needed the work and the money. McGhee did have paying white clients in the civil side of his practice—mainly probate, divorce, and real estate—but these were not big money cases.[16]

The McGhees always had debts. When they bought their house in 1893 they financed just half of the $2,000 price; but a year later remortgaged it for $2,500, and went through three more mortgages before Fred McGhee's death. The McGhees were sued over debts on three occasions between 1893 and 1898; in all cases (one was for medical bills, another for glass work, the third for causes unknown) they either defaulted or stipulated to a judgment against them. They must have had a cash-flow problem.[17]

Lawsuits ended after 1898, and financially, things improved sufficiently that McGhee began to take summer vacations, mostly for fishing. His main angling pal was the physician Val Do Turner, who had come to St. Paul in 1898, also from Tennessee, as Minnesota's first black doctor. He and McGhee began taking fishing trips, mostly in central and northern Minnesota—Lake Pokegama and Sturgeon Lake—in the early years of the twentieth century.[18]

It was probably his love for fishing that led Fred McGhee to one of the last, and most fateful, purchases of his life. He discovered the beauty of Polk County in western Wisconsin, less than 100 miles northeast of St. Paul and easily accessible in those days by train. This rolling country of farms, hardwood forests, lakes, and streams is still prime fishing country today, and a century ago it must have been an angler's paradise. The region's main waterway is the upper Apple River. Near its junction with the St. Croix, the lower Apple runs shallow and quick (making it today a popular spot for inner-tubing). But the upper Apple runs deep and tranquil, and it was this stretch that charmed the McGhees most. In September 1909 Fred and Mattie McGhee purchased thirty-nine acres along the upper Apple, near Amery, Wisconsin, for the sum of $1,500; they paid $1,000 cash and financed the rest with a mortgage. The place came with a little, rustic frame house, and the McGhees spent most of the next three summers there.

They called the place Camp DuGhee (the name apparently a combination of Du Bois and McGhee) or simply "the farm." McGhee, a city dweller almost all of his life, became Farmer Fred there on the banks of the Apple. He and Mattie acquired a plow, a cultivator, a grindstone, a churn, two poultry incubators, and a cow and some turkeys. Though the place was exceedingly humble—the furnishings included two iron beds, two tables, eight chairs, and three lamps—the McGhees entertained a parade of visitors, from the Twin Cities and beyond. McGhee's old Chicago friend, the "society prince" and entrepreneur Julius Avendorph, and his wife visited on more than one occasion; so did W. E. B. Du Bois. A great deal of serious race and national politics, including the earliest work of the NAACP, was discussed in McGhee's rowboat on the upper Apple River.[19]

The year 1909 also marked one of the proudest events in the McGhees' family life; on June 8, 1909, Ruth McGhee graduated from high school—the first and last in Fred McGhee's line ever to do so. That year only five African-American students graduated from St. Paul high schools, and Ruth was the only one of them to graduate with honors. Her good grades won her the opportunity to speak at the commencement ceremonies. She chose as her topic, "The Contribution of the Negro to the Nation." According to *The Appeal*, her talk was "full of telling points and stubborn facts, . . . well received by the large audience." The quality of her speech may have had something to do with the resources at her disposal, not only her father, but also the greatest black intellectual figure of the era: W. E. B. Du Bois himself gave her a hand. Fred McGhee was very proud of his daughter, and he sent Du Bois a graduation photo as a gift. Ruth McGhee had the preparation, the intelligence, and the means to attend college, but for reasons unknown she never did so. Later in life she worked as a secretary and stenographer.[20]

McGhee saw very little of his brothers after moving to St. Paul. Brother Matthew paid one visit, in July 1891. He was seven years older than Fredrick, and seems to have followed his younger brother to Chicago in the 1880s, working as a porter, messenger, and bartender. Matthew probably came to St. Paul that summer to say goodbye, for he was suffering from tuberculosis. On July 5 he was chatting with the McGhees at their home when he was stricken with an attack, went upstairs to rest, and within a half hour died; he was thirty-seven years old. He rests now in St. Paul's Oakland Cemetery. So far as we know, brother Barclay McGhee, who had relocated to Lincoln, Nebraska, never visited Fredrick in St. Paul, nor did Fred visit him. When Fredrick died, Barclay arrived too late for the funeral, turned around, and went home. He came to St. Paul once more, in 1919, to say goodbye to Mattie and Ruth. No further trace of him can now be found.[21]

The McGhees, happily, had much more contact with Mattie's family, the Cranes. In 1892 her parents and brother, Charles, left Louisville to join Mattie in St. Paul, and lived there the rest of their lives. Fred, making use of his Democratic Party connections, got his father-in-law, John Crane, work for the city as a jailer and his brother-in-law, Charles Crane, a job in the workhouse as a cook. The McGhees and Cranes are now together forever, buried in the same burial plot.[22]

13

Niagara

The year 1906 proved to be the most eventful and productive of the short life of the Niagara Movement. The movement established itself, at least for a critical moment, as a credible and independent alternative to the Washington-NAAC leadership.

Niagara held its second annual meeting in mid-August 1906 at Storer College in Harper's Ferry, West Virginia, a location chosen for its symbolism. Just as John Brown had attacked slavery there forty-seven years before, the Niagara men now proposed to launch there an attack on slavery's legacy. Fred McGhee attended as Minnesota's representative and, as head of the movement's legal department, played a prominent role at the meeting. He gave an oral report on the "status of the Negro's civil rights in certain states" and likely composed the written report of the Committee of Legal Defense and Civil Rights and in discussions of the Barbara Pope case (about which more later).[1]

As with all such meetings, there were many speeches and committee reports. The speeches reflected Niagara's pugnacious attitude; speakers condemned both President Roosevelt and Secretary of War Taft, and one referred to Booker T. Washington as the "third person of the trinity" (with Taft and Roosevelt) who had sold out the race. In terms of rhetoric and attitude, the conference's finest achievement was its Address to the Nation, a masterpiece of protest literature:

> In the past year the work of the Negro hater has flourished in the land. Step by step the defenders of the rights of American citizens have retreated. The work of stealing the black man's ballot has progressed.... Discrimination in travel and public accommodation has so spread that some of our weaker brethren are actually afraid to thunder against color discrimination as such and are simply whispering for ordinary decencies.
>
> Against this the Niagara Movement eternally protests.... We claim for ourselves every single right that belongs to a freeborn American, political, civil, and social; and until we get these rights we will never cease to protest and assail the ears of America....

Never before in the modern age has a great and civilized folk threatened to adopt so cowardly a creed in the treatment of its fellow-citizens .... Stripped of verbiage and subterfuge ... the new American creed says: Fear to let black men even try to rise lest they become the equals of the white. And this is a land that professes to follow Jesus Christ. The blasphemy of such a course is only matched by its cowardice.

The Address then listed its "clear and unequivocal" demands: full manhood suffrage; the end to Jim Crow accommodations; unfettered freedom of assembly and association; equal application of the laws, especially criminal laws; federal supervision of elections; federal enforcement of the Civil War amendments to the Constitution; equal and compulsory public education for all children.

Critics of Niagara, of which there was no shortage, noted that these goals differed little from those of the NAAC or Booker T. Washington. But Niagara was not solely about goals or means; it was also about dethroning Washington and discrediting the policies of patience and acquiescence to second-class citizenship associated with him. Niagara's Address made this perfectly clear to those who knew how to read it. Niagarites would accomplish their goals by voting, sacrifice, truth-telling, and "persistent, ceaseless agitation" (a tactic not favored by Washington). "We live to tell these dark brothers of ours—scattered in counsel, wavering and weak—that no bribe of money or notoriety, no promise of

Niagara Conference, 1906.
Fredrick McGhee with his trademark piercing stare is positioned in the second row,
almost directly at center. W. E. B. Du Bois is seated in the front row right of center.

wealth or fame, is worth the surrender of a people's manhood or the loss of a man's self-respect. We refuse to surrender the leadership of this race to cowards and trucklers." Cowards and trucklers—that is, Washington and his minions. The choice of words is arrogant, for it suggests to Washington's many followers, "We don't want you and we don't need you."

The Address concludes:

> We appeal to the young men and women of this nation, to those whose nostrils are not yet befouled by greed and racial narrowness: Stand up for the right, prove yourselves worthy of your heritage .... Courage, brothers! The battle for humanity is not lost or losing. All across the skies sit signs of promise.... The morning breaks over blood-stained hills. We must not falter, we may not shrink. Above are the everlasting stars.

One wonders whether Fred McGhee, upon reading this Address, recalled the social equality speeches of Archbishop Ireland and the challenging words of William A. Hazel spoken in St. Paul 14 years before.[2]

Booker T. Washington, who kept close track of Niagara, understood the challenge, and answered it in the many ways he had at his disposal: editorials (though not over his signature) in the black press, the planting of rumors and disinformation, pressure on particular individuals, and the marshaling of his own great popularity. His pressure may well have reached St. Paul, for it is curious that *The Appeal* covered the Harper's Ferry meeting only by noting that McGhee had attended and called it "very successful." John Quincy Adams had in 1905 printed Niagara's Address to the Nation in full; in 1906, not a word.[3]

While Washington worked against Niagara, events during the rest of 1906, some of them tragic, seemed to work for it. In September many innocent black citizens were murdered in a terrible race riot in Atlanta. It was an explosion of race hatred in the South at a time when Washington was speaking publicly of the relatively happy times for southern blacks and their warm relations with white neighbors. The riot, on top of the endless lynchings and the extension of Jim Crow, hurt the credibility of his nonconfrontational approach. And the federal government's persistent refusal to intervene to protect black citizens called into question once again the wisdom of Bookerite loyalty to President Roosevelt and the Republican Party.[4]

In November came the revelation of Roosevelt's decision in the Brownsville incident (described in Chapter 7), ending the military careers of 167 black soldiers without a hearing or the possibility of appeal. This deed—needlessly done, cynically timed, and cowardly announced—provoked anger and bitter protest in black America. People recalled the remarks Roosevelt had made after the Spanish-American War about the cowardice of black soldiers in Cuba. Taft, though he had privately opposed the order, could not avoid sharing the blame. Roosevelt had betrayed Booker T. Washington; Washington had attached his imprimatur of approval to the president, only to be rewarded with seeming treachery. Still, the Wizard would not criticize his friend the president. There were protest meetings across the country, including St. Paul, where McGhee spoke at the Pilgrim Baptist Church and where his Men's Sunday Club sent Roosevelt a telegram of protest. Those, like Fred McGhee, who had long accused the Republican Party of hypocrisy—of reaping bushels of black votes but returning only crumbs—seemed vindicated.[5]

Then in early 1907 the Niagara Movement scored a rare court victory in the fight against Jim Crow. One summer day in 1906 a black woman named Barbara Pope bought a first-class rail ticket in the District of Columbia for travel to the town of Paeonian Springs, Virginia. When the Southern Railway car crossed into Virginia, Miss Pope was directed to leave the first-class car and move to the Jim Crow car, in accordance with Virginia law. She refused, was arrested, found guilty, and fined $10 plus costs. This case attracted the attention of the Niagarites, perhaps because it took place near in time and place to the Harper's Ferry meeting. Fred McGhee supervised the hiring of local counsel and the shaping of Miss Pope's appeal. They lost the first appeal, but pressed on to the Virginia supreme court; on January 9, 1907, her conviction was vacated and the case remanded for a new trial, a trial that probably never took place. W. E. B. Du Bois exulted over this victory. In a letter to his Niagara colleagues he crowed, "this means that the NIAGARA MOVEMENT has established that under the present statute Virginia cannot fine an interstate passenger who refuses to be Jim Crowed."

Du Bois's assessment was accurate, so far as it went, but his exultation misplaced. The victory turned out to be an empty one. On appeal the state of Virginia simply conceded the case on the sensible ground that the statute in question did not provide for criminal penalties to passengers who refused to change rail cars. The statute applied to railroads, not passengers. By confessing error, which was unquestionably the correct legal decision, the state prevented the litigation of any of the real Jim Crow issues. There being no legal question in dispute, there was no supreme court opinion to publish either. The case was a victory, yes, but it had no consequences except saving Barbara Pope ten dollars.[6]

Niagara failed to exploit the opportunities handed it in late 1906. The founders had intended for the national organization to rest on a solid foundation of state organizations, but these were not taking shape. Even in Minnesota, where McGhee had experience and credibility, plus a close relationship with Du Bois, no state organization ever developed. The movement consisted of McGhee and a few others, with no actual structure or work to do—in this respect a reprise of the Afro-American Council experience. The situation was similar in Niagara "strongholds" around the country. Moreover, where the movement took hold at all it divided the northern civil rights community into rival camps, and there were simply not enough people with enough time, energy, and money to carry one to victory over the other.

The leaders pressed ahead just the same. The civil rights division urged members across the country to undertake state and local action on public accommodation ("Have You a Civil Rights Act in your State? . . . If you haven't one, why not get one passed?"), jury service, and collaboration with other like-minded organizations. The legal department, under McGhee, searched for new cases to take and means to take them. McGhee did not attend the movement's 1907 annual meeting in Boston (we do not know why), but he did send a report. The report dealt mainly with the Barbara Pope case, of which McGhee was proud. But the case had been costly; over $600 in legal fees and costs, a good portion of which still remained unpaid in June 1907. One delegate suggested that taking the case might have been a mistake after all. Du Bois, perhaps defending McGhee's judgment in the matter, disagreed, pointing out that in bringing such cases one can never be sure of the outcome. "We must not expect that we are going to find quickly just the case we want." He was glad that Niagara had taken the case; it had been "more successful than we had any right to expect." McGhee had found another possible case in Kentucky, and the delegates directed him to proceed with the case if it looked promising. That is the last we hear of that case. Either it turned out to be not so promising or McGhee, recalling the Hardy case and others, determined not to take any case without sufficient resources—it would be "tomfoolery."[7]

Just two years old, Niagara faced severe money troubles. At the end of 1907 its treasurer, J. Milton Waldron, reported that it had income of just $741.76 for the period August 1, 1906, through July 31, 1907, of which $279 had been contributed for the Pope case specifically. Dues of $2650 remained unpaid. Niagara owed Du Bois $90, lawyers in the Pope case $240, and McGhee $156. Cash on hand, the entire assets of the treasury, came to $5.[8]

The dire state of the treasury did not affect the organization's rhetoric. The 1907 Address to the Nation restated Niagara's goals and means just as assertively as ever, and added something new:

We call on the 500,000 black voters of the North: Use your ballots to defeat Theodore Roosevelt, William Taft, or any man named by the present
dictatorship. Better vote for avowed enemies than for false friends. But, better still, vote with the white laboring class, remembering that the cause of
labor is the cause of black men, and the black man's cause is labor's own.[9]

These three sentences must have pleased Fred McGhee a great deal, and,
given his closeness with Du Bois, he probably influenced them. William Jennings Bryan would be a candidate again in 1908, and the one message of his
that might make sense to black voters was a class message. This seemed to be
the message that McGhee had tried to make in his St. Paul speech for Bryan in
1896, when he called the election (then Bryan running against McKinley) a
contest between the common people and the moneyed classes. At this moment
in history, only an economic message could cut across racial and regional lines
and bring blacks into the Democratic Party. Unfortunately for McGhee, he did
not live to see this happen.

Though the meeting in Boston was fairly well attended, the historian Elliot
Rudwick calls it the beginning of Niagara's end. One of the causes was internal discord, mostly centering round James Monroe Trotter. Niagara's biggest
and strongest affiliate was in Boston, the Boston Civil Rights League, which
Trotter abrasively led. He excelled at division and could not long tolerate anything less than the top spot; conflict with Du Bois, no great uniter either, was
inevitable. It came in the fall and winter of 1907, over membership. Did people
come into Niagara through Trotter's League or directly? If they came through
the League, then Niagara would be controlled from the periphery, by its
strongest chapters, rather than by the central authority. Trotter made accommodation impossible.

On December 6, 1907, an exasperated Du Bois, general secretary of the
Niagara, prepared a letter to J. Milton Waldron, Niagara's treasurer, that began,
"I have just sent a copy of the enclosed resignation to Mr. McGhee, who as
chairman of the legal department, will on the 28th of December become the
acting General Secretary of the Niagara Movement." Doubtless to McGhee's
relief, Du Bois never sent the resignation letter; it was either a ploy—without
him Niagara was nothing—or a venting of frustration. The letter shows how
central McGhee was to the movement: Du Bois had set it up so that his friend
and chief legal adviser would take over if he left. McGhee did not become acting general secretary, but he did preside over the executive committee meetings the last three days of 1907, which had been convened to resolve the
Boston dispute. The conflict was papered over for the moment.[10]

Niagara business kept Fred McGhee busy in 1908. Early in the year Booker T. Washington brought the leadership battle to McGhee's home territory. On January 18 *The Appeal* announced that Washington would arrive on February 10 for Lincoln Day celebrations. In the next issue it reported that Edward H. Morris, "the leading Afro-American lawyer in the United States," would visit the city, and specifically its black Odd Fellows, of which he was a national leader, the same week. Morris was a signer of the first Niagara call, a friend of McGhee's, and a long-time critic of Washington's. Was the timing of his visit coincidental, or part of the battle? We will never know.[11]

During the second week of February 1908, McGhee, Washington, Morris, and others played out a little drama of estrangement in St. Paul. The Odd Fellows met first. McGhee made a speech to them entitled "Organization." As we know which organization dominated his attention at the time, we can guess (but only guess) what may have been the subject of his remarks. Niagara had recently, and rather successfully, opened its ranks to women. Mrs. Val Do Turner addressed the Odd Fellows on "Organization of Women of the Race." McGhee's friend, William T. Francis, introduced the main speaker, McGhee's old mentor and law partner, E. H. Morris. *The Appeal* reported that "there was a large crowd present and every person was glad to be there."[12]

Washington, befitting his station, enjoyed a much grander gathering, held at the old State Capitol, site of the Wizard's victory at the 1902 NAAC meeting. The event began with a procession from Washington's lodgings, to the office of Governor John A. Johnson. According to John Quincy Adams's *Appeal*, "for about an hour these two great men talked of matters of interest, both giving and receiving valuable information, and the interview was reluctantly concluded when Dr. Washington had to leave to go to the reception." Some 500 or 600 people awaited him in the old House of Representatives' chambers, where upon his appearance they "rose en masse and gave him the Chautauqua salute."

Whether intended or not, the reception surely reminded McGhee and his allies of the enormous esteem the great man continued to enjoy among white citizens and black, and how little so far Niagara had done to wound him. At best the Niagarites were chipping away at the edges of his power. William T. Francis, who had introduced E. H. Morris to the Odd Fellows gathering, now introduced Washington to his much bigger audience. His speech "lasted for more than an hour and was replete with words of wisdom and good, sound advice, which fell upon willing ears and was roundly applauded as the speaker proceeded." Then followed a reception with refreshments, another talk at

People's Church, then more entertainment at Francis's house, with J. Q. Adams, McGhee's friend Val Do Turner, McGhee's fellow Catholic and Democrat Owen Howell, and Thomas Lyles. Since 1890, Fred McGhee had been a regular speaker at Lincoln Day programs, and would have been a principal player, speaker, and socializer at an event such as this one; in February 1908 he was nowhere to be seen.

He was busy snubbing, or being snubbed, and arranging a very different event. Twenty-four hours after the conclusion of Washington's capitol reception, another soiree began, this one McGhee's tribute to his old mentor Morris. McGhee served as toastmaster of this six-course, alcohol-free banquet. Local Niagarite Harvey Burk, plus Dr. Turner, William Morris, and the suddenly ubiquitous William Francis (among others) attended.[13]

To judge from who participated in these various functions, the great majority of politically conscious Twin Cities African Americans saw no conflict at all in honoring both Washington and one of his well-known critics. Most people probably saw no reason not to associate with Bookerites and Niagarites alike; it was only those in the upper levels of leadership who could not stand to be together in the same room.

Three weeks after the Morris and Washington visits W. E. B. Du Bois came to town. He stayed with the McGhees at their University Avenue home, where they also held a reception for him; he made speeches at St. James AME and St. Peter Claver Churches. He and McGhee must have talked a lot of Niagara politics, too. Despite the continuing financial problems, some good things were happening. As Du Bois reported to the movement's members two weeks later, long-time Washington man and NAAC stalwart (and current president) Bishop Alexander Walters had joined the District of Columbia branch of Niagara! Niagara was sending out letters to black voters in the South urging them to vote against Taft in the coming presidential election. He reported also that "another Jim-Crow car case, involving the Pullman service in the south, has been brought in Minnesota by the Legal Department under Secretary McGhee." This case has never been found, and most likely went nowhere. It would be interesting to know how McGhee proposed to challenge a southern transportation practice in a Minnesota court.[14]

Soon after Du Bois's visit the patch-up between him and Trotter over which McGhee had presided the previous December came apart; Trotter left Niagara in April to found the rival Negro American Political League. This move split the vital Massachusetts delegation and cost Niagara one of its most prominent voices, Trotter's *Boston Guardian*. In mid-June Du Bois returned to St. Paul, os-

tensibly to speak at a dinner honoring black graduates of local high schools
and colleges. More likely his stronger reasons for the visit were to confer about
the state of Niagara with his friend McGhee, and also to get in a little fishing.
Mattie and Ruth were spending part of the summer in Apple River country,
probably at the property the McGhees would purchase a year later. Du Bois arrived three weeks before his scheduled appearances, and then never made
them. It is likely that when he and McGhee were supposed to be attending
banquets in St. Paul, they were fishing on the Apple River, and talking about
Niagara.[15]

From St. Paul Du Bois sent out letters to the Niagarites across the country
urging them to attend the fourth annual meeting, this year to be held at Oberlin, Ohio. Comparatively few did—estimates range from nineteen to fifty delegates. McGhee and Du Bois attended, along with fellow founder C.E. Bentley.
From the sketchy accounts of this meeting that survive, one can discern either
McGhee's strong influence or a general turning of opinion in his direction. In
the deliberations leading up to the annual statement to the nation Du Bois and
others spoke for McGhee's political hero, the Democratic candidate William
Jennings Bryan. Though the final communiqué, signed first by McGhee, endorsed no one, it urged African Americans to vote against Taft; thus, Niagara
had now completed the rejection of the Republican Party that McGhee had so
long urged. McGhee must have been particularly pleased by the call to "establish next November the principle of Negro independence in voting, not only
for punishing enemies, but for rebuking false friends." The sentiment resem-
bled that of McGhee's 1903 speech proposing that the NAAC become a political
action group to "take care of certain districts" and use voting power to discard
unfriendly or unresponsive officeholders.

The meeting's final resolution also endorsed violent self-defense: "Obey
the law, defend no crime, conceal no criminal, seek no quarrel; but arm your-
selves, and when the mob invades your home, shoot, and shoot to kill." Had
anyone been paying attention, the phrase, "shoot, and shoot to kill" might have
made headlines in the daily press across the country. But not even the black
press paid much attention to this meeting, for lack of interest, or Booker T.
Washington's influence, or both.[16]

The lack of response shows how little influence the Niagara Movement ex-
erted by then. Born with such energy and high hopes just three years before,
the movement was seriously ill, a victim of the familiar plagues—not enough
people, not enough money, and opposing forces too powerful. The demands
on its general secretary were also unsustainable. Du Bois had many claims on

his time and attention, including his job at Atlanta University. To try to keep Niagara going, encourage its growth, and get it solvent, while publishing his magazine, *Horizon,* and performing his duties at Atlanta, was too much even for the titanically energetic Du Bois.

Niagara's troubles apparently did not deter Fred McGhee from pursuing his work as head of the movement's legal department. He continued to try to raise money, to look for test cases, and to give advice to African-American lawyers around the country. In summer 1909 he prepared what would be his final report to Niagara membership, for presentation at its fifth annual meeting, held at Sea Island City, New Jersey. The report brims with pride over accomplishments (unfortunately, none of the cases McGhee refers to in the report can be found), determination, and frustration over lack of money:

> In the First declaration made by this organization at Niagara, we declared an unceasing war against the denial of suffrage and for civil rights. . . . [W]henever we have had the opportunity we have not failed to carry out this *declaration*; and it is the belief of the department that we have just reason to be proud of the record we have made. . . . But this record, though it be the best, does not bring satisfaction, it inspires us to do more. It is true at the same time the recollection of how small it is when compared with the great deal there is to do . . . caused us to hesitate in sending the report at this conference.
>
> During the past year the department has been unable to do anything owing to the lack of funds, except to offer advice and assistance in the preparation of briefs that have come to us. . . .
>
> Looking to the future we are not discouraged; indeed we have much reason for encouragement. The one thing we most need is a fund so we may prepare cases and present them under the best and most favorable conditions.

This report gives us a bare glimpse of what Fred McGhee did as head of Niagara's legal department, just enough to provoke the imagination. One sees him at his desk in the Globe Building in downtown St. Paul, reviewing letters, trial records, and appellate briefs from around the country, and dictating letters of advice. The report also shows that in some respects nothing had changed since the 1890 failure of McGhee's Minnesota Civil Rights Committee: the war against Jim Crow was being poorly fought in the courts, not for lack of will or lack of lawyers, but for lack of money.[17]

Paradoxically, events were in motion that would soon end Niagara once and for all, but also over time lead to the creation of precisely the kind of legal defense fund for which McGhee pleaded. A race riot in Springfield, Illinois, in

1908 shocked the nation for various reasons. The city's black population had been relatively prosperous and Springfield was Abraham Lincoln's adopted hometown. When a supposed rape of a white woman by a black man touched off lynchings and riots there, it crystallized for an important group of white supporters of racial justice that things were going disastrously wrong and that the Booker T. Washington approach had failed. The event dislodged some of the white intellectual and philanthropic community from its loyalty to Washington and moved it toward Du Bois.

This shift ultimately led to the calling of what came to be known as the National Negro Conference of 1909 in New York City. The promoters were reporter and reformer Mary Ovington, millionaire socialist Wright Walling, and Du Bois. Held in late May, the conference brought together most of the high-profile black leaders, including Du Bois, his rival-antagonist-ally Trotter, Ida B. Wells Barnett, Alexander Walters, and others. McGhee did not attend; nor do we know if he was invited. Booker T. Washington did not attend because he was not invited. More important, the organizers brought in a large group of white reformers and money-men.

Historians trace the beginning of the NAACP to this meeting. The conference created a Committee of Forty, composed of black citizens and white, women and men, to put together a new civil rights organization in which people of both races would work together as equals. With people such as Walling, the industrialist Jacob Schiff, and other wealthy and well-known people behind it, the new organization would begin with money and credibility. Not surprisingly, this prospect engaged Du Bois's imagination and attention far more than penniless and powerless Niagara. The northern civil rights movement did not have room for an additional national organization, and Niagara was nothing without Du Bois, so his commitment to the Committee of Forty sunk Niagara forever.[18]

The genius of the new organization lay in its cross-racial alliance, which gave it money and a vaster potential constituency. Some of the money would eventually be used for court cases and the creation, decades later, of the NAACP Legal Defense Fund. Fred McGhee would not live to see this dream of his come true, but he did live long enough to bring the NAACP to Minnesota. His beloved Niagara Movement failed, but it served as the transition between the amateur and ineffective civil rights organizations of the nineteenth century and the professional, productive bodies of the twentieth century.

14

The Civil Rights Cases

Fred McGhee's four years as head of Niagara's legal department were a fitting culmination, but not the end, of a long career of civil rights litigation. For twenty years McGhee used his lawyer's skills and training to bring cases, or defend cases, on behalf of black clients who were victims of discrimination or accused of crime where race may have been a factor. The record of this aspect of his career is of course incomplete: certainly many cases and causes will never be found. But enough information has survived to permit the reconstruction of at least a fair idea of McGhee's work in this area.

The story begins with his defense in 1889 of the white woman Jennie Hendrickson, described in Chapter 3. There McGhee used a *habeas corpus* proceeding to free the young woman placed in detention without charges or trial; he forced the district court to agree that this "custom," apparently established to protect the detainee's morals, had no basis in law. In a way the case exemplifies the lawyerly and essentially conservative approach that McGhee took on such matters, legal and political, all his life—urging the authorities simply to apply the law fairly and equally to all; not to follow custom or popular desire, in which many prejudices and errors may lurk, but the law. The same approach shows up consistently in the appeals and protests of the Afro-American League, the Afro-American Council, the Minnesota Civil Rights Committee, the Law Enforcement League, and the Niagara Movement, when they requested or demanded of the courts and Congress that they enforce the Constitution and the Civil War amendments. Effective and evenhanded enforcement of state and federal laws, as they were written, would have been a tremendous boon to African Americans.

The *Hendrickson* case also illustrates a lesson that civil rights workers had to learn and keep learning: that victories are never secure. Her victory in 1889 did not have much impact on the day-to-day workings of the police and municipal court in St. Paul, which kept sending women to the House of the Good Shepherd or the county workhouse on suspicion of prostitution. McGhee brought the very same issue to court in 1895 in a *habeas corpus* proceeding on behalf of Jennie McKenzie. She had been sent to the House of the Good Shepherd for violating an ordinance that made it a misdemeanor to "resort around a disorderly house." Judge Willis ruled that "a person might resort around such a place and still be guilty of no offense." In other words, an ordinance that authorized a conviction based on proximity or association alone was invalid; some actual crime, or step toward crime (for Judge Willis, "evil intent" was enough) had to be shown. We do not know if Fred McGhee saw this as a civil rights case. He may simply have been paid to get McKenzie, who almost certainly was a prostitute, out of confinement. But it was precisely this sort of chipping away at overbroad laws and established customs that laid the groundwork for the great civil rights appellate court cases of the twentieth century.[1]

The *Lewis Carter* case, in 1890, did not have civil rights implications, except to the extent that any case involving a black man accused of raping a white woman does. Carter had the good fortune of being accused and arrested in the far North; had it happened in, say, Georgia, he might not have lived to face trial. The case illustrates a lesson still being learned and relearned: the tremendous importance for any defendant, but especially the most vulnerable, of having a skilled advocate, preferably one with some political smarts. Lewis got out of prison because a black lawyer showed up in St. Paul, and the lawyer zealously did his job. Readers will recall that Carter's request for presidential clemency had two key elements. First, McGhee hunted up Carter's accuser and persuaded her to sign a statement supporting his release. Second, the local Republican congressman recommended the clemency to the Republican president; the fact that McGhee was a prominent state Republican leader at the time no doubt made access to Congressman Snider easier. There was nothing brilliant about McGhee's work; it was just energetic and effective advocacy. Countless African Americans accused of crime have suffered dreadfully for lack of this basic protection.

In 1903 McGhee took another ordinary criminal case with similar implications. A black man named James Haynes was accused of attempted rape in Minneapolis. He had, or so the accusation

James Haynes,
inmate #IIII.

went, equipped himself with a vial of chloroform, hoisted himself onto a shed, then cut the screen to a second-floor window, entered, and used the chloroform to try to subdue a fourteen-year-old girl for the purpose of rape. He bungled the attempt, she yelled, the girl's mother appeared, and Haynes then grabbed the girl and carried her with him as he fled. He hid with the girl in a nearby barn until caught by the police. Black citizens of Minneapolis, rightly sensitive to the explosive potential of such cases, rushed to condemn Haynes and disassociate themselves from him. At a mass meeting chaired by lawyer William R. Morris they adopted a resolution stating "in official form" that

> they deplore with unspeakable horror the brutal crime, and condemn it with all earnestness and as law-abiding citizens, offer their services, and; if necessity requires, their lives, in running down and putting into the strong arms of the law any person guilty of, or any person charged with such a crime.

Who could be more contemptible than a cunning, calculating black violator of innocent white girlhood? And who more in need of a defender? Fred McGhee took the case. In one sense, of course, he was just doing his job as a lawyer, but there was more to it than that. Haynes stood condemned before trial, most conspicuously by his black brethren. McGhee had nothing to gain personally or professionally by being the lawyer for the rapist; quite the contrary; respectable blacks had made their position clear, went the thinking. But the protection of the accused's rights in such cases is the very beginning of civil rights. Civil rights are vindicated only when people, often lawyers, undertake to do so.[2]

The *Samuel Hardy* case, in 1892, introduced McGhee to a different and less satisfying area of advocacy, the fight against Jim Crow in the civil courts. This defeat—McGhee and Hardy did not even show up in Chattanooga for the trial—was ignominious. As a criminal defense attorney McGhee relied on his wits and his legwork. He presumably learned from the Hardy case that attacking institutional forces in civil court requires a different kind of advocacy than does criminal defense. Cases must be carefully chosen, the right local counsel selected, and enough money gathered to withstand a war of attrition. McGhee spent the rest of his life—especially during his Niagara years—trying to put those elements together, and never really succeeded. The time was not right; it took the NAACP until the 1940s and 1950s to learn how to bring such cases and win.

McGhee had more success in smaller civil cases in Minnesota courts. We know from his 1897 letter to *The Appeal*, described in Chapter 5, that he regu-

larly brought civil damages cases on behalf of black citizens who claimed discrimination in public accommodations. He claimed then that $25 was an or-
dinary jury award.[3] This was not a huge amount of money, but enough (along
with legal expenses) to sting the owner of a cafe or a small hotel. In part because all issues of *The Appeal* from December 1892 to February of 1897 are lost,
we do not know to which cases McGhee referred. We have details of just five
of his public accommodations cases.

Readers may recall that in 1891, a week after blasting McGhee and the Afro-
American League for their spinelessness, William A. Hazel had been refused
service at the Delicatessen restaurant. Hazel quickly either forgave McGhee or
revised his opinion, for when it came time to sue, he hired Fred McGhee. After pretrial proceedings revealed a weakness in the case, Hazel settled his
$5,000 claim for just his costs. Three years later Rosa Hazel sued the same
restaurant. This one went to trial and McGhee got Mrs. Hazel a verdict of
$25.00. After that, maybe the Delicatessen's proprietors learned to treat the
Hazels right.

In fall 1896 George Hunton arranged with J. H. Mayall to rent an apartment
for $15 per month. He paid the first month in advance, then made moving
arrangements. But when he showed up to move in, Mayall refused to let him
in. Hunton, who was African American, engaged McGhee, who sued Mayall,
white, for $1,000. His pleadings did not cite the civil rights statute, which did
not cover rental property. He based the claim for damages instead on a race-
based breach of contract that subjected his client to distress and humiliation,
just as he had in the Samuel Hardy case. Mayall denied that race played any
part in his decision, and the jury believed him. It awarded Hunton just $38, a
sum that represented precisely his out-of-pocket expenses, $15 in rent and $23
in moving costs. This was a defeat.[4]

In February 1906 the African-American orator Eugene Marshall visited
St. Paul to speak, along with Fred McGhee, at a Lincoln Day celebration. During the visit Marshall accompanied a newly minted black St. Paul lawyer
named Samuel Thompson to the Union Depot for breakfast at its restaurant.

The restaurant refused them service. Let us pause for a moment to examine this event. The Union Depot was at this time one of the nation's great transportation hubs. Hundreds of thousands of passengers passed through it yearly,
many of them doubtless grimy, uncouth, illiterate. Now came two articulate
and well-dressed black gentlemen seeking a simple breakfast at the depot cafe,
and they were insultingly turned away. 1906 was, to be sure, a very dark time
in our nation's race history, but Minnesota escaped the worst of it. This little

act of arrogance still carries a shock. Marshall returned to his home in Michigan, but Thompson hired Fred McGhee to sue the restaurant's owner, George R. Kibbe. He did so, and without trial secured a settlement of $125, a substantial sum for the time.[5]

Later that year McGhee tried a case that probably made Kibbe wish he had taken his case to trial, too. On July 16, 1906, a black citizen named Richard Clark tried to buy a meal at a "chop suey restaurant" on Wabasha Street in downtown St. Paul owned by one Moy Hee. Clark claimed that he had been refused service because of his race, and hired McGhee to sue on his behalf. McGhee did so in November, alleging that "the plaintiff was humiliated and much injured in mind and caused great suffering and pain on account of the humiliation, insult, and contumely thus cast upon him." He asked for damages of $500. The case went to trial in January and resulted in an ambiguous and unsatisfactory verdict: the jury found for Clark but awarded him just one dollar in damages. McGhee had wasted his time, at least from a financial standpoint. On the other hand, if Moy Hee had wronged Richard Clark, he did not escape without cost; the court assessed him costs of $35.80, and presumably he had to pay his two lawyers as well. *The Appeal* put the best face on the case: "Of course this was not enough damages but the principle was maintained that distinctions on account of color will not go in St. Paul."[6]

The Appeal may have had it right. Damages in such cases were often disappointing, but African-American citizens never stopped pressing the principle of open accommodations. From William A. Hazel in 1885, through all of McGhee's years in St. Paul, and ever since, the court cases kept coming. Juries seemed to accept the principle, as the reported verdicts much favored the plaintiffs. This far, at least, the law was doing its proper work. The small damages may have been slaps in the face; or they may have reflected all-white juries' difficulty in appreciating the severity of the humiliations inflicted.

So far as the record permits us to conclude, during 1890–1910, no Minnesota attorney initiated more public accommodations cases than Fredrick McGhee. Such activity of course had always been a part of his mission. He also had personal experience of the "humiliation, insult, and contumely" his clients endured. *The Appeal* reported this story in June 1899:

> Attorney McGhee went into Neumann's restaurant a few days ago and the
> waiters filled his order with red pepper but he promptly called them down
> and sat there until he was properly served. He has been in the same place
> several times and each time some act of discrimination more or less ob-

noxious has been committed, but Mr. McGhee says he will continue to go until he is properly served.

It is a picture that piques the imagination—a man accustomed to working with judges, governors, mayors, and archbishops putting himself, all alone, through humiliation at the hands of waiters. Was he trying to break down the color line one restaurant at a time? We can only imagine, unfortunately, because nothing more about this story has come to light.[7]

The *Harry Summers* case, of 1901, was in its legal form a simple and not very interesting extradition matter, but for McGhee and other black Minnesotans it was a civil rights case. They feared that if Summers were returned to Tennessee his due process rights would be exterminated by a mob, perhaps with the acquiescence of legal authority. Minnesota's civil rights bar—McGhee, William Morris, Frank Wheaton (now departed), and Charles Scrutchin—had used the civil law for redress and criminal procedure in defense, but never before had any faced a situation requiring emergency action to save a client from possible lynching.

McGhee and his non-lawyer collaborators managed the *Summers* case with considerable sophistication, using the law, the press, and political pressure in coordination. McGhee used the courts primarily for delay; his appeal of Governor Van Sant's extradition order bought Summers six weeks of safety in the Ramsey County jail. From its very beginning, Summers's St. Paul allies got his case played prominently in the local press. At a time when southern lynchings were ho-hum news in the northern press, the Summers affair and accompanying protests appeared more than 20 times (including three times on the front page and one editorial) in St. Paul dailies between November 1 and December 1, 1901. This, plus McGhee's agents snooping around Hardeman County, put the Tennesseeans on notice that the fate of Henry Summers would be closely watched. St. Paul's African Americans also made conspicuous use of such political strength as they had. Here their almost-unanimous Republicanism worked for them, for when Governor Van Sant looked out over the throng assembled to hear Fred McGhee's argument against Summers's extradition, he saw hundreds of people he knew had voted for him. There could be no escaping political accountability for his decision. McGhee of course had not voted for Van Sant, but the *Summers* case nevertheless vindicated, in a way, McGhee's political choice. For had the case occurred under the previous governor, a Democrat, McGhee's service to that party would have given the black community political entree.

Though McGhee and his friends did not prevent the extradition of Harry Summers, they got some important work done just the same. The delay and the attention paid to the case may have helped Summers get a fairer, and safer, reception back in Tennessee (he ended up with just an eight-year prison term.) The Minnesotans, for their part, learned to, and showed they could, act swiftly and effectively in an emergency. Should another fugitive from southern justice come along, black Minnesotans would be ready. It did not happen, so far as we know, but no one at the time could know that. Being prepared to act in defense of individual life and liberty is part of civil rights work.[8]

Ten years later McGhee intervened in a very different kind of civil rights matter involving two subjects close to his heart, orphans and education. He had been involved with the Crispus Attucks Home, a residence for black orphans, neglected children, and the elderly, from its earliest days. In 1908 the home had moved from a railroad district to open land on the edge of the city and quite near the Mattocks public school. Attucks at the time housed fifteen to twenty mostly school-age children, so these kids brought some dramatic changes to the one-room Mattocks school. In summer 1909 some white parents of Mattocks students proposed to the school officials that Mattocks be divided into two rooms, or a room be added, so that black and white students could be taught separately. Some public school administration officials seemed to give the proposal serious consideration. The *Pioneer Press* quoted an unnamed school official as saying, "It would be illogical to take half the colored orphans and put them under the same teacher. In fact, the natural thing to do would be to have all the orphans in one room under one teacher."[9]

The leaders of St. Paul's black community were keenly attuned to the progress of Jim Crow across the country, and few knew more about it than McGhee. What is more, McGhee had long been on record as a passionate opponent of school segregation. In an 1892 speech in Philadelphia he had denounced "the evil of the caste school." He identified race segregation in the public schools as an infection that threatened every aspect of national life. "We cannot hope that our country's institutions will remain safe when in the public school we foster and keep alive the very thing that threatens our government most." All of Ruth McGhee's schooling had been integrated.[10]

In 1897 Fred McGhee had spoken in St. Paul at a rally protesting a school segregation controversy in Alton, Illinois. He took the position that in the United States the great institutions, and by extension the country as a whole, could achieve and maintain health only through racial integration:

In church and society and in schools we are our brother's keeper....What affects him in one section, affects him all over the country; what breaks down in one place helps tear down what is built in another. A breaking down one of the links destroys the whole chain....I warn you, don't let even one rotten apple into the barrel.[11]

McGhee's strong feelings about segregated schooling thus compelled him to cancel his plans to attend the 1909 Niagara Movement's annual meeting that summer, and instead focus on the controversy over the Mattocks school integration. When the St. Paul school board convened on September 1, 1909, to consider the Mattocks issue, it found present a large delegation of black citizens, led by McGhee and Mrs. Lillian Turner, president of the Federation of Colored Women's Clubs. The proposal to separate the students by race collapsed. Now it was the turn of white citizens to protest. "Would you have colored children steal pencils from your children?" one woman asked rhetorically. "Would you? Would you? We won't put up with it, that's all." Others claimed that the so-called orphans were not orphans at all, but had parents living in other states and so were not eligible for the services of St. Paul's public schools. The board promised to investigate, but the battle was over; Mattocks school would remain integrated.

According to the superintendent of schools, the exertions of McGhee, Mrs. Turner, and others were unnecessary. He explained at the board meeting that Minnesota law forbade race segregation in public schools. But Fred McGhee might have answered him that in his twenty years of civil rights work in Minnesota and around the country he had learned a few things. One of them was that African Americans could never afford to assume that the law would be enforced to protect their rights and privileges. Experience had taught him that black citizens must assert, not assume, even in Minnesota. That is what he had come to St. Paul in 1889 to do; and that was why, twenty years later, he was doing it still.[12]

15

Who Was Fred McGhee?

What we know of Fred McGhee we know from his public acts and deeds: almost nothing of a personal nature, by him or about him, has survived. We cannot know intimate aspects of his personality. What was he like to live with?—did he brood, was he silent at the dinner table, did he fidget? Did he speak sharply to his wife, hector his daughter about boyfriends, or kick the dog? We will never know. Still, enough evidence exists to permit conclusions about some facets of his personality.

He was a nineteenth-century gentleman, a master of social graces from the formal toast to the grand march. He was a true believer: in the Roman Catholic Church, in the United States Constitution, in the leadership of William Jennings Bryan and W. E. B. Du Bois, in the bright future of his race, and in the power of political organization. And for him, belief was inseparable from action. He was an optimist. Though we do not know his emotional reactions to his many defeats, especially in civil rights affairs—the "sun of our perfect freedom" never did shine—we do know that defeat did not get in the way of action, for he followed every loss with another try at victory. He was self-sacrificing, possibly to a fault: all of his travels and unpaid appearances deprived him, his wife, and his daughter of money and time together. Fred McGhee was a loyal friend and powerful ally; but those who competed with him, in politics and especially in court, saw other qualities, too.

In court McGhee sometimes behaved shamelessly, even ruthlessly. Reporters covering his trials regularly commented on his excessively long, and seemingly pointless, *voir dires* and cross-examinations—as though he sometimes made things difficult just to be difficult. More important, McGhee was not squeamish about using baser human feelings to his advantage. In the 1894 *Henry Johnson* case, as we saw, he appealed openly to the jury's presumed race stereotypes by portraying the dead victim not just as a bad man but as a bad black man, as if this somehow were the lowest of the low. Two similar performances have come to light.

In late 1905 a young man named Henry Sussman shot his wife through the head as she dozed in their Minneapolis hotel room. Sussman tried to avoid trial and punishment by gassing himself, but the police found him first. The state charged him with first-degree murder and sought to finish Sussman's work with a hanging. Fred McGhee undertook his defense.

He had a bad case based on the facts. The prosecution easily proved that Sussman had been a dissolute and irresponsible husband, that he shot his wife, and that he admitted doing so. He denied only having planned the crime, but the prosecutor produced a letter Sussman had written not long before the crime threatening his wife with death. The gallows beckoned.

McGhee pursued a respectable courtroom defense by pounding away at the essential element of first-degree murder, premeditation. He showed that the couple had been getting along well early on the day of the murder, and that both Sussmans were drunk at the fateful moment. But he had another, less honorable, strategy, too: blame the victim. In his opening statement he hinted at his plan:

> I would not raise that veil over Fannie Sussman: I would not let the people look beyond it and see beyond that veil. Oh! I would not do it! But duty calls me, as it calls you, to look without sympathy, to banish pity from our breasts and look as the cold, stern men should look beyond the veil and see what she [Fannie] told him [Henry], and when he heard that story and realized its truth, drank in from the fountain of iniquity and the darkness and bitterness of the cup filled to its overflowing.

McGhee then proved that even after marriage Fannie Sussman sometimes worked as a prostitute: amazingly, he brought to court two men who had been her customers. (Here his long familiarity with the St. Paul sex trade probably came in handy.) On one level, McGhee's theory of the case was that Sussman learned of his wife's infidelities the day of the crime, casting him into a sudden and murderous rage. But the defense attorney admitted openly that he relied just as much or more on extra-legal (and legally indefensible) reactions from the all-male jury: a promiscuous wife brings her fate

Henry Sussman, inmate #2016.

upon herself. "The 'unwritten law,'" proclaimed McGhee, "will guide in this case." The jury convicted Sussman of second-degree murder; instead of death, he got life.[1]

It suited Fred McGhee to appeal again to race stereotypes in his 1907 defense of John Webster. Webster, black, had killed John Sterrett, also black, in the course of a late night brawl at a Minneapolis saloon. Webster had a good defense to the murder charge: he worked at the saloon and had been trying to stop the brawl when his gun went off by accident. McGhee used that defense, but in the course of his final argument also asked the jury once more to divide the black American into two categories, "good" (meaning the defendant Webster) and "bad" (meaning the dead man Sterrett and his kind). "The decent Negro must pay the penalty for the loose living of the colored prizefighter and piano player. It is this dissolute class of Negroes that makes it difficult to solve the race question. If you white men will drive every colored prizefighter and piano-player from your city, I will indorse your action and see that they do not stop in St. Paul." In other words, he was saying, We're all better off (blacks even more so than whites) without the Sterretts of this world. The jury found Webster not guilty.[2]

McGhee was not interested in being an African-American attorney who set a higher standard of propriety than his peers, or in being a "credit to his race" by transcending race in his work. He burned to win, and if exploiting hates and irrationalities helped him to do so, he did not hesitate. Fred McGhee could be a hard, hard man.

The vast majority of trial lawyers go through their entire careers without being assaulted by a witness, receiving citations for contempt of court, or getting into a courthouse fight. McGhee, in contrast, racked up an impressive number of tiffs, from almost the beginning of his St. Paul career to near its end.

In 1893 McGhee had represented Anna Davis in a rent dispute with her landlord, Joseph Smythe. To secure payment of rent, Smythe had locked up Davis's furniture, but someone broke into the warehouse and removed her belongings. Smythe sued Davis, a cohort named Kendal, and McGhee, for damages to cover his loss. McGhee got his trial severed from his codefendants', but it did not help. The jury found that Fredrick McGhee, churchgoer, civil rights leader, and officer of the court, had participated in theft, and awarded Smythe a judgment of $50.[3]

Eighteen years later, in a similar case, McGhee was accused of a different form of dishonesty. He had represented Mary Roberts in a dispute with her former landlords, Mr. and Mrs. Thomas Morgan. Roberts had moved out of their boarding house owing $15.50, and the Morgans had retained a trunk of hers as security for payment. McGhee sued the Morgans, demanding return of the trunk, and while the case was pending he secured release of the trunk in return for a $25 security bond. Roberts lost the case, but when the Morgans tried to collect on the bond the bondsmen could not be found, or so they said. The Morgans now had a judgment but no way to collect it. They sued Lawyer McGhee, claiming that the so-called bondsmen were fictitious; their charge, in other words, was fraud, fraud in a petty case. No resolution of their suit, unfortunately, can be found.[4]

The most spectacular courthouse confrontation of Fred McGhee's career took place not in the courtroom but in the corridor. In 1897 he and lawyer Michael J. Costello (a Republican politician with whom McGhee had shared a speaking engagement in 1891) had gotten into competition over a client in a murder case, the upshot of which was that both lost the client and the fee, leaving bitter feelings. In late September that same year, the two got into conflict over clients in a theft case. As they argued outside a courtroom, Costello said something that set McGhee off, whereupon he "straightened out his right arm, rubbed his thumb and forefinger together, and deliberately reached over and tweaked Costello's nose." The astonished and enraged Costello came back punching so hard and fast that McGhee had to be rescued by police, who shoved him out of the building.

Round one went to Costello, but the fight had just begun. Fifteen minutes later, after the police had left, McGhee came looking for his adversary. "About that trouble of which we were speaking," Costello began. "Go to hell with your troubles," responded McGhee, and Costello attacked again, landing two or three solid shots to the head. Perhaps anticipating by eighty years Muhammad Ali's "rope-a-dope" strategy against George Foreman, McGhee let Costello attack and use up energy and self-control. Then, as the angry Republican rushed him once more, McGhee "hit him a terrible smash in the mouth. Costello's feet flew up and he measured his length on the floor." But the game Irishman was soon up and had McGhee by the throat for a moment, before McGhee tossed him to the floor. "End of round two," shouted a spectator.

By now a crowd had gathered, but both lawyers were beyond embarrassment. Costello staggered McGhee with a right to the chin, but when he tried the same again McGhee sat him down with a combination to the forehead and belly. "Round three," sounded the wag.

Costello stayed game, but he had been hurt. As he staggered forward on the attack, McGhee just laughed. Then he grabbed his sparring partner by the throat and pressed him against a radiator until he stopped punching. A police officer arrived at last, separated the two, and held them at arm's length for a moment. Costello then broke free and landed still another right, his last, to McGhee's mouth. "Take that, you big buck nigger!" The police now stopped the fight for good. "Draw ... because of the interference of the police," yelled the courthouse wit.[5]

Only a wisp of folk memory of Fred McGhee remains in St. Paul. He once spat in another lawyer's face for calling him a nigger. The memory is accurate. Amazingly, however, it is not the Costello fight that is remembered, but still another.

It happened on August 14, 1901, in the Hennepin County courthouse in downtown Minneapolis. McGhee had tried a civil case against a white Minneapolis lawyer named J. M. Dunn, and after it concluded the two had to deal with an allocation of court costs. They disagreed, argued, tempers flared, and Dunn muttered something about "doing business with a d—n nigger." This was too much for McGhee, who responded "What's that?" Then he spat three times, squarely in Dunn's face. Dunn was too shocked to respond other than by employing his handkerchief and saying that he wanted no more trouble. McGhee, for his part, did want more trouble; Dunn's response disappointed him. "You're a contemptible coward, you are," he told Dunn. "I claim to be a gentleman of honor. If a man spat in my face, he'd quit walking." At this point the clerk of court intervened, and the men went their separate ways. *The Appeal* pointed out dryly that "Mr. Dunn has been taught a lesson he will not soon forget."[6]

McGhee did not confine his courthouse disagreements to other lawyers: witnesses and judges got in on the action, too. In an 1897 trial he offended a witness (and former client), "Jersey Lilly" Green with a caustic remark about her lack of good sense. Taking a glass of water from the judge's desk, she dashed it in the lawyer's face. McGhee kept his composure, saying, "This is without exception the most audacious action I ever witnessed in a courtroom, but considering the passions actuating this woman, I would respectfully submit that the court take no cognizance of her conduct." The judge threatened Jersey Lilly with contempt, to which she responded, from the clutches of the bailiffs now restraining her, that she wished she had hit McGhee not just with the water but with the glass as well.[7]

McGhee held his temper on that occasion, but lost it in court at least twice. In a 1904 case he was defending a man on a charge of spouse abuse, and during trial was seen conferring with the complaining witness. The judge, suspecting McGhee of trying to persuade her to drop the charges, ordered him to desist. McGhee took offense and replied that he would talk to her if he saw fit. His reply must have been hot, for the judge immediately held him in contempt of court and fined him $10. Later both judge and lawyer cooled down, and the fine and contempt were rescinded. McGhee emerged the ultimate winner—the woman did not appear to testify and the charge against McGhee's client, her husband, was dismissed.[8]

McGhee probably put his client at risk in a 1908 incident. During a trial he looks to have been pressing a dubious technical point—something he was known to do—getting nowhere, and getting steamed. With his emotions about to boil, he commented, "I hardly think I am at liberty to say what I feel in regard to this matter." Judge Finehout of the Municipal Court invited (or dared) him to do so: "You may say whatever you like." McGhee took the bait and accused the Finehout of "prostituting the ends of this court for the purpose of pandering to public clamor." The judge, possibly surprised to learn there was any clamor at all about this routine assault case, responded to the insult by looking for a way to boost the charge against McGhee's client from a misdemeanor to a felony. Lawyer McGhee did well to get out of court that day with just a fine for his client and none for himself.[9]

In March 1911 he represented three Russian immigrant brothers in a minor theft case: they were accused of cheating a man out of $35 in a poker game. When the case came up for trial, the complaining witness did not appear— excellent good fortune for McGhee's clients. The investigating officer claimed that McGhee had induced the man to disappear. McGhee protested, but Judge Hanft replied, "I have information from other sources that you are defending these men and that you are representing the complaining witness in an attempt to get his money back." This was an extremely serious charge—not only conflict of interest but obstruction of justice as well. McGhee demanded to know more: "I think I should be allowed to know who makes a charge like this against an attorney in this court." The judge refused to reveal his sources; he would conduct a "personal investigation" and McGhee would learn the results in time. So far as we know, nothing came of the investigation, and McGhee continued to practice in the Ramsey County courts.[10]

Race clearly paid a part in some of these incidents, but only some. There were so many of them (and these are just the ones that we know about; there were probably more) that they tell us something about the man himself: he brimmed with competitive intensity. Most of the time he governed it and channeled it into his work, but every now and then it boiled into anger and grew too strong to control.

The incidents described so far took place in racially mixed company. It is striking that in what were surely equally stressful disputes of race politics, McGhee kept himself under control, indeed, tried to avoid confrontations. At the 1902 and 1903 NAAC conventions, for example, he felt intensely aggrieved, tricked, and insulted by the Booker T. Washington men, yet he did not attack or break with them in public. He kept his criticisms within parliamentary bounds and his warfare behind the scenes. Perhaps McGhee felt, as have many others, that in race issues the dirty laundry should not be exposed to the general public.

There was one exception, however. In the early 1900s, McGhee had become involved with an African-American fraternal organization called the United Brotherhood of Friendship and Sisters of the Mysterious Ten. It is not clear that he actually joined; he may have served more in a professional capacity, as legal adviser. In 1908 he became the organizer for its national meeting, or "Grand Lodge," in St. Paul. Relations within the Brotherhood were not at this moment entirely friendly. Disagreements over leadership, between Grand Master W. A. Gaines and the dissident forces of Walter Farmer, threatened to split the organization along regional lines. Stakes were high, as the UBF/SMT claimed over 150,000 members in more than 2,000 lodges, mostly in the Midwest and South. The split had reached St. Paul, where McGhee led the Gaines majority and the Rev. J. A. White the Farmerite faction.[11]

W. A. Gaines, from The Appeal, *July 24, 1909.*

McGhee served as chief organizer of the 1909 Grand Lodge—a job even bigger and more fraught with political tensions than the 1902 NAAC meeting. Despite the divisions within the UBF/SMT, or perhaps because of them, both factions attended in force, each spoiling for a fight. Around a thousand delegates came to town the last weekend of the month, with business set to begin on Monday, July 26, at 9 A.M. at the old State Capitol (site of the 1902 NAAC meeting).[12]

The Farmerites, knowing that they lacked the votes to block Gaines's reelection as Grand Master, plotted a coup. On their way to taking power, however, they ran into McGhee. They planned to seize control of the meeting site, then manage the elections by admitting only friendly delegates. So early that morning of July 26, eighteen Farmerites, led by Mrs. J. A. White, their local leader's wife, entered the capitol, found the custodian, claimed to be in charge, and asked him to unlock the door to the old house chambers. The custodian was about to comply when McGhee—had he been warned?—showed up. To prevent losing control of the meeting hall, he blocked the door with his body so that the custodian could not use the key. The custodian, a Civil War veteran called Captain Prendergast, summoned janitors to help, but McGhee would not yield. He, not these usurpers, was the true convention organizer. The Farmerites, egged on by Mrs. White, gathered round McGhee and Prendergast, who now were exchanging insulting words. Mrs. White then joined in; she and McGhee had a confrontation that may have gone beyond words. At last the police arrived, sorted out who had rented the hall (McGhee), and the doors were duly opened to all delegates. McGhee's obstructions had worked, and Gaines was reelected.

The Farmerites promptly split into a separate convention in St. Paul and issued a resolution condemning McGhee for threatening to spit in Prendergast's face and to hit Mrs. White. "We condemn the attempt of F. L. McGhee to strike the wife of Rev. White, whose mother was an army nurse and herself a woman of distinction of McGhee's own race."

McGhee responded with sharp and insulting words of his own. Prendergast had called him a vile name, one that "reflected upon my color." Mrs. White was the "prime mover of all the trouble and disturbance. It was she who urged the men on and rushed me out of the hall." He had not struck her, nor would he think of doing such a thing. But he was not surprised at the behavior of the Farmerites: "They are mainly from that part of the country where the Negroes . . . grin and fawn." The incident was regrettable, but "I am pleased to know that I have the approval of the better element of my home people." Those concerned with the image of black people in the white press, which covered this incident in gleeful detail, surely wished that McGhee had held his tongue.[13]

Though McGhee had won, his blood was up, and he was not done with the Farmerites. The two factions had engaged in bitter litigation in Texas three years earlier. One of the claims there had been that the Farmerite treasurer, W. F. Bledsoe, had appropriated $1,300 in UBF dues money and turned it over to the illegitimate Farmerite leaders. Bledsoe had attended the St. Paul meeting, and as he prepared to leave town McGhee had him served with a summons and complaint demanding judgment against him for $1,400. None of the facts alleged in the complaint occurred in Minnesota, so suing Bledsoe in Ramsey County was clearly done for Bledsoe's inconvenience. McGhee surely knew that the chances of collecting the money were poor, but he pressed ahead just the same. He got a default judgment for the UBF against Bledsoe in March 1910. Bledsoe appealed, and hearings went on into July before the judgment, for $1,375, was confirmed. Many hours of legal work and a great deal of energy went into these proceedings, all for nothing of consequence. The judgment still stands today, futile and uncollected.[14]

We have seen that in criminal cases McGhee sometimes drew a bright line between "good Negro" and "bad Negro." He may have done this purely for effect in the service of advocacy, but there is evidence, too, that his comments reflected his own belief. In his 1897 denial of the "niggers and blacklegs" quotation, he denied the words but not the sentiment. John Q. Adams may have believed the *Dispatch* quotes precisely because he knew Fred McGhee so well. It is not at all uncommon for people who have risen from misery to achievement to look down upon those have not. Fred McGhee was a middle-class striver, a self-made man, religious and socially conservative. His remark in the 1907 Webster trial—that if the white man would drive all the Negro prizefighters and piano players from Minneapolis he would make sure that they stayed out of St. Paul—has the ring of personal conviction.

The longer a man carries on a public career, the more he reveals himself and delivers ammunition to his critics. The judgmental and censorious Fred McGhee certainly did so. In July 1910 he made a speech at the Bethesda Baptist Church of Minneapolis covering a host of topics: the heroism of John Brown; the virtues of the Democratic Party; the evils of Booker T. Washington; and the sins of Jack Johnson. Johnson was an athletic hero, the first black heavyweight boxing champion, and also a womanizer, a drinker, and in many ways a thoroughly unsavory character. Being the first black champion made him, whether he wished it or not, a "representative of his race," and thus a controversial subject of debate. McGhee, the teetotalling straight arrow, disapproved. In his speech he called Johnson a "disgrace to his race."

The Minneapolis black weekly, *Twin City Star,* took the opportunity to blast McGhee for his politics, his religion, and his judgment. According to the editorial, McGhee's speech revealed him a hypocrite several times over. His real interest in denouncing Johnson was politics, not morality: Booker T. Washington had praised Johnson as a representative of his race; therefore, "Fred L. McGhee must say he is not." Rather, the acolytes of Du Bois "by their fulsomeness and insolence seek to defame ... anything that is identified with Booker T. Washington." But Johnson had accomplished something great, he "has given to us a WORLD'S CHAMPION." This made him a far superior race representative than McGhee, whom the *Star* accused of consorting with the odious South Carolina Democrat, "Pitchfork" Ben Tillman. McGhee claimed to be a religious man, yet he used a church forum to denounce a fellow African American. "Hypocrisy personified!"[15]

The *Star* had it wrong. The speech revealed not McGhee's hypocrisy but something more fundamental: his lack of concern for other people's opinions of him. He was a complicated man—intense, combative, gracious, social, devout, zealous, caustic, loyal. In his public life one characteristic shone strongest: Fred McGhee did not need the approval of others. This surely cost him, in criticism absorbed, political support sacrificed, influence lost, even friendships endangered. A fundamental part of who he was, it also made him a superior advocate and a natural, if sometimes perplexing, leader.

16

I Will Need No Monument

On May 25, 1911, thirty-eight gentlemen, leaders of Twin Cities African Americans, held a testimonial dinner in honor of Fredrick McGhee. They held the event in the grand style of the time. The invitations—printed by *The Appeal*—"consisted of an embossed gilt eagle and U.S. flag on the cover and a four page insert stitched with blue silk." The Newport Restaurant served a four-course meal featuring baked lake trout and Philadelphia capon. The participants prepared lengthy toasts: Attorney Brown S. Smith, "Why We Are Here"; the Rev. A. H. Lealtad, "The Duty of the Community to the Individual"; and Mr. Joseph Strong, "Bettering the Condition of the Negro"; and each guest made brief remarks at least. The guests included most (though by no means all) of the leading black male citizens of the time: in addition to Brown and Lealtad (pastor of St. Philip's Episcopal Church), John Quincy Adams, Dr. Val Do Turner, William R. Morris, John Charleston, and John Dillingham.

The most imaginative and touching presentation came from Arthur Hall, who wrote a poem for the occasion. Its motif was that a "spirit guide" had brought the poem's narrator up to heaven for a tour of the celestial city, of which Frederick Douglass was mayor:

> "And," said the guide, "there's one down here we've got to have on high,
> We've offered him inducements but we can't get him to die.
> We want him for chief justice, police chief and president,
> In fact we'll let him run things if he'll just give his consent."
>
> His voice broke and in his eye I saw a ghostly tear—
> "He's a big man now down yonder, but we'll make him bigger here."
> "His name," I ask, "this Negro great, what might his name be?"
> "His name," they all said reverently, "is Fredrick L. McGhee."

On one level the dinner was simply what its organizers said it was, a heartfelt tribute to a man who had served his community long and well. But just as McGhee's life in St. Paul had been touched so often by controversy, this dinner was motivated in part by two controversies that deeply affected, even threatened, the local black community, and in which McGhee was directly involved.[1]

The more acutely serious matter had to do with McGhee's friend Dr. Val Do Turner. Dr. Turner had come to St. Paul in 1898 from Tennessee, where he had been trained at Nashville's Meharry Medical College. He had probably been recruited, as McGhee was, to build a black professional class in the area. He was the state's first African-American physician.[2] Turner and McGhee soon became friends and, in time, fishing buddies. Though Turner was less political than McGhee—a shyer man, perhaps—the two collaborated often in civic and civil rights work. By 1910 both Minneapolis and St. Paul had several black attorneys and physicians, but these two were the respected elders and leaders, pillars of the community.

In November 1910, however, Ramsey County prosecutors brought charges against Dr. Turner that threatened not only his standing in the community but his livelihood and liberty as well. A young woman from Stillwater, Minnesota, named Anna Anderson had become pregnant out of wedlock and gotten an abortion. But the abortion had been botched and she took ill from infection. As she lay dying she made a statement to police and prosecutors that a "colored doctor" in St. Paul had performed the operation. Upon her death St. Paul police arrested Dr. Val Do Turner and charged him with manslaughter. The pillar of his community faced ruin, prison, and disgrace. The community faced the potential loss of its senior physician, and the shame of having one of its most respected leaders exposed as an incompetent abortionist. Turner's conviction would be a disaster.

His friends rallied. The court set his bail at $3,000: supporters pledged more than twice that amount (including $1,000 from the McGhees) to secure his release. Fred McGhee undertook Dr. Turner's legal defense. It is an irony of McGhee's career that of all the clients he had in criminal cases, the one most able to pay a substantial fee, his friend Val Do Turner, was the one client McGhee was least likely to ask for payment.

Dr. Turner required a first-class defense, for the state had a good case

Val Do Turner from The Appeal, *April 16, 1898.*

against him. It was a sordid and compelling story. Anna Louise Anderson, age seventeen when she died, had come to Stillwater due to tragic circumstances: her father had murdered her mother and been sentenced to the state penitentiary there. The girl found work as a servant in a private home. She had become involved with and pregnant by a young man named Tom Quinnehan, of nearby Oak Park, who had some local fame as a left-handed pitcher for the Stillwater baseball team. In her dying declaration—which would certainly come into evidence at Dr. Turner's trial—Anna Anderson said that Quinnehan had brought her to an African-American doctor in St. Paul for an abortion (or "illegal operation" in the newspaper euphemism of the time). She did not know his name, but she said that his office was on the second floor of an office building downtown, on the same floor as an employment bureau. Investigators quickly learned that Dr. Turner had his office on the second floor of the Kendrick block, Number 206; his neighbor at Number 207 was L. M. Pierce's employment agency. Was it not believable that the town's black doctor might make some money on the side providing abortions for white people? Dr. Turner might deny the accusation, but a jury would have to ask itself why Anna Anderson, on her deathbed, would falsely accuse Dr. Turner. How could she know the location of his office if he were not the abortionist?

Fred McGhee had had more complex cases than this one, and cases more difficult to try, but never a case with graver personal and community implications. Anything less than acquittal would be intolerable. The key to the case had to be the only other person with personal knowledge of the facts, Tom Quinnehan. Turner's and Quinnehan's interests coincided. If Turner was guilty of performing the operation, Quinnehan was equally guilty for arranging it. But if Turner were acquitted, any case against Quinnehan would be weak. The same grand jury that indicted Turner had also indicted the young left-hander, but the authorities, not really needing Quinnehan to get at Turner, had not pursued him. As Turner's trial approached, Quinnehan could not be found.

McGhee worked the same tools of advocacy that characterized his entire career as a trial lawyer: legwork and persuasion. He needed Quinnehan, so he pursued him through the young man's parents. When the trouble broke out, Tom Quinnehan took off for the Minnesota north woods and spent the next few months working in a lumber camp. The police had not tracked him down, so it must have taken all of McGhee's persuasive powers to get Mr. and Mrs. Quinnehan to help. One can only imagine the scene: the small-town Irish couple asked by the big-city black lawyer to make contact with their son, for the benefit of the accused doctor. Why would they consent? Yet consent they did.

McGhee met with Tom Quinnehan at the family home in Oak Park on the Friday before testimony began, and secured his promise to attend the trial—though his mother begged him not to, saying that she feared she would never see him again.

McGhee had set up what turned out to be a most dramatic moment. Quinnehan came to the Ramsey County courthouse on April 10, 1911, and took a seat, unrecognized, among the spectators in Judge Grier Orr's courtroom. On the stand that morning was Anna Anderson's former employer, Mrs. Ida Welshmars. In her testimony, Quinnehan's name came up, and when it did she pointed him out in the courtroom: every head in the courtroom (except McGhee's) must have spun. The clerk of court then hurried to the sheriff's office, located the old bench warrant for Quinnehan's arrest, and brought it and a deputy back to court. The deputy then called Quinnehan into the lobby and placed him under arrest for manslaughter.

Though it might have appeared to Quinnehan's mother at that moment that her fears had been realized, in time both she and her son would have reason to thank Fred McGhee for what he had done. At trial Quinnehan and Turner put up a solid front of denial, leaving Anna Anderson's dying declaration the only evidence against them. And owing to inept questioning by the authorities, her declaration was very brief and lacking in detail. Rather than taking her through the facts systematically, which might have led to additional evidence and corroboration, the investigator covered only the basic points. With Anna Anderson dead and both Turner and Quinnehan denying everything, the prosecution found itself with an incomplete story. Despite the strong points—the African-American doctor and his office location—it was not enough. The jury acquitted Dr. Turner on April 13. Though the Ramsey County attorney threatened to bring Quinnehan to justice despite the acquittal, he did not do so, and that summer the Stillwater ballclub had lefty Quinnehan back on the mound.[3]

Turner's acquittal resolved the threat to him and to the community (though some stayed away from the testimonial, presumably because they believed Turner guilty), and it was probably the immediate inspiration for McGhee's testimonial. But there was another, more chronic threat to local black solidarity going on which played a part as well. This one had to do with McGhee and William T. Francis, personally and as local representatives of the contending national Du Bois and Washington forces.

William Trevane Francis had come to St. Paul as a youth and started in the working world as an office boy for the Northern Pacific Railroad. He rose to clerk and then, after getting a law degree in 1904, to attorney in the railroad's legal department. This was a position of great prestige. All the other black professionals were independent and relied on black patronage, whereas Francis enjoyed a responsible position within an enormous, white-owned corporation. At a time when it was a plum for a black man to be appointed courthouse janitor or statehouse messenger, Francis's achievement was unprecedented. Northern Pacific also permitted him to practice law privately on the side.

Francis was young, fair, a talented singer, a busy member of Pilgrim Baptist Church, an active Republican, and a follower of Booker T. Washington. These qualities enabled him to move into the partial vacuum left by McGhee's religion and politics. Within a short time after becoming a lawyer, Francis seemed to be everywhere—making speeches, chairing committees, presiding over events of all kinds.[4]

Francis and McGhee had been friends for years, dating back to the 1890s, and they remained so as the younger man's star rose and despite their political differences. But at some time around 1910 they had a falling out. Precisely what happened is not at all clear, but there are three likely contributing factors. One is politics, both racial and electoral. At this time McGhee had been a Democrat for seventeen years and a Du Bois man for five. Both were distinct minority positions among Minnesota African Americans. The young and popular Francis seemed to be a leading Republican and Washington man; he was on the inside and with the majority—in some ways, he was the man many had wanted Fred McGhee to be. A second is simple rivalry, with perhaps a dash of generational jealousy. Until Francis came along, no St. Paul black attorney remotely approached McGhee in prominence. But Francis was ten years younger, had grown up in St. Paul, and had a local reputation before he became a lawyer. He participated in the founding of several black-owned business enterprises and, unlike McGhee, had support from white business, so he may have posed something of a professional threat. Third, and related to the second, the two had recently opposed each other in a trial that illustrated their competing legal fortunes. It may have been the first civil trial in Minnesota in which both attorneys were black. McGhee represented James Campbell in a lawsuit against the Cosmopolitan Mutual Casualty Company (a local, black-owned enterprise of which he was a director and legal counsel) to recover unpaid disability benefits. Francis represented the insurer and won. Perhaps McGhee took it hard.[5]

Whatever may have been the precise cause for the breakdown of friendship between the two men, others had noticed it and worked to effect a rec-

onciliation. People were pained not only by the loss of a friendship but also by
what it represented: the intensifying divisions between the Washington and
Du Bois factions in the Twin Cities, which were creating tensions and unpro-
ductive disputes. Healing the rift between Francis and McGhee might help
unite the community as a whole. The reconcilers succeeded, at least at the personal level. When Fred McGhee rose to speak that evening at the Newport, after the dinner and the toasts and all the other speeches, he first thanked the
sponsors and guests for bringing him back together with his old friend "Billy."

On that occasion, fourteen months before his untimely death, Fred McGhee
had his own legacy very much in mind. After thanking his listeners and others
for their support during the Val Do Turner trial and for all their kind words
that evening (his wife, he said, would be very pleased), he looked ahead to the
time when people would regard him not in life but in memory. His words give
a rare example of McGhee reflecting publicly about himself:

> I am sure that when the time shall come that I am no more, when that time
> will come when life is o'er, happy will be the thoughts of tonight. And now
> that I know your thoughts about me I realize the responsibility which rests
> upon me. . . .
>
> And so I ask your aid, your help and your prayers; encourage me when
> I am right and tell me of my faults; tell me when I am wrong. Help me in
> everything you can, for in all that I strive to do I shall ask not for treasure,
> but for this I would strive—when the lips now speaking are laid in the
> grave, that my brothers will gather themselves as you are gathered tonight
> and say, "He lived; tried to be right; tried to help the race; and trying to be
> right and trying to help the race he died."
>
> Then I will need no monument; then I will need not flowers, for I will
> have built in your hearts and memories a monument more lasting than any
> monument in gold or in bronze, in brass or in stone could be . . . . And you
> need bring no flowers then, for I will be gone. The flowers I want as I lay
> on death's bed are these words: That I deserved well of my fellow man.

The personal reconciliation between McGhee and William Francis seems
to have lasted the rest of McGhee's life. The political unity of rival black leadership factions also seemed promising. The *Twin City Star* wrote after the testimonial dinner, "The harmonious effect of this meeting will tend to advance
our race's best interest." The event had produced "a chord of perfect harmony . . . and Blest be the ties that now bind us into concerted effort for the
welfare of our race." Within a year, however, the very same *Star* was blasting
McGhee for his support of Du Bois and accusing him of stealing from black
orphans. And even Billy Francis himself, whatever his personal feelings for

McGhee, could not hold back when it came to his friend's loyalty to the Democratic Party. In January 1912 he published a letter that concluded:

> How prominent members of our race who pose as leaders and tell us they have our interest at heart can advise us to wallow in the political pig pen with Vardaman, Tillman ... et al, without blushing for shame is more than good citizens can understand.

Anyone who took interest in that letter knew that he referred to the leading black Democrat, Fredrick McGhee.[6]

No dinner, no honors, no warmth of personal feelings could change the destiny that Fred McGhee had fashioned for himself. When it came to the two beliefs that seemed to isolate him the most from his fellow African Americans—that their political future lay with the Democratic Party and that their civil rights future lay with Du Bois—he would not compromise. Time would prove him correct, but not until long after he was dead.

No one at the Newport Restaurant dinner that May 1911 evening could have had an inkling that the next time they met to honor Fred McGhee would be at his memorial service, or that it would come so soon. Only in retrospect do the events of that evening take on a tinge of sadness, and McGhee's speech an aura of prophecy. He wanted people to say that he lived trying to serve others and to help the race, and that is how in fact he spent the rest of his days. He did not know that from then on many of the things he did, he did for the last time.

17

The Lottery of Life

Fred McGhee spent the last year and a half of his life doing what he had done for the previous twenty: trying criminal cases, doing political work, and assisting at the endings and beginnings of civil rights organizations. Only late in his life had he added a new element, summers at the vacation home on the Apple River in Wisconsin. The purchase of the cabin, the weekend escapes, and the weeks of fishing and puttering in midsummer were the most characteristically Minnesotan behaviors that McGhee ever adopted. It was the final irony of his life that it was there, at the summer place, Camp DuGhee, that his death began. But of course McGhee had no idea in 1910 or 1911 that he had so little time left—and even had he known, it seems unlikely he would have acted differently.

The Niagara Movement quietly came to its end in early 1910. W. E. B. Du Bois finished it off by transferring his energies to a new venture, one which took shape in May 1909 with the National Negro Conference in New York City. The conference brought together an impressive group of African-American leaders—Du Bois, Ida B. Wells Barnett, William Monroe Trotter, Bishop Alexander Walters, and others—with a much larger group of white reformers and philanthropists. It turned out to be one of the most important meetings in American history. A seismic shift had occurred in the civil rights movement; a big share of white money, energy, and credibility, heretofore almost entirely aligned with Booker T. Washington, was now transferred to Du Bois. Washington's monopoly was broken; the radicals' insistence on political rights gained not only legitimacy but also powerful white advocates.

The National Association for the Advancement of Colored People (NAACP) began at this meeting. The conference created a Committee of Forty, including members both black and white, women and men, to assemble a national biracial civil rights organization in which blacks and whites would work together for common goals. Late in 1909 the new organization was incorporated as the National Association for the Advancement of Colored People, with Oswald Villard as president and Du Bois as Director of Publicity and Research.[1]

Fred McGhee did not participate in the National Negro Conference or the Committee of Forty. We do not know why, though we can make some educated guesses. It may have been a question of national stature; unlike Trotter and Walters, he had never been the top man in any organization; and unlike Trotter and Wells Barnett and Cleveland's Harry Smith, he had never had a newspaper voice. It might have been geographical: the other participants all "represented" much larger black populations. He may have been too closely identified with his good friend Du Bois to have been considered useful. It may be that McGhee made it clear to Du Bois that he did not wish to be invited because he was too busy. In spring 1909 he was preparing for the *Campbell v. Cosmopolitan Mutual* trial against William T. Francis, organizing the UBF/SMT Grand Lodge, and getting ready for daughter Ruth's high school graduation. He may simply have preferred to stay home.

Still, Fred McGhee was by no means done with national race politics. Though not a named member of the National Negro Committee, he lent his name to that Committee's 1910 attack on Booker T. Washington's leadership. Washington had made a tour of Great Britain and Europe to raise money for his causes, and he had made his standard, optimistic speeches. The National Negro Committee responded with an open letter to the "People of Great Britain and Europe," contradicting the Wizard.

They had heard, they wrote, of Washington's attempt to assure Europeans that the condition of African Americans was "satisfactory." The truth, sadly, was very much to the contrary. The letter then summarized the 1910 realities of disfranchisement, Jim Crow, lynchings, employment discrimination, and deplorable circumstances of health, housing, and education. Washington of course had a right to his opinions, but his opinions were distorted by his financial dependence on powerful white donors: "... he has for years been compelled to tell, not the whole truth, but that part of it which certain powerful interests in America wish to appear as the whole truth." The letter concluded, "it is one thing to be optimistic ... but it is quite a different thing, consciously or unconsciously, to misrepresent the truth." The letter was signed by twenty-three African-American leaders, including Alexander Walters, William Trotter, Du Bois, E. H. Morris, and McGhee.[2]

The law practice continued the same as always, a mixture of small cases and well-publicized murder trials, none of them paying very well. McGhee's courtroom successes never brought him, so to speak, the best class of criminals. His greatest victory had been the acquittals of his two white clients in the *Raverty* case, but so far as we know he never again represented a white person in a major case. His last murder trial, in early 1912, typified the circumstances that McGhee faced: impecunious black defendants, low pay (he was probably court-appointed), and very limited resources for mounting a defense. McGhee did the best he could.

McGhee's last murder case, and his very last trial, brought him together, in an odd way, with his two friends William T. Francis and Val Do Turner. It was the only time, so far as is known, that McGhee employed an insanity defense.

George Parker was a medical student from Omaha who also worked as a waiter on the Soo Line Railroad. He was engaged to marry Marguerite DeTienne, who lived at the home of Andrew and Celestine Jackson at 603 St. Anthony Avenue in St. Paul. On December 24, 1911, Parker came to St. Paul to visit Miss DeTienne for Christmas. It was clear from the beginning of his visit that Parker was not his usual self; the first time his fiancée saw him was when she picked him up at the downtown jail. Police had brought him there when they found him raving on the street. After a night in jail he had calmed down, so the police released him to Miss DeTienne. She brought him to the Jacksons' house.

At first Parker had a pleasant visit. He had lunch, conversed with the invalid Mrs. Jackson, took a rest, then shared supper with Marguerite and the housekeeper. But after supper he began to fall apart, laughing in an unnatural way at everything said. Mrs. Jackson gave permission for Parker to spend the night, but she called a neighbor, Edward Thomas, to come and stay also "because there wasn't any menfolks in the house." Thomas and Parker conversed well into the night, until Parker at last fell asleep.

From a room upstairs Marguerite DeTienne called William T. Francis, who lived across the street, to discuss how to secure the return of money that the police had supposedly taken from Parker while he was in jail. Francis said he would come right over, and a few minutes later DeTienne and Thomas heard sounds on the stairway, which they took to be Francis arriving, "but in place of Mr. Francis it was Mr. Parker, a raving maniac. He came upstairs, well, he didn't look like a human being at all, his face was drawn and his eyes were all blood-shot, and his face all pulled up, he came upstairs calling for everyone to ... 'Get out of here.'"

In the meantime, Francis arrived and joined the others in trying to persuade Parker to come downstairs. Parker was dressed in his nightshirt, body held rigid, eyes bulging, raving and quoting scripture incoherently. After several minutes of urging and cajoling he began to follow the others downstairs, with them leading him single file down the stairway. When all but Parker had

Fredrick McGhee, about 1910.

reached the bottom and gone through the doorway Parker shouted, "Get out of here," then closed and locked the stairway door. He then dashed back up into Mrs. Jackson's room. The next time anyone saw Mrs. Jackson, she had managed to get out of bed, open her window, and crawl through it onto an upstairs porch, but it was too late. Parker had stabbed her over forty times with a knife, and she died the following day.

William Francis called the police, then got an ax to smash open the stairway door. The police arrived immediately and subdued Parker with force. The arresting officer said that while Parker looked insane, he talked quite rationally. Dr. Val Do Turner examined Parker the next day in jail, and found him looking "rather wild," but lying calmly on his cot.

On January 11, 1912, the grand jury indicted Parker for first-degree murder. His attorney, Fred McGhee, had already been at work; he brought his client's father, Abraham Parker, in from Omaha to have him ready at the arraignment on January 12. McGhee refused to enter a plea for Parker, arguing that the man was incapable of understanding the charge against him. McGhee then had Abraham Parker testify about his son's history of periods of raving and delusion. The court summarily committed George Parker to the state hospital for the insane at St. Peter. The case seemed to have come quickly to an end that satisfied everyone except, perhaps, Celestine Jackson's relatives and friends.

But George Parker did not stay in St. Peter for long. After a little more than three months, the hospital superintendent sent him back to St. Paul, certifying that he was now sane enough to stand trial. On May 10, 1912, Fred McGhee began the last jury trial of his life; he had to persuade twelve white men that his client had been legally insane when he killed Celestine Jackson.

The trial dealt with one issue of fact: Parker's condition of mind on the night of December 26, 1911. McGhee painted the jurors a lurid picture. The day before the crime his client had been hallucinating, seeing red streaks staining the moon; he had been delusional, claiming that he could adjust the images in a moving picture show with his mind. The next day he had deteriorated further, mentally and physically: his eyes bulged, he gritted his teeth and stared, and laughed wildly. In that condition he had brutally killed a woman whom he knew and with whom he had long been friendly.

Then McGhee called on his "expert" witness, Dr. Val Do Turner. The use of Dr. Turner illustrates the potentially disastrous lack of resources available to McGhee in the case. Turner was a general practitioner and surgeon, with no special training or experience in psychiatry. What is more, he had examined Parker only once. McGhee had to use a very long hypothetical question (one that asks the witness to assume the truth of certain evidence previously intro-

duced at trial but not personally known to him) to give Turner enough information upon which to base a medical conclusion. It was an extremely thin
foundation for an expert opinion, utterly inadequate by today's standards, but
McGhee got it past the judge, and Turner gave the needed response: Parker
was insane on the night of December 26. On cross-examination, Dr. Turner revealed the weakness of his evidence; when asked to give a more precise diag-
nosis than "insane," he admitted, "I didn't study it long enough to judge the
form of insanity it was." Nor could he give a prognosis. To make the trial a little stranger still, McGhee then put himself on the witness stand to testify about
his own observations of Parker in late December and early January.

Fortunately for George Parker, the prosecution did not seem to fight his insanity plea very hard, and the jury got the message. He was quickly acquitted
by reason of insanity and returned to St. Peter, this time for an indefinite
period. Fred McGhee had won his last case.[3]

In the four months between George Parker's first and second commitments
to the state hospital, Fred McGhee took the lead in creating yet another local
civil rights organization. It was his sixth, after the local Afro-American League,
the Minnesota Civil Rights Committee, the Law Enforcement League, the local
National Afro-American Council, and the Minnesota chapter of the Niagara
Movement. It would prove to be the only one to last, for it became, after
McGhee's death, the local chapter of the NAACP.

McGhee's NAACP organizing efforts went back at least to fall 1911, when he
sponsored a fund-raising musical performance by the African-American
violinist Clarence Cameron White, who performed solo and in ensemble with
local musicians. Those in the audience received not only entertainment—
a mixture of classical and popular pieces—but copies of *The Crisis,* the NAACP's
monthly magazine edited by Du Bois. The event raised $6.75.[4]

Local organizing began in earnest the following March, when McGhee convened a meeting of leading black citizens to consider creating a local organization to affiliate with the national NAACP and to send delegates to its convention in late April. The meeting drew most of the local male leaders, including
John Q. Adams, Val Do Turner, John Dillingham, Owen Howell, A. H. Lealtad,
Brown S. Smith, and Charles Sumner Smith, editor of the *Twin City Star.*[5]

McGhee was chosen meeting chairman and Adams secretary, suggesting a
possible unity among local Du Bois and Washington forces. All agreed on the
need to organize once again in defense of civil rights. Some, however, Editor
Smith among them, resisted affiliation with the NAACP precisely because Du
Bois's leadership implied rejection of Washington's. In the *Star* Smith

obliquely blasted McGhee, announcing that he would never identify himself "with any proposition to send a negro [McGhee] who signed that 'Appeal to Europe' [the National Negro Committee letter] as a delegate to any gathering convened for race betterment." As previously noted, McGhee had in 1910 signed, along with Du Bois and many others, an open letter to race allies in England and elsewhere in Europe. The letter charged Washington with misleading the world about the condition of African Americans in the United States. Beholden financially to his white benefactors, "he has been compelled to tell, not the whole truth, but that part of it which certain powerful interest in American wish to appear as the whole truth." The letter had gone out under the name of the National Negro Committee, whose members comprised also many of the African-American founders of the NAACP. So Smith had it exactly right: joining the national NAACP did imply rejection of Washington, though this was probably not clear to everyone at the time.

Perhaps as a gesture to local independence, the organizers did not call the new entity the Minnesota NAACP, or anything similar, but rather the Twin Cities Protective League. McGhee was the first signer of the new league's constitution and bylaws. Two of the League's very first acts were to affiliate with the national NAACP and to name McGhee and Dr. Turner its delegates to the national convention in Chicago. About a month later the two old friends left for Chicago, passing through Milwaukee, so that McGhee could make an anti-lynching speech at a Catholic gathering. We do not know what the St. Paulites did at the NAACP meeting. McGhee reported that the convention had been "very fine in every way," and he was elected to its National Committee, the first Minnesotan to be so honored. Fred McGhee's national civil rights career had begun in Chicago in 1890 when he served as Minnesota's delegate to the Afro-American Council convention. It ended in Chicago twenty-two years later.[6]

Not long after returning from Chicago, McGhee attended his last political convention, the state Democratic Party convention in Duluth. He had been very busy in St. Paul that spring mobilizing black Democrats for the coming city elections. According to the *Twin City Star*, the Ramsey County Colored Democrats meeting in March drew 150 people. McGhee gave a speech, naturally, and was selected "National Democratic representative for Minnesota."[7]

On July 4, Mattie, Ruth, and Fred McGhee closed up their house on University Avenue for a long summer vacation. Ruth journeyed north to spend the season with friends in Winnipeg, while Fred and Mattie made the short jaunt northeast to the Apple River and Camp DuGhee. There they entertained a succession of guests: their old Chicago friend Julius Avendorph, and his friend, surgeon Daniel Williams; in August St. Paul's new black dentist, Dr. W. F. Watkins, paid a visit; and in the same month Mrs. George Sleet and her infant son joined the McGhees, prompting *The Appeal* to ask rhetorically, "Wonder what Baby Sleet will look like when he comes home from fresh cow's milk and country fare."[8]

Fred McGhee came back to St. Paul from time to time for business, but always briefly. It came as a surprise, then, to Father Stephen Theobald, pastor of St. Peter Claver, when McGhee showed up at mass one Sunday in mid-August—and a greater surprise still that he walked with crutches. McGhee explained that he had bruised or perhaps sprained his right leg chasing his turkeys at Camp DuGhee. He made a joke of the resulting hobble, calling it his "Turkey Trot," after a popular dance of the time.[9]

The joke was funny, but the injury was not. It refused to heal. Eventually a blood clot formed at the spot of the injury, then dislodged and traveled to McGhee's lung, where an infection developed. In late August that infection nearly killed him, but he rallied. On September 7, *The Appeal* reported that McGhee was "in a fair way for an early recovery." But in this age before antibiotics, his physician, Dr. Turner, had no real treatment available to him. McGhee remained bedridden at home, waiting for his body to defeat the infectious attack.

On September 19, after over a month of illness, Fred McGhee took a rapid turn for the worse, and it became clear that he would not recover. Reported *The Appeal*, "At the time of his death he was surrounded by the immediate members of his family, his physician, and a few intimate friends; he fought well, as he had always done, but when he found his strength going, he said, 'Let God's will be done,' and calmly, peacefully yielded up the ghost and passed into that other, brighter world." McGhee died six weeks shy of his fifty-first birthday. Dr. Turner reported the cause of death to be "injury by fall to the right leg. Thrombosis in leg to lung causing pneumonia."[10]

The Twin Cities African-American community felt and expressed a terrible jolt of grief. "No death that has occurred in St. Paul in a quarter of a century has been more sadly and generally deplored," commented *The Appeal*. St. Peter Claver Church could not accommodate the great throng of mourners, black and white, who came to McGhee's funeral service on September 23. They filled the sanctuary and hundreds more had to stand outside. Father Stephen Theobald, Minnesota's first black priest and, like McGhee had once been, a protégé of Archbishop Ireland's, gave the eulogy. McGhee was buried at Calvary Cemetery, where his grave marker may easily be found today.

The funeral service fell far short of meeting the needs of McGhee's many friends and admirers to express their sense of loss. A great memorial service took place a week later, on September 29, at the much larger Pilgrim Baptist Church. The mourners once again filled the sanctuary to overflowing, and the long program reflected how much people wanted to say and hear about their late friend.

Seven eulogies were given that day. Master of ceremonies Orrington Hall set the tone. "We have met today to honor a great man.... Out of the lottery of life Fredrick McGhee drew a black skin, a slave's miserable hut, ragged clothes, moral and educational disadvantages. What he put into the world will be told to you by the speakers who are to follow. We meet to honor Fredrick L. McGhee but we cannot honor him .... His honor was in his acts."

The Reverend A. H. Lealtad spoke on "McGhee as a Churchman," stressing that he was a truly catholic Christian, giving aid "to any Christian congregation in this city and in the city of Minneapolis." Mrs. Val Do Turner spoke of "McGhee as a Friend," telling of the many deeds of private charity McGhee had done, for wayward boys and girls, for countless "little clubs, church organizations and social societies," all at a cost to him of time and energy. "'Greater love hath no man than this; that a man lay down his life for his friends,' and I feel as I know many others of you feel that this really applies to Mr. McGhee, for if he had rested after business hours ... he might be with us in the flesh today; but every hour, nay, every moment that he could not only spare but steal from his personal affairs was devoted to the advancement of his race, his people, his friends, of the community."

Two white men spoke at the service. Former prosecutor and former St. Paul Mayor C. D. O'Brien drew the topic, "McGhee as a Man," and focused on how much McGhee had achieved against great odds. "How he overcame all of it, educated himself for the forensic battles of his profession, cultivated his intellect ... is amazing, marvelous.... There must have been much in him that we only now feebly commence to recognize. How proud any man might be who could have the record left by him, the memory of his life, the memory of his achievements, all for the betterment of his race and of his fellow men."

McGhee's old Democratic colleague and courtroom adversary (in the *Raverty* case, for one), former Ramsey county attorney Thomas P. Kane, had the theme "McGhee as a Lawyer," but spoke more about McGhee's character as a man and as a race man. "During the long years I have known him ... I learned to appreciate the charitable, generous and silent, thoughtful man who never made much ostentation about his good and generous acts.... He was always watchful and vigilant in any movement that made for increase in the development of his race .... For long years his smile will be remembered, his enthusiasm and liberality will be felt."

William T. Francis gave the address, "McGhee as a Citizen," three sentences of which summarize Fred McGhee's public life exceedingly well: "Public spirited in the highest degree, his whole soul wrapped up in the interests of this community and of the race at large, he was born to leadership, born to the purple; and it was as natural for him to lead as it was for most men to follow. The greatest fighter I have ever known; he grew to know greatness but never rest. Success was his, yes, to a high degree, but never ease."

The final speaker, attorney Brown S. Smith of Minneapolis, speaking on "McGhee as a Race Man," gave the most eloquent tribute of all.

> It was indeed a godsend that a person of [the] moral and intellectual worth of Fred McGhee was located in Minnesota. Many of us have no impression of the real standing, of the importance of this man to the Negro race in America. I say—and I speak advisedly—that there is not another man of the Negro race that really stands higher or stands for more than our dead chieftain. He was a race man in all that the term implies. Broadminded, courageous, and fearless. As at the bar of justice so he was at the court of last resort, the bar of public opinion. For us he set an example. Today in New York, in Texas, in Missouri, in Kansas, in Kentucky, and wherever there is a black face, their heads are bowed in grief over the loss of this man....We feel his loss, God knows. There will always be a certain void, a certain vacuum that cannot be filled. I know of nothing that would inspire a little Negro boy more than to hold up before his face the picture of Fred McGhee. May I say in conclusion, "Good night, sweet prince, and may the angels guide thy rest."

From New York, W. E. B. Du Bois eulogized McGhee in the pages of *Crisis:* "When the twenty-nine colored men met at Niagara Falls in 1905 and stemmed the tide of abject surrender to oppression among Negroes, Frederick L. McGhee of St. Paul was a central figure, and he is the first of that faithful group to die. He was a staunch advocate of democracy, and because he knew by bitter experience how his own dark face had served as an excuse for discouraging him and discriminating unfairly against him, he became especially an advocate of the rights of colored men. He stood like a wall against the encroachment of color caste in the Northwest." Of all the tributes that his death inspired, Fred McGhee probably would have preferred this one, written by Du Bois twenty-one years later: "McGhee was a Catholic ... and an unswerving and self-sacrificing champion of the colored race."[11]

In his adopted home city of St. Paul and his adopted state of Minnesota, Fred McGhee seems to have been forgotten. No monument, except his gravestone, bears his name. His deeds are recalled only by a handful of local history enthusiasts and older African-American citizens. In that sense he has no living legacy.

But what he did and how he lived his life have consequences still today. He was the state's first black attorney, but being first, by itself, was no great accomplishment. What made him outstanding was the way he carried out the mission he had taken on. He knew that all would judge him not just for himself but as a representative of his race: he had to show the people of St. Paul and Minnesota that a black attorney could perform not just adequately but at the highest professional level. This he did from the moment of his arrival in 1889 and for the next twenty-three years. The many African-American attorneys, and now judges and appellate judges, that have followed in his path might thank him for the high standards that he set.

In his civil rights work Fred McGhee knew almost nothing but failure, but these failures laid the necessary groundwork for later success. McGhee's destiny was akin to that of a field commander in George Washington's revolutionary army, which won very few victories but ultimately won the war. In the early years its greatest service was simply to keep the struggle going, to survive as a symbol of resistance and hope. It was much the same with civil rights work in the era of Jim Crow. Victories were rare because the most powerful forces—political, social, intellectual, and economic—were aligned against the fortunes of black people in America. Fred McGhee was one of the national leaders, and the pre-eminent Minnesota leader, who took the battle to the enemy, absorbed the defeats without despair, and kept the struggle alive.

More than any other person, Fredrick McGhee brought the NAACP to Minnesota. Roy Wilkins, who grew up in St. Paul and later went on to become the executive director of the NAACP, remembered in his autobiography, "We knew McGhee, and it was through him that the National Association for the Advancement of Colored People reached St. Paul and [our house at] 906 Galtier Street." Under the guidance of men like Wilkins, the NAACP became precisely the organization that McGhee worked his whole life to bring into being, an organization of national power in public opinion, in Congress, and in the courts. Its achievements, in Minnesota and nationwide, are Fred McGhee's living legacy.[12]

The color line limited Fred McGhee's possibilities in life. Without it he might have been a judge, a member of Congress, at the very least well-to-do.

The color line also made him extraordinary. It gave him powerful forces against which to develop and exert his energies and gifts. This was an irony that he shared with his comrades in the war against race division in the United States. Booker T. Washington, W. E. B. Du Bois, T. Thomas Fortune, James Monroe Trotter, like McGhee, were men of great ability; but what would they have done with their lives in a land without race prejudice? Would they be remembered today?

Race and the color line made Fred McGhee one of the great Minnesotans of his time, the state's most nationally prominent African American of the Jim Crow era. But to think of him only as a race figure does not do him justice. Just as every other human being does, Fred McGhee faced one great question: how to live a good life in the circumstances presented to him. Judging from his deeds, this was a question to which he gave more thought and planning than most people do. All of his adult life he made choices to take on responsibilities, to act based on his beliefs, and to do so publicly.

The most fateful of all his decisions was moving to St. Paul. Coming to Minnesota as its first black attorney, and as a trial lawyer, meant embracing a role where his successes and failures would be public, where he would be seen as a representative of his people, where he would be expected to take leadership in many issues, and where the public eye would never blink. McGhee made this choice and never permitted its consequences, nor the unexpected changes in his life, notably conversion to Catholicism and Democracy, to deflect him in his pursuit of a life of leadership and responsibility. The consequences included public criticism, constant travel, endless hours of unpaid work, many defeats, and estrangement from comrades. McGhee bore these with only occasional lapses in grace and composure. He not only bore them, but never ceased creating new responsibilities for himself, which meant additional work and risk of failure.

One of the things biography can do—maybe the only useful thing it can do—is offer the public examples of people who led good lives. Fredrick Lamar McGhee took his own talents and the hard circumstances of his origins and his time, and from them constructed a courageous and exemplary life.

Epilogue

Lawyer McGhee died without a will. This caused no legal problems with his estate: all property passed by law to his widow. The problem was that he had so little property to pass. The McGhees lived comfortably, probably a little better than most citizens of St. Paul. McGhee earned enough to buy the house at 665 University Avenue and the Wisconsin "farm," to travel a great deal and do a mountain of unpaid work, to contribute to church and charity—but not enough to accumulate real wealth in land, money, or investments.

The probate proceedings that followed McGhee's death show him owning the family homestead, valued at $6,000 (but subject to two mortgages); the Wisconsin land, worth $1,500, but also mortgaged; $375 in bank deposits; accounts receivable of $875, only $100 of which was deemed collectable; and law books worth $900. His tangible personal property consisted of four suits, two overcoats, one ruby ring, one gold watch and chain, one stickpin, plus household furnishings at home and in Wisconsin. It seems probable that he also had some life insurance, though this does not appear (as it would not) in the probate records.[1]

Fred McGhee's death had a devastating financial impact on his wife and daughter. Mattie, at age forty-three, had not worked outside of the home since her Chicago days over a quarter-century earlier. If Ruth, age twenty-three, had any hopes of further education, they were now dashed. It appears that for most of the next several years she supported herself and her mother working as a typist and stenographer for an advertising agency in downtown St. Paul. Mattie never took a job, but she did pay off both the mortgages on the homestead (an $1,800 mortgage from 1904 and a $500 one from 1905) in the two years after her husband's death. Perhaps life insurance made this possible.[2]

Mattie and Ruth stayed in the family home for seven years after Fred McGhee's death. For a while, they continued to be recognized as a prominent African American family. On Sunday, September 19, 1913, all the black churches in the Twin Cities were asked to honor the memory of Fredrick L. McGhee, "agitator for civil rights," on the anniversary of his death. Near the time of the second anniversary, W. E. B. Du Bois paid Mattie a brief visit in St. Paul. On July 19, 1916, when Booker T. Washington's wife addressed the annual picnic of the Sunday Schools Union at Minnehaha Park in Minneapolis, Mattie was invited as a special guest along with William T. Francis's wife, Nellie. In time, however, as new leaders emerged in the Twin Cities's African-American community, Fred McGhee's memory began to fade—and the esteem with which Mattie and Ruth were regarded faded with it.[3]

In September of 1919 Ruth left St. Paul for Washington, D.C., to take a job with the federal government. Mattie followed her in November. She apparently sold the family home to Mr. and Mrs. Hugh Schuck, a black couple, who lived and operated a real estate business there for several years. The house was lost to foreclosure in 1926 and demolished in 1933. A bank parking lot now occupies the site. Mattie made no attempt to hold on to the Wisconsin land, which was lost to foreclosure in 1913.[4]

Mattie and Ruth settled eventually in New York City, where Mattie died of stomach cancer on January 30, 1933. Ruth returned to St. Paul in 1955, alone, unmarried, and childless, and died there in 1957. It is a measure of how thoroughly the McGhees had been forgotten that when the local black paper printed the notice of her death it misspelled their family name (as "McGee"); and though it mentioned her father said nothing of his and the family's stature a half century earlier. Even Ruth's death certificate seemed to conspire to forget her distinguished heritage; it misspells her surname too, and gives her race as white. She died of cardio-respiratory pneumonia and malnutrition at age sixty-eight. Ruth and Mattie are buried in unmarked graves next to husband and father in Calvary Cemetery.[5]

McGhee's brother Matthew died unmarried in St. Paul in 1892. His eldest and last surviving brother, Barclay, paid a final visit to Mattie in St. Paul in 1919, apparently alone, and then disappeared. No further record of him, or any wife or children, can be found. So far as anyone knows today, the genetic line begun by Abraham and Sarah McGhee on the John A. Walker farm in northern Mississippi lasted just one generation.[6]

It goes without saying, however, that others—many other too numerous to mention—continued McGhee's struggle. Below is a brief account of what became of some of McGhee's closest associates:

John Quincy Adams continued to edit and publish *The Appeal*, though with declining energy and quality, for ten more years. He was killed September 3, 1922, when struck by a car as he stepped off a streetcar. The family hired as his successor a young University of Minnesota journalism student named Roy

Wilkins. Wilkins ran the paper for just a few months before moving to Kansas City and eventually becoming executive director of the NAACP.[7]

Antonio Calderone served his full term, minus good time, in Stillwater prison. In 1911 he got another lawyer and petitioned the court for a new trial on the grounds that his confession had been coerced, but the motion failed. He was released from prison in 1917 at age thirty-seven. No one knows what became of him after that.[8]

W. E. B. DuBois outlived his friend McGhee by over fifty years. He stayed with the NAACP as editor of *The Crisis* until the mid-1930s. He became increasingly radical politically, and disillusioned, and eventually left the organization he had done so much to create and build. His lifelong quest for African American rights and pan-Africanism led him eventually to Ghana, where he died in 1963, on the eve of the great U.S. civil rights march on Washington. The announcement of his death that day was made by another civil rights pioneer who had known Fred McGhee, Roy Wilkins.[9]

William T. Francis emerged as Fred McGhee's legitimate successor. He took over McGhee's law practice and made himself a very distinguished career as a trial lawyer and local civil rights leader. His loyalty and service to the Republican Party paid off in 1927 when Calvin Coolidge appointed him United States ambassador to Liberia. That reward, however, proved fatal: Francis died of yellow fever in Monrovia, Liberia, in July 1929.[10]

James Haynes (or *Hayes*), whom McGhee defended on burglary and attempted rape charges in 1903, was sentenced to twenty-five years at Stillwater, where he suffered an all-too common fate: he died there of tuberculosis on March 8, 1906, at the age of twenty-five or twenty-six.[11]

William A. Hazel left St. Paul around the turn of the century. He moved first to Cambridge, Massachusetts, then to Alabama, where he taught at Booker T. Washington's Tuskegee Institute from 1909 to 1919. From there he moved on to Howard University in Washington, D.C., where he taught and designed campus buildings, some of which still stand. He left Howard for private architectural practice in the 1920s, and died in 1929.[12]

Archbishop John Ireland completed the last great works of his life, the construction of St. Paul's magnificent Cathedral and Minneapolis's equally beautiful Basilica, in 1915. He died three years later.[13]

Henry Johnson, whom McGhee defended in his second murder trial, in 1894, did not live long in prison. He died there of tuberculosis on March 15, 1896.[14]

William R. Morris, who came to Minnesota just weeks after McGhee and set up his practice in Minneapolis, practiced law there for over forty years. Unlike McGhee he remained a stalwart Republican and a Protestant all his life.

Morris participated actively in race politics too, but less prominently than McGhee did. He devoted a great deal of time to fraternal lodge matters, serving as an officer in the Scottish Rite Masons, the Odd Fellows, and the Knights of Pythias. For reasons now unknown, Morris took his own life by jumping from the eighth floor of the interior court of the Metropolitan Life Building, where he had his office, on December 29, 1929. He was seventy years old. His estate listed his entire assets as bank deposits of $107.46.[15]

George Parker, acquitted in 1912 by reason of insanity, was committed to the state hospital for the criminally insane at St. Peter and given little chance of living much longer. Shortly after arriving at St. Peter, he became involved in an escape plot, in which one prisoner succeeded. Despite everything, Parker recovered his health and was certified cured in April of 1914. The trial judge, Grier Orr, ordered him released on the condition that he "not come to the city of St. Paul and that he shall immediately leave the state of Minnesota and not return hereto." Parker ignored these conditions, came back to St. Paul, and resumed work as a railroad dining car waiter, a job he held for the next thirty years. He married, bought a house just down the street from the scene of his crime, and lived there until his death in 1947.[16]

Philip Rice was the defendant in McGhee's first, and probably least successful, murder trial. Sentenced to life in prison in 1894, he adjusted poorly to Stillwater; twelve times his jailers put him in solitary confinement, for such offenses as fighting, talking back, refusing to work, and sneering. Near the end of his life he was transferred to the State Hospital for the Criminally Insane at St. Peter, where he died March 25, 1930.[17]

Henry Sussman, who tried to kill himself before the police caught him, then escaped execution with a second-degree murder conviction, finally took his own life in prison on February 28, 1909.[18]

Dr. Val Do Turner remained very active in race matters after McGhee's death, serving for many years as secretary of the St. Paul branch of the NAACP. He continued to practice medicine in downtown St. Paul until 1928, when he was forced to retire after once again being accused of committing criminal abortion. The evidence against him was strong, but the judge mild: he suspended the criminal proceedings on the condition that Turner give up his medical license and leave town. Turner soon returned to his native Tennessee, and his ultimate fate is unknown.[19]

Booker T. Washington continued his work at Tuskegee and his battle against DuBois until his untimely death in 1915 at the age of fifty-eight. His Tuskegee Institute is now Tuskegee University.[20]

Notes

Notes to the Introduction

1. Herbert Aptheker, ed., *A Documentary History of the Negro People in the United States* (New York: Citadel Press, 1968), 904.

2. W. E. B. Du Bois, "A Great Advocate," *Crisis*, Oct. 1912, 15-16.

3. Du Bois, "The McGhee's of St. Paul," *Crisis*, June 1933, 130.

Notes to Chapter One

1. *Appeal*, June 22, 1889, p. 1; *Pioneer Press*, June 18, 1889, p. 7. The four dailies were the *Pioneer Press*, the *St. Paul Dispatch*, the *St. Paul Globe*, and the *St. Paul Daily News*.

2. Bessie Pierce, *A History of Chicago*, vol. 3 (New York: Alfred A. Knopf, 1947), 391-392 (Chicago generally); Allen Spear, *Black Chicago, the Making of an Urban Ghetto, 1870-1930* (Chicago: Univ. of Chicago Press, 1967), 12; Harold F. Gosnell, *Negro Politicians* (Chicago: Univ. of Chicago Press, 1935), 66, 73, 86, 111 (E. H. Morris); *Appeal*, Feb. 11, 1888, p. 1 (running for office and president of Autumn Social Club).

3. A. R. Fenwick, *Sturdy Sons of Saint Paul* (St. Paul, Minn.: Junior Pioneer Association, 1899(?), 95; W. B. Hennessy, *Past and Present of Saint Paul* (St. Paul, Minn.: 1906), 632 (McGhee's birth); Joretta Kidd Markham Flaherty et al., *History of Monroe County, Mississippi* (Dallas: Curtis Media Corp., 1988), 856-866; Manuscript U.S. Census, Slave Inhabitants of the Western Division of Monroe County, Mississippi, 121 (John A. Walker).

4. Shelby Foote, *The Civil War, a Narrative* vol. 2 (New York: Random House, 1963), 388, 921-934 (quote, 928); William C. Harris, *Presidential Reconstruction in Mississippi* (Baton Rouge: Louisiana State Univ. Press, 1988), 856-866 (location of rail line); *War of the Rebellion. A Compilation of the Official Records of the Union and Confederate Armies*, vol. XXXII, pt. 2 (Washington, D.C.: Government Printing Office, 1880-1901) 787; Flaherty, *History of Monroe County*, 865 (camped at Walker plantation); *Official Records*, vol. XXXII, pt. 1, 252, 257 (slaves left with Union army).

5. Fenwick, *Sturdy Sons of Saint Paul*, 95; Hennessy, *Past and Present of Saint Paul*, 632; *Helms's Knoxville City Directory* (Knoxville, Tenn.: 1869), 97 (McGhees went to Knoxville); Lucile Deaderick, ed., *Heart of the Valley, A History of Knoxville, Tennessee* (Knoxville, Tenn.: East Tennessee Historical Society, 1976), 42 (the white McGhees); *Knoxville City Directory*, 97 (Abraham McGhee a blacksmith).

6. Fenwick, *Sturdy Sons of Saint Paul*, 632 (enrolled in school); Hennessy, *Past and Present of Saint Paul*, 95 (deaths of parents); Manuscript U.S. Census, Population Schedule for Knox County, Tennessee, 1870, p. 376 (death of Abraham and ages of brothers).

7. Robert J. Booker, *And There Was Light! The 120-Year History of Knoxville College*, Knoxville, Tennessee (Virginia Beach, Va.: Donning Co., 1994), 11-12; Mary U. Ruthrock, ed., *The French Broad-Holston Country, A History of Knox County, Tennessee* (Knoxville, Tenn.: East Tennessee Historical Society, 1946), 317-318.

8. *Knoxville City Directory 1880* (Knoxville, Tenn.: 1880), 96.

9. Fenwick, *Sturdy Sons of Saint Paul*, 95; *Appeal*, June 22, 1889, p. 1 (moved to Chicago); Pierce, *A History of Chicago*, vol. 3, 391-392 (Chicago generally); Spear,

Black Chicago, 12 (black Chicago); *Lakeside Directory of Chicago* (Chicago: R.R. Donnelly & Son, 1876, 1877, and 1881) (arrivals and occupations of McGhee brothers).

10. Fenwick, *Sturdy Sons of Saint Paul,* 95; Hennessy, *Past and Present of Saint Paul,* 632; *Cleveland Gazette,* Oct. 6, 1883, p. 4 (in the first known mention of McGhee in the press, he is president of Chicago's black community's Philosophy Literary Society); Oct. 24, 1885, p. 1 (delegate to the Illinois State Colored Convention) Nov. 24, 1883, p. 1 (in law school); *New York Globe,* Aug. 2, 1884, p. 2 (president of Autumn Social Club); Aug. 9, 1884, p. 2 (Waiters Union); Fredrick L. McGhee Illinois attorney registration card, Illinois State Archives, Springfield, Illinois; *Lakeside Directory of Chicago* 1886 p. 958 (in practice with Morris); It has not been possible so far to determine which law school McGhee attended. The *Detroit Plaindealer* asserted in 1892 that he had attended the Union College of Law, *Plaindealer* (Detroit, Michigan), April 22, 1892, p. 1, but this appears not to be true. Union College of Law later became Northwestern University. Northwestern's archives for that period include the Union College records, and show no student named McGhee ever enrolled. Letter to the author from Patrick Quinn, Northwestern University archivist, Feb. 28, 1994. Gosnell, *Negro Politicians,* 66 (E. H. Morris).

11. Fenwick, *Sturdy Sons of Saint Paul,* 95; Hennessy, *Past and Present of Saint Paul,* 632 (Abraham McGhee). Both authors report that Sarah McGhee's mother had been born in Africa. Fredrick McGhee himself must have been the source of this information. Peter Kolchin, *American Slavery, 1619-1877* (New York: Hill & Wang, 1993), 105-111, 128-129, 141-148 (restrictions on slaves generally).

12. Robert J. Booker, *Two Hundred Years of Black Culture in Knoxville, Tennessee, 1791-1991* (Virginia Beach, Va.: Donning Co., 1993), 60-63; Deaderick, *Heart of the Valley,* 41.

13. Fenwick, *Sturdy Sons of Saint Paul,* 95; *Appeal,* June 22, 1889, p. 1 (marriage); Fredrick's and Mattie's paths might have crossed in the travels between work and

home. According to the 1886 *Lakeside Directory of Chicago,* Fred lived at 3623 Butterfield and worked at 193 Clark St., while Mattie lived at 2807 Butterfield and worked, as a clerk, at 279 Clark St; *Appeal,* Feb. 11, 1888, p. 1 (running for office and president of Autumn Social Club).

14. David V. Taylor, *Pilgrim's Progress: Black St. Paul and the Making of an Urban Ghetto, 1870-1939* (Ph.D. dissertation, University of Minnesota, 1977), 22-23, 84-90 (black population figures and community information); *Eleventh Census of the United States: 1890, Part I, Population* (Washington, D.C.: Government Printing Office, 1897) 386, 538 (city population figures, black population of Minneapolis.) David V. Taylor concurs that Adams was the key figure in recruiting McGhee to St. Paul, *Pilgrim's Progress,* 85-86.

15. David V. Taylor, "John Quincy Adams: St. Paul Editor and Black Leader," *Minnesota History* 43 (Winter 1973): 282-297.

16. *Id.* (*Appeal* in Chicago); *Appeal,* Jan. 7, 1888, p. 1 (McGhee seeking to leave Chicago for Omaha); Feb. 25, 1888, p. 1 (banquet); March 17, 1888, p. 1 (March visit); June 9, 1888, p. 2 (quotation); May 1, 1889, p. 1, May 25, 1889, p. 1 (Autumn Social Club).

17. *Appeal,* June 22, 1889, p. 1; June 29, 1899, p. 1, and Aug. 2, 1889, p. 1 (Morris arrives).

Notes to Chapter Two

1. *Appeal,* July 13, 1889, p. 3. Alice Finerty fared the worst from the altercation; she ended up with 60 days in the workhouse for engaging in prostitution. *Pioneer Press,* July 10, 1889, p. 7. The *Appeal*'s version of the case differed somewhat from the *Pioneer Press*'s: it said that Stafford and Warner lived in the same house.

2. *Appeal,* Sept. 7, 1889, p. 1 (*Aker* and Minton case); *Appeal,* Oct. 28, 1889, p. 1; *Pioneer Press,* Oct. 23, 1889, p. 7; Oct. 24, 1889, p. 7; (Hendrickson). The named petitioner in Hendrickson's *habeas corpus* case was a black barber named Lewis Jackson. His connection with Hendrickson is unknown, but as McGhee needed to be paid by someone, and Hendrickson was in no

position to do so, it is possible that Jackson and the woman had a business relationship. Ramsey County District Court criminal case file no. 2097, State ex rel *Lewis S. Jackson v St. Valeria, Warden of the House of the Good Shepherd*, MHS.

3. *Appeal*, Nov. 9, 1889, p. 2.

4. *Pioneer Press*, March 29, 1890, p. 5.

5. Record of proceedings of the court martial of Private Lewis Carter, National Archives and Records Center, Washington, D.C., microfilm copy in possession of MHS.

6. *Western Appeal*, Aug. 18, 1888, p. 1; *Minneapolis Journal*, Sept. 25, 1928, p. 1; U.S. Army pension application of Samuel P. Snider, National Archives and Records Center, Washington, D.C., copy in author's possession.

7. Pardon petition, affidavit of Lewis Carter, and letter from Samuel P. Snider to President Harrison, proceedings of the court martial of Private Lewis Carter.

8. *St. Paul Globe*, March 14, 1890, p. 1; *Appeal*, March 22, 1890, p. 2; *Pioneer Press*, March 29, 1890, p. 5; Statement of Maria Scholls (undated), Record of proceedings of the court martial of Private Lewis Carter.

9. *St. Paul Globe*, March 14, 1890, p. 1; *Pioneer Press*, March 28, 1890, p. 8.

10. *Appeal*, Oct. 10, 1891, p. 3; Convict record of Frank Conway, Stillwater Prison, MHS; *State v Conway*, 23 Minn. 291 (Minn. Sup. Ct. 1877); *State v Conway* supreme court case file, MHS.

11. Ramsey County District Court criminal case file no. 2364, MHS; *Minneapolis Tribune*, Aug. 6, 1891, p. 5; Oct. 24, 1891, p. 3; Oct. 27, 1891, p. 3; *Minneapolis Journal*, Oct. 27, 1891, p. 6; Oct. 28, 1891, p. 7; *St. Paul Dispatch*, Oct. 23, 1891, p. 3; Oct. 26, 1891, p. 2; Oct. 27, 1891, p. 3; *Pioneer Press*, Oct. 23, 1891, p. 5; Oct. 28, 1891, p. 7; *Appeal*, Oct. 31, 1891, p. 3.

Notes to Chapter Three

1. The federal civil rights act of 1866 outlawed discrimination based on race in many kinds of public accommodations. The Supreme Court ruled this statute unconstitutional in the Civil Rights Cases.

Congress passed no similar statute until the Civil Rights Act of 1965.

2. These events are described in many books. An excellent one is Rayford W. Logan's *The Negro in American Life and Thought: The Nadir, 1877-1901* (New York: Dial Press, 1954).

3. *Statutes of Minnesota 1879-1888*, vol. 2, ch. 124, secs. 203 & 204.

4. Emma Lou Thornbrough, *T. Thomas Fortune, Militant Journalist* (Chicago: Univ. of Chicago Press, 1972); Emma Lou Thornbrough, "The National Afro-American League, 1887-1908," *Journal of Southern History* 27 (Nov. 1961): 494-512, quote at 496.

5. *Appeal*, Nov. 9, 1889, p. 1.

6. Thornbrough, "The National Afro-American League," 494-512.

7. *Pioneer Press*, Aug. 28, 1890, p. 2; *Appeal*, Aug. 30, 1890, p. 3 (first foray into politics); Nov. 1, 1890, p. 1 (speech); Jan. 24, 1891, p. 3 (state committee).

8. *Appeal*, Jan. 3, 1891, p. 3; *Northwestern Chronicle*, Jan. 9, 1891, p. 1. The *Chronicle*, founded by Archbishop Ireland, was the weekly paper of his archdiocese.

9. *St. Paul Globe*, Jan. 2, 1891, p. 2; *Pioneer Press*, Jan. 2, 1891, p. 8.

10. *Appeal*, Jan. 31, 1891, p. 3 (Hazel's letter); Jan. 10, 1891, p. 3 (dispute with restaurant); Louise Daniel Hutchinson, "Building on a Heritage," *American Visions* (Aug. 1989): 11; *Appeal*, Feb. 8, 1890, pp. 1, 3 (Hazel's life and career generally).

11. Thornbrough, "The National Afro-American League," 500-501 (the League's organizational troubles and failures).

12. *Appeal*, May 16, 1891, p. 1; May 23, 1891, p. 3.

13. *Appeal*, June 20, 1891, pp. 1, 3; June 27, 1891, p. 1 (notice of and protests regarding Tennessee act); July 18, 1891, p. 3 (Hardy elected delegate); Sept. 12, 1891, p. 2 (formation of Civil Rights Committee and text of Tennessee statute); Thornbrough, "National Afro-American League," 501 ("tomfoolery").

14. *Appeal*, Sept. 12, 1891, p. 2 (text of manifesto); Oct. 3, 1891, p. 3; Oct. 10, 1891, p. 2; Oct. 17, 1891, p. 2 (fundraising). The Committee quickly received pledges of over $200, including $100 from *The Appeal*,

$15 from St. Peter Claver Sodality, $10 from Samuel Hardy, and $5 each from McGhee, William R. Morris, and W. A. Hazel. This was enough to begin. Case file, *Samuel E. Hardy v East Tennessee, Georgia & Virginia Railway Co.*, U.S. Circuit Court, Chattanooga, Tennessee, law case no. 312, National Archives and Records Administration, Southeast Region, Atlanta, copy in author's possession.

15. *Appeal*, Jan. 2, 1892, p. 3; Jan. 30, 1892, p. 3 (trip east and adoption of Ruth). If Ruth was indeed around two-and-a-half years old in Jan. 1892, she would have been born in summer 1889. Her death certificate gives her date of birth as Aug. 12, 1887. This date must be wrong—there is no mistaking a two-year-old for a four-year-old. Aug. 12, 1889, however, is possible. Death certificate of Ruth McGhee, Ramsey County, Minnesota, Department of Health, St. Paul, copy in author's possession. *Appeal*, Nov. 28, 1891, pp. 1, 3 (announcement of Republican Convention).

16. Case file, *Hardy v East Tennessee, Georgia, and Virginia Railway.*

17. Sarah H. Lemmon, "Transportation Segregation in the Federal Courts Since 1865," *Journal of Negro History* 38 (April 1953): 174-193; Stanley J. Folmsbee, "The Origin of the First 'Jim Crow' Law," *Journal of Southern History* 15 (1949): 235-247 (pre-*Hardy* railroad cases); *Appeal*, April 2, 1892, p. 3 (McGhee leaves for Chattanooga); case file, *Hardy v East Tennessee, Georgia & Virginia Railway.*

18. *Pioneer Press*, April 24, 1892, p. 5.

19. *Pioneer Press*, Jan. 28, 1892, p. 5; *Appeal*, March 19, 1892, p. 3 (agitation for black delegate); April 2, 1892, p. 3 (McGhee recommended); *Pioneer Press*, May 5, 1892, p. 5 (McGhee not chosen); *Appeal*, May 28, 1892, p. 3 ("the Negro a power"); June 4, 1892, p. 5; June 11, 1892, p. 3 (meeting of black Republicans); *Chicago InterOcean*, June 15, 1892, p. 10 (McGhee supports Reed, but is satisfied with Harrison); Harry J. Sievers, *Benjamin Harrison, Hoosier President: The White House and After* (Indianapolis: Bobbs-Merrill, 1968), 227-233 (account of 1892 Convention).

20. *Svenska Amerikanska Posten*, May 10, 1892, p. 4, translated in Peg Meier, *Bring Warm Clothes, Letters and Photos from Minnesota's Past* (Minneapolis: Neighbors Publishing, 1981), 189.

21. *Appeal*, July 23, 1892, p. 3 (McGhee in Wisconsin); July 30, 1892, p. 3 (state Republican Convention—*The Appeal* commented that there had been "not one Afro-American delegate . . . we won't forget it."); *Negro World*, July 30, 1892, p. 1 (official explanation); *Appeal*, Aug., 6, 1892, p. 5 (McGhee angry); Sept. 17, 1892, p. 4 (protest meeting); Sept. 24, 1892, p. 3 (satisfactory assurances; McGhee back on the stump); Nov. 19, 1892, p. 3 (election results—"a regular Waterloo" for local Republicans).

22. Telephone conversation between Mary Ann Hawkins of National Archives, Southeast Region, and the author, Feb. 16, 1996 (dismissal of case); *Plessy v Ferguson*, 163 U.S. 537 (1895).

Notes to Chapter Four

1. *St. Peter Claver Church, St. Paul, Minnesota, 1892-1967 Diamond Jubilee* (St. Paul: St. Peter Claver Church, 1967) 6.

2. Sharon M. Howell, "The Consecrated Blizzard of the Northwest: Archbishop John Ireland of St. Paul and His Relationship with the Black Catholic Community," NCCB Secretariat for Black Catholics, University of St. Thomas, St. Paul, Minnesota, 1989; Marvin R. O'Connell, *John Ireland and the American Catholic Church* (St. Paul: Minnesota Historical Society Press, 1988).

3. *Western Appeal*, April 28, 1888, p. 4 (Slattery in town); Dec. 1, 1888, p. 2 (large crowd gathered to hear Father Shanley speak on Catholic doctrine); Feb. 15, 1890, p. 3; March 1, 1890, p. 3; March 22, 1890, p. 3; April 19, 1890, p. 3 (Father Harrison's articles); *Northwestern Chronicle*, April 11, 1890, p. 1 (Ireland's interest in converting black Americans).

4. *Appeal*, March 1, 1890, p. 3; April 19, 1890, p. 2; *Northwestern Chronicle*, May 16, 1890, p. 1; *Washington Post*, May 5, 1890, p. 5.

5. *Appeal*, Feb. 8, 1890, p. 2; July 4, 1890, p. 3; *Northwestern Chronicle*, July 4, 1890, pp. 1, 5. Albert S. Foley, *God's Men of Color, the Colored Catholic Priests of the United*

States 1854–1954 (New York: Farrar, Straus & Co., 1955), 32–41 (Father Tolton).

6. Fredrick L. McGhee, "What the Catholic Church Means for the Negro," *Howard's American Magazine* 5 (1900): 361, 366; *Cleveland Gazette,* June 29, 1901, p. 2 ("one common brotherhood").

7. *Appeal,* March 14, 1891, p. 3 (John Rudd in town); David Spalding, "The Negro Catholic Congresses, 1889–1894," *Catholic Historical Review* 55 (Oct. 1969): 337–357; *St. Joseph's Advocate* (April 1889): 592–599 (first Congress); *Appeal,* July 12, 1890, p. 1 (account of second Congress); *Appeal,* Jan. 2, 1892, p. 3 (McGhee leaves for Philadelphia); *Three Catholic Afro-American Congresses* (Cincinnati: American Catholic Tribune, 1893), 137.

8. *Three Catholic Afro-American Congresses,* 136–160; Cyprian Davis, *A History of Black Catholics in the United States* (New York: Crossroad, 1990), 180–181; Spalding, "The Negro Catholic Congresses," 346–347.

9. Spalding, "The Negro Catholic Congresses," 348–352; Davis, *A History of Black Catholics,* 187–193; *Appeal,* Feb. 15, 1890, p. 2 (defense of separate churches).

10. O'Connell, *John Ireland and the American Catholic Church,* 375–401.

11. Davis, *A History of Black Catholics,* 193; Spalding, "The Negro Catholic Congresses," 352–357; Letter from Fredrick McGhee and James Lofton to Father Joseph Slattery, Jan. 20, 1900, Archives of the Josephite Fathers, Baltimore, Maryland.

12. *Cleveland Gazette,* June 29, 1901, p. 2; St. Peter Claver Registrum Baptizarum Ecclesiae, St. Peter Claver parish offices, St. Paul, Minnesota. The records show that Fredrick was godfather to sixteen, of whom six were adults; Mattie was godmother to eight. *St. Peter Claver Church, St. Paul, Minnesota, 1892–1967 Diamond Jubilee,* 6, 10; Foley, *God's Men of Color,* 95–103 (Theobald).

Notes to Chapter Five

1. *St. Paul Globe,* April 20, 1895, p. 2.

2. Ramsey County District Court criminal case file no. 3865, *State v John Costello;* Ramsey County District Court criminal case file no. 3868, *State v Henry West and*

Florence Young; Ramsey County District Court criminal case file no. 3887, *State v Henry West,* MHS.

3. Ramsey County District Court civil case file no. 62069, *Lucy Coleman v James Ross; St. Paul Globe,* Dec. 6, 1895, p. 8; Dec. 7, 1895, p. 2 (Coleman); Feb. 15, 1895, p. 8; Feb. 19, 1895, p. 2; March 26, 1895, p. 2; *Pioneer Press,* Feb. 19, 1895, p. 8 (Allen).

4. *Pioneer Press,* Dec. 16, 1893, p. 5 (the Johnson-Rollins crime); Dec. 19, 1893, p. 5 (flight); March 13, 1894, p. 8 (trial begins); March 14, 1894, p. 2 (trial); March 15, 1894, p. 8 (Johnson testifies); *St. Paul Globe,* March 14, 1894, p. 2 (trial); *St. Paul Dispatch,* March 15, 1894, p. 2, *St. Paul Globe,* March 15, 1894, p. 8 (closing arguments); March 16, 1894, p. 1 (verdict). *Pioneer Press,* Nov. 10, 1891, p. 2 (Blackstone shot); Nov. 17, 1891, p. 2 (Blackstone dies, Davis arrested); March 29, 1892, p. 5 (trial begins); March 30, 1892, p. 3 (Davis testifies); March 31, 1892, p. 8 (Davis acquitted).

5. *St. Paul Globe,* Jan. 19, 1894, p. 2; Jan. 20, 1894, p. 2; Jan. 21, 1894, p. 2; *St. Paul Dispatch,* Jan. 22, 1894, p. 3 (Philip Rice case). David V. Taylor, "Transcript of an Oral History Interview with Adina Gibbs, Dec. 18, 1970." Audio-Visual Library of the Minnesota Historical Society (Adina Gibbs).

6. *St. Paul Globe,* April 15, 1895, p. 2.

7. *Pioneer Press,* June 3, 1895, p. 1; St. Paul Globe, June 3, 1895, p. 1 (near-lynching); June 4, 1895, p. 8 (McGhee represents); June 12, 1895, p. 2 (preliminary hearing); June 22, 1895, p. 2 (indicted); June 25, 1895, p. 2 (plea and sentence); Ramsey County District Court criminal case files nos. 3096 and 3013, *State v Houston Osborn.* At the preliminary hearing, Anton Kachel denied that Osborn had been "strung up." Convict record of Houston Osborn, Stillwater Prison, Book G, p. 569 (died in prison).

8. *Statutes of Minnesota 1879–1888,* vol. 2, ch. 124, secs. 203 & 204.

9. *Appeal,* April 24, 1897, p. 3 (text of the amendments and Morris and Wheaton as drafters).

10. *St. Paul Dispatch,* April 9, 1897, p. 9. The term "blackleg" apparently meant, "one who systematically tries to win by

cheating." It has its origin in English horse-racing, where sporting men "were in the habit of wearing black top boots." *South St. Paul Daily Reporter,* June 17, 1912, p. 2, quoting *London Evening Standard.*

11. *Appeal,* April 24, 1897, p. 2.

12. *Rhone v Loomis,* 74 Minn. Rep. 200, 203, 207 (1898).

13. Minnesota supreme court case file, *Rhone v Loomis,* MHS.

14. *Appeal,* April 22, 1899, p. 4 (bill enacted); April 29, 1999, Minnesota Law Supplement, p. 2. (full text of statute as amended); *Bemidji Pioneer,* Feb. 20, 1902, p. 1 (circumstances of drafting the legislation).

15. The story of black America's reaction to the Spanish-American War is told brilliantly in Willard B. Gatewood Jr.'s *Black America and the White Man's Burden, 1898-1903* (Urbana: University of Illinois Press, 1975) and in George P. Marks III's *The Black Press Views White Imperialism* (New York: Arno Press, 1971).

16. *Appeal,* April 23, 1898, p. 3 (big rally, no McGhee); Sept. 10, 1898, p. 3 (concert); Oct. 1, 1898, p. 3 (Minn. volunteers).

17. *Appeal,* Nov. 12, 1898, p. 3; *Pioneer Press,* Nov. 26, 1898, p. 4. For a complete description of the *Cuba* extravaganza, see Dave Riehle, "The Great Cuba Pageant of 1898: St. Paul's Citizens Support the Struggle for Civil Rights," *Ramsey County History* 33 (Winter, 1999): 15-20.

18. Philip S. Foner, *Antonio Maceo: the "Bronze Titan" of Cuba's Struggle for Independence* (New York: Monthly Review Press, 1977).

19. Lynne Farley Emery, *Black Dance in the United States* (New York: Dance Horizons, 1980), 26; Thomas Morgan and William Barlow, *From Cakewalkers to Concert Halls, An Illustrated History of American Popular Music from 1865 to 1930* (Washington, D.C.: Elliot & Clark, 1992), 26; Edward Thorp, *Black Dance* (Woodstock, N.Y.: Overlook Press, 1980), 55 (history of the cakewalk generally). *Appeal,* April 10, 1892, p. 3 (cakewalk comes to St. Paul).

20. Mark Sullivan, *In Our Times,* vol. 4 (New York: Scribner's, 1932), 242.

21. James Weldon Johnson, *Black Manhattan* (New York: Atheneum, 1986), 105.

22. Chicago *Broad Ax,* March 25, 1899, p. 2, quoting *Odd Fellows Journal; Appeal,* March 12, 1892, p. 3.

23. *Appeal,* Dec. 3, 1898, p. 4.

24. *Appeal,* Dec. 10, 1898, p. 4.

25. *Appeal,* Dec. 24, 1898, p. 3.

26. *Appeal,* Feb. 11, 1899, p. 4.

27. *Appeal,* May 6, 1899, p. 3.

Notes to Chapter Six

1. Most historians date Washington's ascendancy to his famous "Atlanta Compromise" speech of 1895, which was interpreted as black acceptance of permanent social segregation, in return for limited economic and political rights. In Louis R. Harlan, *Booker T. Washington, Wizard of Tuskegee, 1901-1915* (New York: Oxford University Press, 1983), 217-220. The full text of the speech may be found in Booker T. Washington, *Up From Slavery* (Garden City, New York: Doubleday, 1963), 157-162.

2. *Appeal,* June 18, 1898, p. 3 (1st meeting); July 2, 1898, p. 3; July 9, 1898, p. 3; July 23, 1898, p. 4 (organizing meetings).

3. *Appeal,* Sept. 17, 1898, pp. 3-4.

4. Thornbrough, "The National Afro-American League," (AAC organized); *Appeal,* Jan. 7, 1899, p. 2 (McGhee and Adams delegates).

5. *Appeal,* Jan. 7, 1899, pp. 2-3 (full text of Address).

6. *Appeal,* Jan. 21, 1899, p. 3 (Jan. meeting); Feb. 25, 1899, p. 3 (Douglass day event).

7. *Appeal,* April 22, 1899, p. 3.

8. Emma Thornbrough, *T. Thomas Fortune, Militant Journalist,* 191-192; David Levering Lewis, *W. E. B. Du Bois, Biography of a Race, 1869-1919* (New York: Henry Holt & Co., 1993), 230-231; Thornbrough, "The National Afro-American League," 503-504 (Chicago meeting); George E. Cunningham, "The Italian: A Hindrance to White Solidarity in Louisiana, 1890-1898," *Journal of Negro History* 50 (Jan. 1965): 35-36 (lynching of Italians); George B. Tindall, *South Carolina Negroes, 1877-1900* (Louisiana State University Press: Baton Rouge, 1966), 255-256 (facts of Baker case); *Appeal,* March 26, 1898, p. 1 (Baker case protest); Sept. 9, 1899, pp. 1-2 (text of Address).

9. *Appeal*, Sept. 9, 1899, p. 1. McGhee and Du Bois undoubtedly met during the meeting. We also have record of a social event at which both men spoke—a "stag banquet" held after conclusion of the Council's Friday business. McGhee's old Chicago friends E. H. Morris and Julius Avendorph attended as well. *Afro-American Advance*, Aug. 26, 1899, p. 1.

10. *Appeal*, Jan. 6, 1900, p. 3; Chicago *Broad Ax*, Jan. 6, 1900, p. 1 (McGhee at D.C. meeting); *Appeal*, Jan. 13, 1900, p. 3 (Jan. meeting); Jan. 20, 1900, p. 3 (McGhee presided); Feb. 3, 1900, pp. 3-4 (meeting at Morris's office); Dec. 16, 1899, p. 3; Dec. 23, 1899, p. 5 (*A Social Glass*). McGhee and his wife also played in *The Last Loaf*, for St. Peter Claver, in Oct. 1894. *Appeal*, Sept. 29, 1894, p. 3.

11. *Appeal*, Jan. 20, 1900, p. 3; *Pioneer Press*, Jan. 18, 1900, p. 5. Back in 1897, at the time of the controversy over amendments to the state civil rights statute, McGhee had complained that the $500 maximum in damages would be far too little for a man of Washington's ("the embodiment of the highest type of Afro-American manhood") stature. *Appeal*, April 24, 1897, p. 2.

12. The prevailing assessments of Washington are expressed very well in Harlan, *Booker T. Washington, Wizard of Tuskegee*, and David Levering Lewis, *W. E. B. Du Bois*.

13. *Appeal*, Aug. 18, 1900, p. 1; Washington, D.C., *Colored American*, Sept. 1, 1900, p. 5; Sept. 8, 1900, pp. 1, 9; *Cleveland Gazette*, Sept. 8, 1900, p. 1 (accounts of Indianapolis meeting).

14. Thornbrough, "The National Afro-American League," 504. Ida B. Wells Barnett, who attended the meeting, later voiced the same suspicion. Alfreda M. Duster, ed., *Crusade for Justice, the Autobiography of Ida B. Wells* (University of Chicago Press: Chicago, 1970), 264-265.

15. *Appeal*, Sept. 8, 1900, p. 3; Oct. 20, 1900, p. 3 (two brief mentions of the Council).

16. *Appeal*, March 16, 1901, p. 3 (back from Eastern speaking tour); Aug. 3, 1901, p. 3 (Harry Shepherd, Minnesota's delegate); Aug. 17, 1901, p. 2 (McGhee head of legislative bureau).

17. *Appeal*, Oct. 5, 1901, p. 3 (McGhee to represent Summers; Oct. 12, 1901, p. 2 (Summers loses in district court); Nov. 23, 1901, p. 3 (case set for supreme court); Nov. 30, 1901, p. 3 (loss at supreme court); *Pioneer Press*, Oct. 5, 1901, p. 10; *St. Paul Dispatch*, Oct. 4, 1901, p. 11; Oct. 12, 1901, p. 7 (accounts of the crime); *St. Paul Globe*, Oct. 11, 1901, p. 2 (hearing with governor); Oct. 12, 1901, p. 2 (Van Sant's decision); Ramsey County District Court case file, State ex rel. *Summers v Justus*, MHS; *Appeal*, March 29, 1902, p. 3 (Summers in jail in Tennessee); Sept. 20, 1902, p 3 (sentence).

Notes to Chapter Seven

1. *Pioneer Press*, May 4, 1892, p. 1, May 5, 1892, p. 1 (election results) (Frederick Wright defeated incumbent mayor Robert Smith by nearly 4,000 votes out of 24,500 cast); *St. Paul Dispatch*, June 22, 1894, p. 5 (pay of third assistant city attorney); *Pioneer Press*, March 11, 1893, p. 4 (Chamberlain appointed); *St. Paul Daily News*, March 15, 1893, p. 5 (Walter Chapin appointed); *St. Paul Globe*, March 19, 1893, p. 3 (analysis of Chapin's appointment and quotation.) McGhee's defection may also have been spurred by the way the party treated his friend, client, and fellow-Catholic Samuel Hardy when the Republicans got control of St. Paul city government in the spring of 1892: Hardy was replaced as city hall janitor by Republican John Dillingham. *Appeal*, Aug. 20, 1892, p. 4.

2. Logan, *The Negro in American Life and Thought*, 37-51.

3. Paolo E. Coletta, *William Jennings Bryan, Political Evangelist, 1869-1908* (Lincoln: University of Nebraska Press, 1964), 99-160 (1896 convention and events leading to Bryan's nomination.)

4. *St. Paul Globe*, Oct. 11, 1896, p. 2; *Pioneer Press*, Oct. 11, 1896, p. 2.

5. *Appeal*, June 23, 1900, p. 3 (McGhee selected alternate delegate); Chicago *Broad Ax*, July 7, 1900, p. 1 (account of Negro Democrats' meeting); *St. Paul Globe*, July 1, 1900, p. 5 (candidate for presidency of Negro Democrats); July 6, 1900, p. 4 (defeated, made chair of committee on address).

6. Chicago *Broad Ax*, July 21, 1900, p. 1 (text of Address).

7. Gatewood, *Black America and the White Man's Burden*, 55-59 (black soldiers in combat in Cuba), 241-244 (Roosevelt's remarks and resulting controversy); Topeka *Colored Citizen*, Aug. 3, 1901, p. 1 (Roosevelt's remarks); Chicago *Broad Ax*, July 21, 1900 p. 1 (contents of Address).

8. Fredrick L. McGhee, "Another View," *Howard's American Magazine* 5 (Oct. 1900): 94. McGhee's article follows and supplements a longer anti-imperialism piece by Howard University Professor Kelly Miller entitled, "The Effect of Imperialism Upon the Negro Race." Miller argued there that "the acquiescence of the negro in the political rape of the Filipino would give ground of justification to the assaults upon his rights at home.... The Negro would show himself unworthy of the rights he claims should he deny the same to a struggling people under another sky." McGhee's title, "Another View," seems to imply that he differed with Miller, but the opposite was true.

9. *St. Paul Globe*, Oct. 2, 1900, p. 1. The Democratic platform of 1900 took no position on any civil rights issues. Willard B. Gatewood Jr., *Black Americans and the White Man's Burden*, 238-242 (Bryan's courting of black voters).

10. *Pioneer Press*, Oct. 2, 1900, p. 4.

11. *Pioneer Press*, Oct. 3, 1900, p. 4; Oct. 5, 1900, p. 4. The *Pioneer Press* probably had it right that Bryan considered the addition of nonwhite peoples to the American polity to be harmful to the nation. The 1900 Democratic platform stated that "Filipinos cannot be citizens without endangering our civilization," and supported continued exclusion of the Chinese and "all Asiatic races." "The Democratic Platform," *The Outlook* 65 (July 14, 1900): 635-637.

12. Gatewood, *Black America and the White Man's Burden*, 257-258 (black voting 1900).

13. *The Commoner*, Nov. 1, 1901, pp. 1-3.

14. Fredrick McGhee to Booker T. Washington, Sept. 14, 1904. Booker T. Washington Papers, Library of Congress.

15. Washington, D.C., *Bee*, Sept. 10, 1904, p. 4 (text of Address). Judge Parker received 5,084,491 votes, nearly

1,300,000 fewer than Bryan got in 1900. *The World Almanac and Book of Facts 1999* (Mahwah, New Jersey: PRIMEDIA Reference Inc., 1998), 494.

16. Ann J. Lane, *The Brownsville Affair, National Crisis and Black Reaction* (Port Washington, N.Y.: National University Publications, 1971).

17. Lewis, *W. E. B. Du Bois*, 341.

18. *Appeal*, Nov. 7, 1908, p. 3 (McGhee campaigns for Bryan); Bryan received 6,467,946 votes in 1896, 6,358,071 in 1900, and 6,409,106 in 1908. *The World Almanac and Book of Facts 1999*, 494.

19. *Pioneer Press*, July 10, 1912, p. 6.

20. *Pioneer Press*, July 12, 1912, p. 6.

Notes to Chapter Eight

1. Fredrick L. McGhee to Emmett Scott, March 25, 1902; McGhee to Scott, March 29, 1902. Booker T. Washington Papers, Library of Congress.

2. McGhee to Washington, April 5, 1902. Booker T. Washington Papers.

3. *Appeal*, July 5, 1902 p. 3 (complete meeting program).

4. McGhee to Scott, March 29, 1902. Booker T. Washington Papers.

5. *Appeal*, July 19, 1902, p. 2.

6. *Appeal*, July 19, 1902, p. 2 (Van Sant's speech); *Pioneer Press*, July 10, 1902, p. 2 (Washington's arrival). That Washington came was no surprise to readers of the *Pioneer Press*; it printed on July 9 that he was expected to arrive that day. *Pioneer Press*, July 9, 1902, p. 3.

7. *Pioneer Press*, July 10, 1902, p. 2.

8. *St. Paul Globe*, July 10, 1902, p. 10.

9. Ibid.

10. *Pioneer Press*, July 11, 1902, p. 3 (Wells Barnett's speech); *Dictionary of American Negro Biography*, 30-31; Darlene Clark Hine, ed., *Black Women in America* (Brooklyn: Carlson Publishing Co., 1993), 1242-1244 (Wells Barnett's life and career generally). The story of lynching in all its horror is told compellingly in Leon Litwack, *Trouble in Mind, Black Southerners in the Age of Jim Crow* (New York: Alfred A. Knopf, 1998).

11. *Appeal*, July 19, 1902, p. 2.

12. *Pioneer Press*, July 10, 1902, p. 2 (predicted fight over officers); July 11, 1902,

p. 3; *St. Paul Globe*, July 11, 1902, p. 10 (accounts of the controversy).

13. *St. Paul Globe*, July 11, 1902, p. 10.

14. *Appeal*, July 5, 1902, p. 3 (musical selections); *St. Paul Dispatch*, July 11, 1902, p. 3 (Washington's speech).

15. *Pioneer Press*, July 11, 1902, p. 3; Thornbrough, *T. Thomas Fortune*, 226-228.

16. *St. Paul Dispatch*, July 11, 1902, p. 3.

17. *Appeal*, July 19, 1902, p. 3.

18. *Pioneer Press*, July 12, 1902, p. 3; *St. Paul Dispatch*, July 11, 1902, p. 3; *St. Paul Globe*, July 10, 1902, p. 4 (editorial). The *Globe* commented that "by minimizing the importance to them [black Americans] of the pursuit of political ends ... he [Washington] has shown himself to be at once a profound thinker, a good American and a safe guide for his people."

19. *Cleveland Gazette*, Aug. 16, 1902, p. 1; *Indianapolis Freeman*, Aug. 9, 1902, p. 1; Aug. 16, 1902, p. 1; Washington, D.C., *Colored American*, July 19, 1902, p. 2; *Washington Bee*, July 26, 1902, p. 2.

20. Washington, D.C., *Colored American*, July 26, 1902, p. 2.

21. Emmett Scott to Booker T. Washington, July 17, 1902. Booker T. Washington Papers.

22. Thornbrough, *T. Thomas Fortune*, 234-235 (federal appointment); *Appeal*, Dec. 13, 1902, p. 4 (Fortune's address); Jan. 17, 1903, p. 3 (reorganization plan).

23. *Appeal*, Feb. 7, 1903, p. 3 (local NAAC activities); Feb. 21, 1903, p. 3 (Douglass Day events). An interesting example of civil rights litigation involved the black attorney Charles Scrutchin, who lived and worked in Bemidji, Minnesota. When he was refused a shave in Blackduck, Minnesota, he hired a white lawyer and took the barber to court—and won a verdict of one cent. *Bemidji Pioneer*, Feb. 20, 1902, p. 1 (text of court decision); Steven R. Hoffbeck, "Victories Yet to Win, Charles Scrutchin, Bemidji's Black Activist Attorney," *Minnesota History* 55 (Summer 1996): 59-75.

24. *Appeal*, Jan. 31, 1903, p. 3 (text of NAAC Address); Feb. 7, 1903, p. 3 (McGhee elected local president); Feb. 21, 1903, p. 3 (Douglass Day event). Precisely what role McGhee played in the Council's legal work during this period is not clear. One account

had him elected head of the legal bureau at the 1902 meeting. *Appeal*, July 19, 1902, p. 3. The previous head had been lawyer J. Madison Vance. Before 1901 it appears that the NAAC's legal work was done through its legislative bureau, of which McGhee was selected head in 1900, *Cleveland Gazette*, Sept. 8, 1900, p. 1. Even before then, he had been assisting the Council in attempting a challenge of a Jim Crow voting law in Louisiana. The case, State ex rel. *Ryanes v Gleason*, proved to be a complete failure.

25. Charles Puttkamer & Ruth Worthy, "William Monroe Trotter, 1872-1934," *Journal of Negro History* 43 (Oct. 1958): 301; Stephen R. Fox, *The Guardian of Boston: William Monroe Trotter* (New York: Atheneum, 1970) (Trotter generally); Fredrick McGhee to William M. Trotter, June 15, 1903. W.E.B. DuBois Papers; *St. Paul Daily Globe*, June 28, 1903, p. 2.

26. *Louisville Times*, July 1, 1903, p. 3; July 2, p. 1; July 2, p. 7; July 3, p. 3; Louisville *Courier-Journal*, July 2, 1903, p. 4; July 3, p. 1; July 4, p. 4 (daily press accounts of the meeting); Thornbrough, "The National Afro-American League," 505 (summary account of events and *Guardian* quote); *Washington Bee*, Aug. 12, 1905, p. 3 (McGhee's letter); Lewis, *W. E. B. Du Bois*, 298-299 (brief summary of meeting); Cleveland *Gazette*, July 11, 1903, p. 1; Indianapolis *Freeman*, July 18, 1903, p. 1 (partisan black press accounts of Louisville disputes).

Notes to Chapter Nine

1. *Minneapolis Tribune*, Nov. 19, p. 1; Nov. 20, 1903, pp. 1, 7; *Minneapolis Journal*, Nov. 19, 1903, p. 1; Nov. 20, 1903, p. 1; Nov. 21, 1903, p. 1; Nov. 23, 1903, pp. 1-2; Nov. 24, 1903, pp. 1-2; Nov. 25, 1903, p. 1; *Pioneer Press*, Nov. 22, 1903, pp. 1, 7 (first accounts of crime and search for Calderone); *Minneapolis Tribune*, Jan. 20, 1904, p. 6; *Minneapolis Journal*, Jan. 23, 1904, p. 6 (trails of blood); *Pioneer Press*, Nov. 23, 1903, p. 1; *Minneapolis Journal*, Nov. 23, 1903, p. 2; "The McGhee's of St. Paul," *Crisis*, 40 (June 1933): 130 (versions of carriage stop). McGhee actually testified to still a different version, at the coroner's inquest. He said that the livery through

which he had hired the hack first sent one with not enough fur robes to keep people warm. This was the one with the roan horse. He sent that one back, at which time a detective, revolver drawn, came running and chased it, believing that he was pursuing Calderone. McGhee then ordered a second rig, in which he took his client to Minneapolis. *Minneapolis Tribune,* Nov. 25, 1903, p. 9.

2. *Pioneer Press,* Nov. 22, 1903, p. 1; Nov. 24, 1903, p. 2. Both men were placed under oath and grilled about their actions at the coroner's inquest into Battalia's death. *Minneapolis Journal,* Nov. 24, 1903, p. 1; *Minneapolis Tribune,* Nov. 25, 1903, p. 9.

3. *Pioneer Press,* Nov. 24, 1903, p. 1; *Minneapolis Journal,* Nov. 24, 1903, pp. 1-2 (statement and circumstances of giving it.) In 1911, Calderone got a different lawyer and petitioned the governor for clemency; one of the grounds was that his confession had been coerced. The petition was denied. *Pioneer Press,* April 13, 1911, p. 6.

4. *Minneapolis Tribune,* Jan. 20, 1904, p. 6; Jan. 21, 1904, p. 7 (trial begins and jury selection); Hennepin County District Court criminal case file no. 7558, *State of Minnesota v Antonio Calderone* (indictment and voir dire).

5. *Minneapolis Tribune,* Jan. 22, 1904, p. 6 (opening statements); Jan. 23, 1904, p. 8 (testimony).

6. *Minneapolis Tribune,* Jan. 23, 1904, p. 8 (third man); Jan. 24, 1904, p. 5 (will be hanged); Convict Record, Antonio Calderone, Stillwater State Prison, MHS (Calderone's height and weight). Prosecutors apparently decided against using Henry for fear of muddying what they thought was a straightforward case. Though his testimony could have been devastating to Calderone, Henry would have made a poor witness. According to one account, he was once a St. Paul physician who had fallen into a life a crime through drug addiction. There was even doubt that he was the "third man" at all; the streetcar conductor who had taken the men to the Franklin Ave. Bridge failed to identify Henry. McGhee let it be known in the press that he relished cross-examining Henry, and that he would use him to prove

that a fourth man had been present at the scene. This might have been a ploy to keep Henry off the stand. Or it may have been true. After the trial was over, McGhee told reporters that not long after Calderone's arrest an Italian man had contacted him and offered to produce the real third man, but only if McGhee would give his daughter as a hostage, to protect that third man from prosecution, until the trial was done. McGhee refused. *Minneapolis Journal,* Jan. 22, 1904, pp. 1-2; Jan. 23, 1904, pp. 1, 6; Jan. 27, 1904, p. 1; Jan. 28, 1904, p. 1.

7. *Minneapolis Tribune,* Jan. 26, 1904, p. 7; Jan. 27, 1904, p. 6; *Minneapolis Journal,* Jan. 26, 1904, p. 1 (defense testimony and closing arguments).

8. *Minneapolis Tribune,* Jan. 28, 1904, p. 6; *Minneapolis Journal,* Jan. 28, 1904, p. 1 (verdict); Feb. 2, 1904, p. 1 (sentence). At sentencing, the prosecutor, Fred Boardman, agreed that without the manslaughter option, Calderone would have been convicted of at least second-degree murder. Ibid.

Notes to Chapter Ten

1. W. E. B. Du Bois, *Writings* (New York: Literary Classics of the United States, 1986).

2. Lewis, *W. E. B. Du Bois,* 286-288 ("Of Booker T. Washington"), 297-301 (events leading up to the conference), 304-308 (the conference); Fox, *The Guardian of Boston,* 49-63 (Boston riot and pressure on Atlanta University). W. E. B. Du Bois to Fredrick McGhee, Dec. 28, 1903; McGhee to Du Bois, Dec. 31, 1903, W. E. B. Du Bois Papers.

3. Lewis, *W. E. B. Du Bois,* 304-311; Herbert Aptheker, *Afro-American History: The Modern Era* (New York: Citadel Press, 1971), 119-126; Kelly Miller, "Summary of the Proceedings of the Conference at Carnegie Hall," Booker T. Washington papers.

4. Lewis, *W. E. B. Du Bois,* 307 (chaos quote); McGhee to Washington, Jan. 12, 1904, April 19, 1904, and Sept. 14, 1904. Booker T. Washington Papers; *St. Paul Globe,* April 20, 1904, p. 2, *Appeal,* April 23, 1904, p. 3 (St. Paul meeting supporting Crum); Sept. 17, 1904, p. 2 (NAAC meeting without McGhee); Feb. 25, 1905, p. 3 (Crum confirmed).

5. Lewis, *W. E. B. Du Bois*, 311.

6. *Appeal*, Feb. 25, 1905, p. 3 (Du Bois in St. Paul); Lewis, *W. E. B. Du Bois*, 223-224, 303, 311, 365-366.

7. Elliott Rudwick, "The Niagara Movement," *Journal of Negro History* 42 (April, 1957): 177-182; Herbert Aptheker, ed., *A Documentary History of the Negro People in the United States* (New York: Citadel Press, 1968), 900-901 (Du Bois's circular), 903 (Declaration of Principles), 904 (McGhee's role and need for Niagara. The full quotation is: "The honor of founding the organization belongs to F. L. McGhee, who first suggested it; C. C. Bentley, who planned the method of organization and W. M. Trotter, who put the backbone into the platform."); Lewis, *W. E. B. Du Bois*, 304-311, Fox, *Guardian of Boston*, 89-90 (founding of Niagara); *Appeal*, July 29, 1905, pp. 2, 4 (Niagara manifesto).

8. *Washington Bee*, Aug. 12, 1905, p. 3.

Notes to Chapter Eleven

1. *St. Paul Dispatch*, May 3, 1905, pp. 1-2; May 4, 1905, pp. 1-2; May 5, 1905, p. 1; *St. Paul Daily News*, May 3, 1905, pp. 1-2; May 4, 1905, pp. 1-2; May 5, 1905, p. 1; May 8, 1905, p. 8; *Pioneer Press*, May 4, 1905, pp. 1-2; May 5, 1905, p. 2.

2. Minnesota Statutes of 1905, ch. 95, sec. 4789 (appointment of counsel); Ramsey County Criminal Registers of Actions, Book I, MHS (McGhee appointed); case file, Municipal Court of St. Paul, *State v Harry Laramie and James R. Egan*, MHS (preliminary hearing); *Appeal*, June 10, 1905, p. 3 (other murder case); July 29, 1905, p. 3 (McGhee on vacation).

3. *St. Paul Globe*, Nov. 1, 1898, p. 3 (Rose Ledegar); Ramsey County District Court criminal case file no. 4649, *State of Minnesota v Harry Laramie and James R. Egan*, MHS; *Pioneer Press*, Nov. 17, 1905, p. 3; Nov. 18, 1905, p. 2; Nov. 21, 1905, p. 3; Nov. 22, 1905, p. 3; Nov. 23, 1905, p. 1; *St. Paul Dispatch*, Nov. 22, 1905, pp. 1, 15; Nov. 23, 1905, pp. 1-2; *St. Paul Daily News*, Nov. 23, 1905, p. 6; *Minneapolis Tribune*, Nov. 17, 1905, p. 9; Nov. 18, 1905, p. 3; Nov. 19, 1905, p. 19; Nov. 21, 1905, p. 5; Nov. 22, 1905, p. 8; Nov. 23, 1905, p. 6 (trial).

Notes to Chapter Twelve

1. Barclay was born in Mississippi around 1851 and Matthew 1854. Manuscript U.S. Census, Third Ward, Knoxville, Tennessee, 1870. Barclay appears to have gotten his name from the white McGhees of Tennessee. The elder Barclay McGhee (1750?-1819) was the founder of the white McGhee family in Tennessee. His grandson Barclay (1816-1866) probably owned Abraham McGhee and sold him to John A. Walker of Monroe County, Mississippi. Letter from Steve Cotham, head of McClung Historical Collection, Knox County Public Library, Knoxville, Tennessee, Aug. 8, 1996. How long young Fred McGhee lived with both brothers is not known. Barclay preceded him to Chicago; he was there in 1876, perhaps earlier. *Lakeside Directory of Chicago, 1876*. Matthew followed his brothers to Chicago in 1886. *Lakeside Directory of Chicago, 1886, 958*.

2. Fenwick, *Sturdy Sons of St. Paul*, 95; *Appeal*, June 22, 1889, p. 1; (marriage to Mattie and her origins); Sept. 1, 1888; Oct. 6, 1888 (separation, Galesburg); Nov. 24, 1888 (return to Chicago); Death certificate, Burial permit, Mattie McGhee, City of St. Paul, Department of Health, June 26, 1933 (Mattie's age) (the burial permit gives her age, at her death in 1933, as 63.) We do not know how Fred and Mattie met, but it is easy to see how their paths may have crossed. In 1886 he had his offices at 193 Clark St., and lived at 3623 Butterfield; that year Mattie worked at 279 Clark St. and lived at 2807 Butterfield. 1886 *Lakeside Directory of Chicago*, 381, 958.

3. *Appeal*, Jan. 30, 1892, p. 3 (adoption of Ruth); *Deed*, Thomas and Mary Daly to Fredrick and Mattie McGhee, Feb. 9, 1893, document no. 170685, 245 Deeds 486, Ramsey County Recorder, St. Paul. *Pioneer Press*, Jan. 15, 1896, p. 8 (Washington's visit; this was probably his first visit to St. Paul, and McGhee likely arranged it).

4. Willard B. Gatewood, *Aristocrats of Color: The Black Elite, 1880-1920* (Bloomington: Indiana University Press, 1990), 129; Taylor, *Pilgrim's Progress* (general social situation, etc.); Samuel Hardy (often known as Colonel Hardy) was a janitor; James Kidd Hilyard, one of the most loved

and honored early black citizens, ran a laundry; Owen Howell ran a tailoring and tobacco establishment. The McGhees retained some friends from their Chicago days, most notably the entrepreneur and "society prince" Julius Avendorph, who was a regular visitor. They entertained visiting guests a great deal, people such as attorney James Guy of Topeka. One of the interesting aspects of the social life of the times, so well chronicled by *The Appeal*, was how much long-distance visiting took place. Northern middle-class blacks of the turn-of-the-century were great travelers.

5. Gatewood, *Aristocrats of Color*; Lewis, *W. E. B. Du Bois*; Fox, *The Guardian of Boston*; Thornbrough, *T. Thomas Fortune*.

6. Articles of incorporation, St. Peter Claver Church, Ramsey County Recorder, St. Paul; *Appeal*, June 20, 1891, p. 3 (Mattie directs Little Red Riding Hood); Sept. 1, 1894, p. 3 (Fred fries chicken at Claver picnic); July 3, 1897, p. 3 (Fred chaperones Claver choir party); Aug. 14, 1897, p. 3 (Fred organizes Claver picnic at Lake Minnetonka); Dec. 22, 1897, p. 3 (Fred is treasurer of Claver Sodality); June 18, 1898, p. 3 (McGhees give lawn social for Claver); Oct. 8, 1898, p. 3 (Fred speaks at Claver reception for Archbishop Ireland); Feb. 11, 1899, p. 3 (Fred organizes masque for Claver); May 6, 1899, p. 3 (Fred directs Claver spring fest); April 17, 1900, p. 3 (McGhees host Claver ladies' musicale); July 7, 1900, p. 3 (Fred on committee for Claver picnic); Dec. 27, 1901, p. 3 (Mattie to sing at Claver Christmas mass and give whist party); Nov. 16, 1907, p. 3 (Mattie a member of Ladies' Home Catholic Club); April 3, 1909, p. 3 (Mattie sings for Ladies' Home Catholic Club); Oct. 15, 1910, p. 3 (McGhees perform with Ladies' Home Catholic Club's Lady Minstrels); *Twin City Star*, June 16, 1910, p. 2 (McGhees host reception for Father Theobald); Registrum Baptizarum Ecclesiae, St. Peter Claver Parish, St. Paul, Minnesota (McGhees as godparents).

7. As part of his ongoing sociological work at Atlanta University, W. E. B. Du Bois published a study in 1907 entitled "Economic Cooperation Among Negro Americans." That paper covered many subjects,

including black fraternal organizations. His national membership figures were: Odd Fellows, 285,931; United Brotherhood of Friendship, 74,400; Knights of Pythias, 69,331; Masons, 45,835; Elks, 3,746. These numbers were probably based on incomplete information. The UBF, for example, claimed membership of 150,000 at around this time. See Chapter 15, n. 7. *The Atlanta University Publications* (New York: Arno Press and New York Times Press, 1969), No. 12, "Economic Cooperation Among Negro Americans," 109–126. David Taylor surveys black clubs and fraternal organizations in St. Paul in *Pilgrim's Progress*, 188–212.

8. *Appeal*, May 18, 1901, p. 3 (Fred participates in mock trial); June 8, 1901, p. 3 (Fred speaks at club meeting); Oct. 11, 1901, p. 3 (Fred is an officer); April 5, 1902, p. 3 (Fred speaks); May 2, 1903, p. 3 (mock trial); Oct. 29, 1904, p. 3 (Mattie sings at benefit for the club); Feb. 25, 1905, p. 3 (Fred speaks at benefit for the club); Jan. 13, 1906, p. 3 (Fred is an officer); April 21, 1907, p. 3 (Fred will speak).

9. McGhee's participation in local party politics spanned his entire life in St. Paul. The first meeting we know of was the local Republican Conclave in summer 1890; the last was the state Democratic Convention in Duluth in summer 1912.

10. *Appeal*, July 14, 1900, p. 3; July 13, 1901, p. 3; Nov. 16, 1901, p. 3.

11. *Appeal*, April 27, 1901, p. 3.

12. *Appeal* Sept. 28, 1894, p. 3; *St. Paul Globe*, Feb. 20, 1895, p. 2 (*Last Loaf*); *Appeal*, Dec. 3, 1898, p. 2 (*Cuba* show); Dec. 16, 1899, p. 3 (*A Social Glass*); June 20, 1891, p. 3 (children's play).

13. *Appeal* Feb. 20, 1904, p. 3; Feb. 18, 1905, p. 3; Feb. 17, 1906, p. 3; Feb. 20, 1909, p. 3; Feb. 24, 1912, p. 3 (Lincoln Day appearances); Feb. 11, 1899, p. 3; Feb. 21, 1903, p. 3; Feb. 11, 1911 (Douglass Day appearances); Jan. 8, 1910, p. 3; Jan. 7, 1911, p. 3; *Twin City Star*, Jan. 14, 1911, p. 1 (Sumner Day appearances); *Appeal*, Feb. 20, 1909, p. 3 (Spokane); Jan. 4, 1890, p. 3 (debate at Lyceum Club); Feb. 8, 1890, p. 3 (speech at Claver Sodality); March 22, 1890, p. 3 (speech to Knights of Pythias); June 21, 1890, p. 3 (talk at testimonial for

James K. Hilyard); July 12, 1890, p. 3 (NEA meeting and Wells, Brown, and Tolton); July 19, 1890, p. 3 (speech at dedication of Odd Fellows' hall); July 26, 1890, p. 3 (speech at Odd Fellows picnic); Aug. 9, 1890, p. 3 (speech at Thomas Lyles birthday celebration); Aug. 30, 1890, p. 3 (speech at GOP Convention); Oct. 11, 1890, p. 3 (speech to Colored Citizens' Union); Oct. 18, 1890, p. 3 (speech to Minneapolis Club of Colored Republicans).

14. The complete text of McGhee's speech, as transcribed by a reporter for *The Appeal*, is contained in the John W. Blair papers, 1867-1915 (P1788), MHS.

15. Paul D. Nelson, "Orphans and Old Folks, St. Paul's Crispus Attucks Home," *Minnesota History* 56 (Fall 1998): 105-106; *Appeal* Oct. 5, 1912, p. 2.

16. *St. Paul Daily News*, February 29, 1908, p. 1. Probably McGhee's most prosperous client was Dr. Val Do Turner (see Ch. 16), and it is unlikely that McGhee charged him.

17. Mortgages: document no. 170703, Feb. 9, 1893 ($1,000 to Joseph Bock); document no. 187660, May 1, 1894 ($2,500 to Connecticut Mutual Life Insurance Co.); document no. 239481, May 1, 1899 ($2,500 to Connecticut Mutual Life Insurance Co.); document no. 297272, May 1, 1904 ($1,800 to Phoenix Mutual Life Insurance Co.); document no. 300173, Aug. 6, 1905 ($400 to Edward Dampier), all documents Ramsey County Recorder, St. Paul. Ramsey County civil case file no. 72051, *Brown & Haywood Co. v F. L. McGhee*, March 17, 1898 (default judgment against McGhee for $68.81 plus $7.50 costs; Brown & Haywood dealt in glass); Ramsey County civil case file no. 73773, *Drs. Fulton & McDevitt v F. L. McGhee*, Nov. 21, 1898 (McGhee stipulated to a judgment against him for $64.50; he paid it off in Jan. 1899); Ramsey County civil case file no. 103140, *L. D. Powell Co. v F. L. McGhee*, (the plaintiff got a default judgment against McGhee in the sum of $50.48) (lawsuits).

18. There is some dispute about whether Turner was indeed the first African-American physician in the state. He arrived in St. Paul in mid-March of 1898. *Appeal*,

March 19, 1898, p. 3. On April 9, *The Appeal* reported that Turner already had his medical practice up and running. *Appeal*, April 9, 1898, p. 3. A week later, *The Appeal* reported that Dr. Thomas Cook was the first black physician to get a license to practice in Minnesota by passing the state exam. *Appeal*, April 16, 1898, p. 3. In all events, Dr. Turner had much the more prominent career as a physician and as a citizen. Fishing: *Appeal*, July 29, 1905, p. 3 (Sturgeon Lake); July 14, 1906, p. 3; May 30, 1908, p. 3 (Lake Pokegama); Aug. 1, 1908, p. 3 (Wisconsin); Aug. 13, 1910, p. 3 (Wisconsin).

19. *Deed*, Nettie & Gilbert Tripp to McGhees, Sept. 25, 1909, 68 Book of Deeds 204, Polk County, Wisconsin, Recorder; Estate of Fredrick L. McGhee, County Court of Polk County, Wisconsin, 5 Book of Records 460; *Appeal*, Aug. 13, 1910, p. 3; Aug. 5, 1911, p. 3; July 6, 1912, p. 3; Aug. 3, 1912, p. 3. In his 1933 remembrance of the McGhees, W. E. B. Du Bois wrote, "I remember camping with him one summer [probably 1908] on the Apple river, Wisconsin, and his clients swarmed over the country-side and with boats invaded the lake where he was fishing in order to consult him. Around the campfire he used to tell us extraordinary stories of his adventures . . . ." "The McGhee's of St. Paul," *Crisis* 40 (June 1933), 130.

20. *Appeal*, June 12, 1909, p. 3; *Pioneer Press*, June 9, 1909, p. 5; McGhee to Du Bois, May 26, 1909, Du Bois Papers (Ruth's graduation); *St. Paul City Directory* (Ruth's occupation).

21. *Appeal*, July 11, 1891, p. 3 (Matthew's death); Sept. 29, 1912, p. 3; June 14, 1919, p. 3 (Barclay's visits); letter to author from Nebraska State Historical Society, Aug. 1, 1995.

22. *Appeal*, Oct. 8, 1892, p. 3 (Cranes move to St. Paul); July 10, 1897, p. 3 (Charles Crane appointed workhouse chef); Jan. 9, 1900, p. 3 (John Crane appointed jailer).

Notes to Chapter Thirteen

1. Rudwick, "The Niagara Movement," 185-189; Lewis, *W. E. B. Du Bois*, 328-330.

2. Herbert Aptheker, ed., *A Documen-*

tary History of the Negro People in the United States (New York: Citadel Press, 1968), 907–909.

3. *Appeal*, Aug. 18, 1906, p. 3.

4. Lewis, *W. E. B. Du Bois*, 330–340.

5. Ann J. Lane, *The Brownsville Affair, National Crisis and Black Reaction* (Port Washington, N.Y.: National University Publications, 1971) (the Affair and reactions generally); *Appeal*, Dec. 1, 1906, p. 3 (local protest).

6. Circular letter, Du Bois to Niagara Movement members, April 10, 1907, Du Bois Papers; Virginia Supreme Court of Appeals Order Book No. 34, p. 83, *Barbara Pope v Commonwealth of Virginia*, Jan. 9, 1907.

7. Undated report (probably early 1908) by J. Milton Waldron, Niagara treasurer; Minutes of Aug. 27, 1907 Niagara meeting, p. 3 (McGhee's report), Du Bois Papers.

8. Undated report of J. Milton Waldon, Niagara treasurer, Du Bois Papers.

9. *Cleveland Gazette*, Sept. 7, 1907, p. __.

10. Rudwick, "The Niagara Movement," 192–194 (account of 1907 meeting and dissension); Du Bois to Milton Waldron, Dec. 6, 1907, Du Bois Papers.

11. *Appeal*, Jan. 18, 1908, p. 3; Jan. 25, 1908, p. 3.

12. *Appeal*, Feb. 15, 1908, p. 3.

13. *Pioneer Press*, Feb. 11, 1908, p. 4; *Appeal*, Feb. 15, 1908, p. 3.

14. *Appeal*, March 7, 1908, p. 3; Du Bois to "Dear Colleagues," March 14, 1908, Du Bois Papers.

15. *Appeal*, April 25, 1908, p. 3; May 9, 1908, p. 3; May 30, 1908, p. 3; June 20, 1908, p. 3; July 11, 1908, p. 3; Aug. 1, 1908, p. 3 (Du Bois in town, fishing with McGhee); Lewis, *W. E. B. Du Bois*, 376–377 (Trotter split).

16. Rudwick, "The Niagara Movement," 196; Lewis, *W. E. B. Du Bois*, 375–376; Du Bois to Niagara members, July 15, 1909, Du Bois Papers; *Oberlin Tribune*, September 4, 1908 (details of deliberations and quotations).

17. Report of the Fifth Annual Niagara Movement Convention, by F. L. McGhee, Aug. 14, 1909, Du Bois Papers.

18. Lewis, *W. E. B. Du Bois*, 386–407.

Notes to Chapter Fourteen

1. *St. Paul Globe*, May 10, 1895, p. 2; Ramsey County District Court criminal case files no. 3059, State ex rel *McGhee v McMahon*, and 3063, State ex rel *McKenzie v Mother Superior of House of the Good Shepherd*, MHS.

2. *Appeal*, Aug. 29, 1903, p. 3; Hennepin County district court criminal case file nos. 7466, 7475, and 7476, *State v James Haynes*, Hennepin County Government Center, Minneapolis, Minnesota.

3. *Appeal*, April 24, 1897, p. 2.

4. Civil case file, William A. Hazel vs. E. W. White, Ramsey County District Court, February 1891, MHS. Civil case file, Rosa Hazzard Hazel vs. J. W. Blau, et al, Ramsey County District Court, December 1894, MHS. *St. Paul Globe*, Oct. 13, 1896, p. 8; Ramsey County District Court civil case file no. 67324, *George Hunton v J. H. Mayall*, MHS.

5. *Appeal*, Feb. 24, 1906, p. 3; Ramsey County District Court civil case file no. 93002, *Samuel Thompson v G.R. Kibbe*, filed March 16, 1906, MHS. *Pioneer Press*, July 14, 1911, p. 14.

6. Ramsey County District Court civil case no. 94559, *Richard C. Clark v Moy Hee, d.b.a. Kong Tong Lo Co.*, filed Nov. 21, 1906, Ramsey County Courthouse, St. Paul, Minnesota; *Appeal*, Jan. 26, 1907, p. 3.

7. *Appeal*, June 17, 1899, p. 3.

8. *Appeal*, Oct. 5, 1901, p. 3 (McGhee to represent Summers); Oct. 12, 1901, p. 2 (Summers loses in district court); Nov. 23, 1901, p. 3 (case set for supreme court); Nov. 30, 1901, p. 3 (loss at supreme court); *St. Paul Dispatch*, Oct. 5, 1901, p. 5; *Pioneer Press*, Oct. 5, 1901, p. 10 (protest meetings); *St. Paul Globe*, Oct. 11, 1901, p. 2 (hearing with governor); *Pioneer Press*, Oct. 12, 1901, p. 4 (editorial supporting Van Sant's decision); Ramsey County District Court criminal case file, State ex rel. *Summers v Justus*, MHS; *Appeal*, March 29, 1902, p. 3 (Summers in jail in Tennessee; Sept. 20, 1902, p. 3 (Summers sentenced to eight years).

9. Nelson, "Orphans and Old Folks," 110–112; *Pioneer Press*, Sept. 1, 1909, p. 14.

10. *Three Catholic Afro-American Congresses*, 153–156.

11. *Appeal*, Nov. 6, 1897, p. 3.

12. Nelson, "Orphans and Old Folks," 110-112; *Pioneer Press*, Sept. 2, 1909, p. 14.

Notes to Chapter Fifteen

1. *Minneapolis Tribune*, Sept. 28, 1906, pp. 1, 6 (the crime); Sept. 29, 1906, pp. 1, 10 (Sussman confesses); Sept. 30, 1906, p. 4 (first court appearance); *Minneapolis Journal*, Dec. 10, 1906, pp. 1-2 (trial begins); Dec. 11, 1906, p. 8; Dec. 11, 1906, pp. 1, 7; Dec. 12, 1906, pp. 1-2 (trial); Dec. 13, 1906, pp. 1, 2, 4 (quotation); Dec. 14, 1906, p. 7 (Fannie a prostitute); Dec. 14, 1906, pp. 1, 2; Dec. 15, 1906, pp. 1, 2 (unwritten law), p. 7 (Sussman testifies); Dec. 17, 1906, p. 7 (closing arguments); Dec. 18, 1906, p. 6 (verdict and sentence).

2. *Minneapolis Journal*, May 14, 1907, p. 13.

3. *St. Paul Globe*, April 29, 1893, p. 2; May 23, 1893, p. 8; June 21, 1893, p. 2; Oct. 7, 1893, p. 7.

4. *St. Paul Dispatch*, March 30, 1911, p. 13.

5. *St. Paul Dispatch*, Oct. 2, 1897, p. 5.

6. *Appeal*, Aug. 17, 1901, p. 3; *St. Paul Globe*, Aug. 15, 1901, p. 2.

7. *Appeal*, July 24, 1897, p. 3.

8. *Appeal*, Feb. 27, 1904, p. 3.

9. *St. Paul Daily News*, February 29, 1908, pp. 1-2.

10. *St. Paul Dispatch*, March 30, 1911, p. 13.

11. *Appeal*, April 25, 1908, p. 4; May 2, 1908, p. 2; *United Brotherhood of Friendship v Bledsoe*, 119 sw Rep. 874 (1911).

12. *Appeal*, Jan. 30, 1909, p. 3 (organizing meeting at McGhee's); July 24, 1909, p. 2 (account of convention).

13. *Pioneer Press*, July 27, 1909, p. 5; July 28, 1909, p. 12; July 29, 1909, p. 5; *Appeal*, July 31, 1909, p. 2.

14. *Grand Lodge of the United Brotherhood of Friendship v W. F. Bledsoe*, Ramsey County District Court civil case file no. 10152, Ramsey County Courthouse, St. Paul.

15. *Twin City Star*, July 7, 1910, p. 4.

Notes to Chapter Sixteen

1. *Appeal*, May 27, 1911, p. 2.

2. *Appeal*, April 9, 1898, p. 3. Another candidate for first black physician is Dr. Thomas Cook, who also arrived in St. Paul in spring 1898. *Appeal*, April 16, 1898, p. 3. He was unquestionably the first black physician to get a license in Minnesota by passing the state exam. He did it in April 1898, whereas Dr. Turner did not get his (he failed the exam six times) until April 1900. However, it appears that Dr. Turner had already been licensed in Tennessee, and practiced in St. Paul based on that license before Dr. Cook set up his practice. Minnesota Board of Medical Examiners, license applications, 1895-1900, MHS.

3. *Stillwater Gazette*, Nov. 30, 1910, pp. 1, 3 (Anderson's death and coroner's inquest); April 12, 1911, p. 1 (Quinnehan arrested); *Pioneer Press*, April 11, 1911, p. 1 (Quinnehan arrested); April 14, 1911, p. 10 (acquittal); Ramsey County District Court criminal case file no. 5397, *State of Minnesota v Val Do Turner*, MHS; and case file no. 5401, *State of Minnesota v Thomas Quinnehan*, MHS; Washington County, Minnesota, coroner's inquest file no. 7460.5, Anna Louise Anderson, MHS. It seems probable that some people declined to attend the McGhee testimonial because they believed that Dr. Turner was in fact an abortionist. And he probably was. In 1936, the state Board of Medical Examiners charged him with performing an abortion, found that he had done so, but declined to revoke his license. Board of Medical Examiners, Minutes and Agenda Book, 1936-1937, In Re: Revocation of License of Val Do Turner, M.D., July 8, 1936, MHS. A month later he was charged with manslaughter for arranging an abortion that resulted in the woman's death. On Sept. 23, 1936, he agreed to surrender his medical license and leave Minnesota in return for no further action on the criminal charges. Ramsey County District Court criminal case file no. 15221, *State of Minnesota v Valdo Turner and George Viger*, MHS.

4. Douglas R. Heidenreich, *With Satisfaction and Honor, William Mitchell College of Law 1900-2000* (St. Paul: William Mitchell College of Law, 1999), 19-20; *Twin City Star*, Dec. 20, 1910, p. 1 (Francis biographical information); McGhee and Francis had known each other at least since 1892, and probably longer, *Appeal*,

April 7, 1892, p. 3. They shared as a mutual friend Julius Avendorph of Chicago. *Appeal*, Sept. 1, 1894, p. 3; Sept. 29, 1894, p. 3. They participated together in the Business Men's Club, *Appeal*, Dec. 15, 1900, p. 3; NAAC events, July 19, 1902, p. 3, Feb. 7 and Feb. 21, 1903, p. 3; and purely social gatherings, Nov. 30, 1901, p. 3 (football game in Chicago); Aug. 8, 1903, p. 3 (dinner honoring Francis); Jan. 2, 1904, p. 3 (annual "family dinner"); Dec. 31, 1904, p. 3 (New Year's calls); Dec. 16, 1905, p. 3 (stag dinner); Dec. 23, 1905, p. 3 (banquet for Bobby Marshall). After finishing law school Francis presided at a Garrison Day event at Pilgrim Baptist, Dec. 16, 1905, p. 3; ran for city assembly, March 10, 1906, p. 3; was elected president of the Men's Sunday Club, Jan. 5, 1907, p. 3; had a place of honor during Booker T. Washington's 1908 visit, Feb. 15, 1908, p. 3.

5. *Appeal*, Sept. 23, 1905, p. 4 (Francis a director); June 6, 1908, p. 3 (counsel for); July 3, 1909, p. 3 *(Campbell v Cosmopolitan Mutual Casualty Co.)*.

6. *Twin City Star*, June 3, 1911, p. 4; *Appeal*, May 27, 1911, p. 2 (long quotation).

7. *Twin City Star*, Jan. 27, 1912, p. 4.

Notes to Chapter Seventeen

1. Charles Flint Kellogg, *NAACP, A History of the National Association for the Advancement of Colored People* (Baltimore: Johns Hopkins University Press, 1967), 31-51.

2. Aptheker, ed., *A Documentary History of the Negro People in the United States*, 884-886.

3. *Pioneer Press*, Dec. 27, 1911, p. 6; Dec. 28, 1911, p. 10; Ramsey County District Court criminal case file no. 5368, *State of Minnesota v George W. Parker*, transcript of hearing, Jan. 12, 1912, and transcript of trial, May 10, 1912, MHS.

4. *Appeal*, Nov. 11, 1911, p. 3; *Twin City Star*, Dec. 2, 1911, p. 1.

5. *Twin City Star*, March 16, 1912, p. 2; *Appeal*, March 30, 1912, p. 3.

6. *Appeal*, March 30, 1912, p. 3 (Protective League formed and associated with NAACP); April 6, 1912, p. 3 (McGhee and Turner will be sent to Chicago); April 20, 1912, p. 2 (they leave for Chicago); April 27,

1912, p. 3; May 4, 1912, p. 3 ("very fine"); *Twin City Star*, March 16, 1912, p. 2; May 4, 1912, p. 2; *Crisis*, Nov. 1911, p. 43 (McGhee on NAACP General Committee).

7. *Appeal*, June 8, 1912, p. 3 (state convention); March 2, 1912, p. 3; March 9, 1912, p. 3 (local black Democrats); *Twin City Star*, March 9, 1912, p. 2 ; April 13, 1912, p. 4 (local Democrats).

8. *Appeal*, July 6, 1912, p. 3; July 27, 1912, p. 3; Aug. 3, 1912, p. 3.

9. *Appeal*, Aug. 10, 1912, p. 3; Aug. 18, 1912, p. 3 (McGhee visits St. Paul); Aug. 24, 1912, p. 3 (Turkey Trot); Oct. 5, 1912, pp. 2, 4 (Theobald's comments).

10. *Appeal*, Aug. 31, 1912, p. 3 (near death); Sept. 7, 1912, p. 3 (rallied); Sept. 21, 1912, p. 3 (death); Death Certificate of Fredrick L. McGhee, St. Paul Department of Health. Three versions of McGhee's last words and moments circulated shortly after his death. The "let God's will be done" quote was printed Sept. 21. On Sept. 28, the *Twin City Star* reported that he had said, "I have fought the good fight." *Twin City Star*, Sept. 28, 1912, p. 1. In his eulogy, Father Theobald, who was there when McGhee died, said only that "he was able to listen to the prayers which commended his soul to Almighty God and to the angels and saints." *Appeal*, Sept. 28, 1912, p. 2.

11. *Appeal*, Oct. 5, 1912, pp. 2, 4; *Twin City Star*, Sept. 28, 1912, p. 1; *Crisis* (June 1933): 130. The complete sentence is, "He was a Catholic, a great friend of the late Bishop Ireland and an unswerving and self-sacrificing champion of the colored race."

12. Roy Wilkins, *Standing Fast: The Autobiography of Roy Wilkins*, with Tom Mathews (New York: Viking, 1982), 35.

Notes to Epilogue

1. Estate of Fredrick L. McGhee, Ramsey County Probate Court file no. 20337, Ramsey County Courthouse, St. Paul, Minnesota.

2. *St. Paul City Directory* 1916, p. 1069 (Ruth a stenographer); *St. Paul City Directory* 1919, p. 777 (Ruth a typist); Satisfaction of Mortgage, document no. 298326; Satisfaction of Mortgage, document no. 300173, Ramsey County Re-

corder, Ramsey County Government Center West, St. Paul, Minnesota.

3. *Twin Cities Star* September 19, 1913, p. 4 (first anniversary commemorations); *Twin Cities Star* September 25, 1914, p. 2 (meets with W.E.B. Du Bois); *Twin Cities Star* July 22, 1916, p. 1 (accompanies Mrs. Booker T. Washington).

4. *Appeal*, August 23, 1919, 3 (Ruth leaves); November 29, 1919, p. 3 (Mattie leaves); December 6, 1919, p. 3 (house sold to Schucks); June 9, 1923, p. 3 (Schucks in real estate business); Estate of Frederick L. McGhee, Polk County Probate Court, Polk County Courthouse, Balsam Lake, Wisconsin (Wisconsin land); File card record for 665 West University Avenue, City of St. Paul office of Licenses and Inspections, St. Paul, Minnesota (demolition).

5. *Twin City Herald*, February 4, 1933, p. 2; "The McGhee's of St. Paul," *Crisis* 40, no. 6 (February 1933), 130 (Mattie's death); *St. Paul Recorder*, January 31, 1958, p. 4 (Ruth's death and residence); Certificate of Death, Ruth L. McGee, St. Paul Department of Health, St. Paul, Minnesota; Burial permits, Ruth and Mattie McGhee, Calvary Cemetery, St. Paul, Minnesota.

6. *Appeal*, June 14, 1919, p. 3 (Barclay's visit); Personal communication between the author and Nebraska Historical Society, July 24 and August 1, 1995 (no further trace of Barclay).

7. David V. Taylor, "John Quincy Adams," 282-297; Roy Wilkins, *Standing Fast: The Autobiography of Roy Wilkins* (New York: Viking, 1982), 47-55 (editor of *Appeal*), 220 (appointed executive secretary of NAACP).

8. Convict Record, Antonio Calderone, Stillwater State Prison, MHS; *Pioneer Press*, April 10, 1911, p. 6.

9. Lewis, *W.E.B. DuBois*, pp. 1-2.

10. *Twin City Star*, October 12, 1912, p. 2 (takes over law practice); *St. Paul Daily News*, July 15, 1929, p. 1 (death).

11. Convict Record of James Hayes, Stillwater Prison, Book K, p. 212, MHS.

12. Louise David Hutchinson, "Building on a Dream," *American Visions* (August 1989), 11.

13. Marvin O'Connell, *John Ireland*, 499-517.

14. Convict Record of Henry Johnson, Stillwater Prison, Book G, p. 246, MHS.

15. *Twin City Star*, June 2, 1910, p. 1 (basic biographical information); *Minneapolis Star*, December 31, 1929, p. 5; *Minneapolis Tribune*, December 31, 1929, p. 7; Certificate of Death no. 4940, William R. Morris, City of Minneapolis Division of Public Health, Hennepin County Government Center, Minneapolis, Minnesota; Hennepin County Probate Court file no. 38215, Estate of William R. Morris, Hennepin County Government Center, Minneapolis; *Northwestern Monitor*, May 27, 1930, p. 1 (death).

16. Ramsey County district court criminal case file no. 5638, State vs. George Parker, MHS; *Minneapolis Journal*, July 25, 1912, p. 1 (escape plot); *St. Paul City Directory 1914*, p. 1307 (back in St. Paul working as a waiter); *St. Paul City Directory 1920*, p. 1116 (working as a waiter for Great Northern); *St. Paul City Directory 1932*, p. 900 (married to Cora); *St. Paul City Directory 1938*, p. 960 (married to Carrie, owners of 761 St. Anthony Ave.); *St. Paul City Directory 1946*, p. 927 (still working for Great Northern); Certificate of Death, George W. Parker, City of St. Paul Department of Health (date of death).

17. Convict Record of Philip Rice, Stillwater Prison, Book G, pp. 330-331, MHS.

18. Convict Record of Henry Sussman, Stillwater Prison, Book L, p. 529, MHS.

19. Taylor, *Pilgrim's Progress*, 119; Wilkins, *Standing Fast*, 36 (Turner and the NAACP); Ramsey County district court criminal case file no. 15221, State vs. Val Do Turner and George Viger; Board of Medical Examiners, Minutes and Agenda Book, 1936-1937, In Re: Revocation of License of Val Do Turner, M.D., July 8, 1936, MHS (criminal charges and action against his medical license).

20. Louis R. Harlan, *Booker T. Washington, the Wizard of Tuskegee, 1901-1915* (New York: Oxford University Press, 1983), 455 (death).

Index

Page numbers in *italics* refer to illustrations. Page numbers followed by n refer to the endnote number on that page.

Adams, Cyrus Field, 10, 98, 100, 105, 111
Adams, John Quincy: *The Appeal*, leadership of, 10–11; background of, 10, 149; death of, 206; and the LEL, 66, 70, 71, 75; at Lincoln Day, St. Paul, 1908, 164; McGhee's relationship with, 10–11, 58, 91; and the Morris-Wheaton bill, 57, 58; and the NAAC, 68, 70, 97, 104; and the NAAL, 26–27; Republican Party, black support of, 35; at testimonial dinner, 186. *See also The Appeal* (St. Paul)
Adams, Mrs. John Quincy, 105
African Americans: aristocracy of, 148–49; and the cakewalk, 62–65; in Chicago, 4, 7, 9–11; clubs and fraternal organizations, 25, 149–50, 220n7; in Minnesota (*see* Minnesota, civil rights in); Republican Party, support of, 28–29, 35, 69, 80–81; and the Spanish-American War, 60–61, 86–87 (*see also Cuba*); suffrage (*see* suffrage); in the Twin Cities, 4, 10, 108, 148, 219n4. *See also* civil rights laws
Afro-American League. *See* National Afro-American League (NAAL)
The Age (New York City), 26. *See also* Fortune, T. Thomas
Aker (Ella) case, 14
Allen (Joseph) case, 52
American Law Enforcement League (LEL): courts Minneapolis whites' support, 70–72; formation of and demands from, 66–68; fund-raising activities, 74–75; Gibbs' dinner for, 70–72; hosts Booker T. Washington, 75–76; as local affiliate of NAAC, 70; McGhee in, 66, 68, 70–71, 74, 75. *See also* National Afro-American Council (NAAC)

Anderson, Anna Louise, 187–89
Andrzejewski, J. T., *48*
anti-imperialism, 87, 88, 89, 216n8(ch 7)
The Appeal (St. Paul): Adams' leadership of, 10–11; announces McGhee's arrival, *3*, 11; on the cakewalk, 63–64; on Catholicism for blacks, 41; Clark (Richard) case, 172; on McGhee in *Cuba*, 62; on McGhee's abilities as lawyer, 24; and the Morris-Wheaton bill, 57, 58; on the NAAC, 77, 105, 106; on the Niagara Movement, 159. *See also* Adams, John Quincy
"Appeal to Europe" letter, National Negro Committee, 194, 199
"Atlanta Compromise" speech, 47, 214n1
Atlanta (Ga.) race riot, 1906, 159
Atlanta University, 128
Autumn Social Club, 7, 9, 11
Avendorph, Julius, 155, 199–200, 219n4

Baily, Henry, *130*
Baker, Frazier, 73
Barber, J. Max, *130*
Barnett, Ferdinand, 77
Barnett, Ida B. Wells: at NAAC convention, Indianapolis, 76–77, 215n14; at NAAC convention, St. Paul, 101, 102, 104; at the National Negro Conference of 1909, 167
Battalia, Salvatore, *113*. *See also* Calderone (Antonio) case
Bentley, C. C., 165, 219n7
Blair, John, 152
Bledsoe, W. F., 183
Boardman, Fred, 116, 120
Bonner, Robert, *130*
Boston Civil Rights League, 162
Boston Riot, 125
Brown, Hallie Q., 152
Brown, Henry ("Whisky"), 54
Browne, Hugh, 127

227

Brownsville affair, 94–95
Bryan, William Jennings, *83*; 1896 election, 83, 85; 1900 election, 89–91; 1908 election, 94–95, 162, 165; anti-imperialism, 87; economic justice platform, 83, 88, 162; election results, 216n18; on racial issues, 83, 89–91, 216n11(ch 7). *See also* presidential elections
Burk, Harvey, 164
Business Men's Club, 150
Butler, Pierce, 52

cakewalk controversy, 62–65
Calderone (Antonio) case, 112–21, *117*; crime, 112–13, 115; jury selection, 115–16; later life of, 207; McGhee outwits police, 113–15, 213n1, 214n2; McGhee's defense, 118–20; prosecution, 116–18, 218n6; verdict, 120–21, 218nn3, 8
Camp DuGhee (Apple River, Wis.), 154–55, 205, 221n19
Campbell (James) case, 190
Carlson, J. S., 36
Carnegie, Andrew, 126
Carnegie Conference, 124–28; eight points statement, 126–27; initiation of, 122, 125–26; McGhee's role in, 122, 125–27
Carr, James, 16, 17
Carter (Lewis) case, 15–19, 169
Catholic Church. *See* Roman Catholic Church
Catholic Order of Foresters, 149–50
Catholic Tribune, 43
Chamberlain, Leon T., 81–82
Chapin, Walter, 82
Charleston, John, 186
Chicago, African Americans in, 4, 7, 9–11
civil rights laws: federal, 25, 211n1; in Minnesota, 26, 55–58, 60; Morris-Wheaton bill, 56–58, 213n10(ch 5); and the NAAC, 107; second amendment to, 60; as Southern cause, 32–33, 38. *See also* education; Jim Crow laws; lynching; suffrage
Civil War, McGhee family in, 5–6
Clark (Richard) case, 172
class justice, Democratic platform of, 83, 88, 162
Cleveland, Grover, 82. *See also* presidential elections
Coleman (Lucy) case, 51
Collins (Justice), 59
Committee of Forty, National Negro Conference, 193

Conley, Detective, 113, 114
Conroy, E. J., 113, 114
The Conservator (Chicago), 10
Conway (Frank) case, 18
Cook, Thomas, 217n18
Cooper, E. E., 76
Costello, Michael, fistfight with, 179–80
Costello (John) case, 50
Crane, Charles, 156
Crane, John, 156
Crane, Mattie. *See* McGhee, Mattie Crane
Crews, Nelson, 103–4
criminal justice system, 1890s, 50–51
Crispus Attucks Home, 153, 174
Crum, W. H., 127
Cuba, 61–62. *See also* cakewalk controversy
Cunningham's club, 64

Davis, Henrietta Vinton, 151
Davis, Kate, 53
Davis (Anna) case, 178
Delicatessen restaurant, 171
Demars, William. *See* Shenk (Ida) case
Democratic Party: and black suffrage, 81; class and economic justice platform, 83, 88, 162; position on racial issues, 89–90, 216nn9, 11(ch 7). *See also* McGhee, Fredrick L., as Democrat; presidential elections
Dillingham, John, 186, 198
disfranchisement. *see* suffrage
Douglass, Frederick, 33, 47, 80
Du Bois, W. E. B., *123, 130*; approach to black progress, 100–101, 122, 124; background of, 149; on the Brownsville affair, 94–95; at Camp DuGhee, 155, 221n19; at Carnegie Conference, 1904, 122, 124–28; death of, 207; eulogizes McGhee, 202; McGhee's friendship with, 74, 95, 128, 215n9; at NAAC convention, Indianapolis, 76; at NAAC convention, St. Paul, 100, 102, 105; and the NAACP, 193; at the National Negro Conference 1909, 167; and the Niagara Movement, 129–32, *130*, 160, 162, 164–65; on the Pope (Barbara) case, 160, 161; *The Souls of Black Folk*, 124; at the Tuskegee Institute, 124; Washington's relationship with, 122, 124–25, 128 (*see also* Carnegie Conference)
Dunbar, Paul Laurence, 150, 151
Dunn, J. M., 180

Eagan, James R. (Dick Taylor), 135, *141*, 142

economic justice, Democratic platform of, 83, 88, 162
education: Carnegie Conference on, 126, 127; NAAC call to action on, 69; Niagara Movement on, 158; and school segregation, 174–75
1890s: criminal justice system, 50–51; race relations, national, 25–26, 46 (*see also* civil rights laws)
Ellis, (Grace May) case, 20–24
Emancipation Day rally, 1891, 29–30
Emery, Lynne, 63

Farmer, Walter, 182
Ferris, William, 111
Finerty (Alice) case, 13, 206n1
Foote, Shelby, 5
Fortune, T. Thomas, 26; background of, 26, 149; in the Boston Riot, 125; at the Carnegie Conference, 126; character of, 102; in the NAAC, 68, 69, 77, 101–2, 103–4, 105; on NAAC's weaknesses, 107; and the NAAL, 26, 27, 32; Trotter's opinion of, 109
franchise. *see* suffrage
Francis, William Trevane, *104*; background of, 149, 189–90; death of, 207; eulogizes McGhee, 202; at Lincoln Day, St. Paul, 1908, 163–64; McGhee's relationship with, 190–92; in the NAAC, 97, 104, 105; and the Parker (George) case, 195, 197
French, Allen, *48*

Gaillard, Nicholas, 43
Gaines, W. A., 182, *182*
Gatewood, Willard, 148
Gibbs, Adina, 53–54
Gibbs, Jasper, 66, 70–72, 75
Glenn, Franc, 151
Godbout, Elzeard, 133, 139, 143
gold standard, 87
Gravelle, Dr., 119
Green, "Jersey Lilly," 180
Guy, James, 215n4

Hackley, E. Azalia, 151
Hale, W. D., 70, 71
Hall, Arthur, 186
Hall, O. C., 93
Hall, Orrington, 201
Hardy, Samuel: civil rights case of, 31–35, 37, 170, 207n14; loses city janitor job, 211n1; and the Negro Catholic

Congresses, 43; and the Summers (Harry) case, 78
Harris, Eva, *48*
Harris, Joseph, *48*
Harrison, Benjamin, 18, 33, 36. *See also* presidential elections
Harrison, J. T., 41, 46
Hart, W. H. H., *130*
Haynes (James) case, *169*, 169–70, 207
Hazel, Mrs. William A., 61, 70, 171
Hazel, William A., *30*, 30–31, 32, 35, 66, 171, 207
Heard, W. H., 32
Henderson, James M., 15, 101
Hendrickson (Jennie) case, 14–15, 168, 206n2
Henry, Francis, 118, 219n6
Herndon, Alonzo F., *130*
Herndon, Norris F., *130*
Hilyard, James Kidd, 219n4
Hoffman, John J., 138, 144
Hope, John, *130*
"Hotfoot" (Alec Williams), 64
Howell, Owen, 164, 198, 219n4
Hunton (George) case, 171

Illinois State Colored Convention, 1895, 7
imperialism, 87, 88, 89, 212n8(ch 7)
Ireland, John, *40*; background of, 39; and the cause of racial justice, 29, 41, 42, 46, 48; at NAAC convention, St. Paul, 105; at the Negro Catholic Congress, 1893, 45; proselytizing efforts, 39, 40–41, 49
Irish voters, St. Paul, 82
Italian murder case. *See* Calderone (Antonio) case

Jackson, Claude, *48*
James, Charles, 35, 148, 149
Jim Crow laws: Carnegie Conference on, 126; enactment, 1890s, 25–26, 46; and the Hardy (William) case, 32–35, 37, 170; LEL call to action on, 67–68; McGhee's public accomodations cases, 171–72; NAAC call to action on, 69; Niagara Movement on, 157, 158, 160; as a Southern problem, 32–33
Johnson, Jack, 184
Johnson, John A., *83*, 163
Johnson (Henry) case, 52–53, *53*, 176, 207
Jones, Percy, 70, 71

Kachel, Anton, 54, 55, 213n7(ch 5)
Kane, Thomas P., 75, 89, 136, 201–2

Kapplinger Scholls, Maria, 16–19
Kemp, Mrs. J. V., 61, 72
Kibbe, George R., 171
Kiefer (Mayor), 75
King, Birdie, 48
Knoxville College, 6

Laramie, Harry, 140, 141, 142
The Last Loaf, 151
Law Enforcement League. See American
   Law Enforcement League (LEL)
Lealtad, A. H., 186, 198, 201
Leary, William, 117
Ledeger, Rose, 138, 144
Lewis, David Levering, 128
Lind, John, 70
Lofton, William, 46, 47
Loomis, James, 93
Lyles, Thomas, 164
lynching: of Baker, Frazier, 73; Carnegie
   Conference on, 126; frequency of,
   1890s, 25–26, 46; LEL call to action on,
   67–68; in Minnesota, 53–54, 213n7(ch
   5); NAAC call to action on, 69, 72–73;
   Osborn (Houston) case, 54–55, 209n7(ch
   5); Summers (Harry) case, 78–79, 172

Maceo, Antonio, 60, 62
Marshall, Eugene, 171, 218n5(ch 14)
Mattocks public school, 174–75
McGhee, Abraham, 5, 6, 7, 9
McGhee, Barclay, 6, 7, 156, 215n1
McGhee, Fredrick L.: acting experiences,
   62, 74–75, 151, 215n10; becomes a
   lawyer, 7, 9, 210n10 (see also McGhee,
   Fredrick L., law practice of); birth and
   youth, 4–5, 6; at Camp DuGhee, 154–55,
   193, 200, 221n19; character of (see
   McGhee, Fredrick L., character of);
   charity work of, 152–53; in Chicago, 7;
   during Civil War, 5–6; daughter of (see
   McGhee, Ruth Lamar); death and funeral, 200, 224nn10, 11; early influences
   on, 7, 9; estrangement from black leaders, 58, 82, 182, 192; friends, social status of, 148, 219n4; income and debts,
   153–54; in Knoxville, 6–7; legacy of,
   203–4; marriage to Mattie Crane, 9, 147,
   210n13; memorial service, 201–2; moves
   to St. Paul, 10–12; and music, 150–51; in
   Neumann's restaurant, 172–73; oratorical skills, 15, 23, 53–54, 93, 144, 152; organizing abilities and experience, 27,
   106, 132, 198; photographs and draw-

ings of, ii, 3, 28, 51, 88, 117, 130, 196; in
   politics (see McGhee, Fredrick L., and
   politics); religion of (see McGhee,
   Fredrick L., as Catholic); residence, University Ave., 147, 148; social life, 149–51;
   social status, 9–10, 147–49; testimonial
   dinner for, 1911, 186–89, 191–92; vacations, 153, 154–55, 193, 200
McGhee, Fredrick L., character of: charity
   work, 152–53; in the courtroom, 146,
   176–78; makes distinctions among
   blacks, 52–53, 56–57, 178, 184–85; non-
   conformist, 4, 185, 192; optimism of,
   176; temper, control of, 178–81
McGhee, Fredrick L., as Catholic, 39–49;
   on the benefits of Catholicism, 31,
   42–43, 47–48; conversion, 39, 41–43;
   and Ireland, John, 41, 42; at the Negro
   Catholic Congresses, 43–47; Protestantism, attitude toward, 42, 47–48;
   spiritual devotion of, 47–48
McGhee, Fredrick L., as Democrat,
   80–95; as alternate convention delegate,
   1900, 95; attraction to Party, 84–85,
   87–88, 92; criticizes Republican Party,
   85–89; defection to Party, 37, 81–82, 95,
   215n1; at Duluth convention, 1912, 199;
   estranged from black Republicans, 82,
   192; gives gift to Bryan, 89–91; in social
   life, 150, 220n9; in St. Paul politics, 92,
   93; supports Bryan, 84–85, 89–91, 92,
   95; wavers in 1904 election, 91–93. See
   also McGhee, Fredrick L., and politics
McGhee, Fredrick L., law practice of,
   13–24, 50–55, 112–21; Aker (Ella) case,
   14; Allen (Joseph) case, 52; Calderone
   (Antonio) case (see Calderone (Antonio)
   case); Campbell (James) case, 190; Carter
   (Lewis) case, 15–19, 169; civil rights, defense of, 168–75 (see also specific cases);
   Clark (Richard) case, 171–72; clients,
   procuring of, 15, 50, 136, 154; Coleman
   (Lucy) case, 51; Conway (Frank) case, 18;
   Costello (John) case, 50; Costello
   (Michael), fistfight with, 179–80; Davis
   (Anna) case, 178; dishonesty, accused of,
   178–79, 181; early career, 13–24; Finerty
   (Alice) case, 13, 206n1; Hardy (Samuel)
   case, 32–35, 37–38, 170, 211n14; Haynes
   (James) case, 169–70; Hendrickson (Jen-
   nie) case, 14–15, 168, 210n2; Hunton
   (George) case, 171; income from, 4, 136,
   153–54, 187, 194–95; Johnson (Henry)
   case, 52–53, 176; jury selection tactics,

115–16, 136; McKenzie (Jennie) case, 169; Minea (George) case, 50; Minton (Hattie) case, 14; NAAC cases, 108, 217n24; for the Niagara Movement, 160, 161, 166; Osborn (Houston) case, 54–55, 213n7(ch 5); Parker (George) case, 195, 197–98; Pope (Barbara) case, 160, 161; race as an issue, use of, 52–53, 178; Raverty (Peter) case (*see* Raverty (Peter) case); respected reputation of, 13, 15, 19, 22, 23–24, 53–54, 121; Rice (Philip) case, 53; Roberts (Mary) case, 178–79; ruthlessness in court, 176–78; Shenk (Ida) case, 20–24; Stafford (William) case, 13, 210n1; Summers (Harry) case, 78–79, 172; Sussman (Henry) case, 177–78; Thompson (Samuel) case, 171, 218n5(ch 14); Turner (Val Do) case, 187–89; Webster (John) case, 178; West (Henry) case, 50–51

McGhee, Fredrick L., and politics: as at-large presidential elector, 1892, 35, 36–37, 81; civil rights law, second amendment to, 60; as a Democrat (*see* McGhee, Fredrick L., as Democrat); denied patronage job, 1892, 81–82; Morris-Wheaton bill, opposition to, 56–58, 209n10(ch 5); and the National Afro-American League, 26–27; on political independence for blacks, 92; as a Republican, 27–28, 35, 36–37; speech to NAAC Chicago meeting, 1899, 72–73

McGhee, Fredrick L., speeches and writings: anti-imperialist, 87, 88, 89, 216n8(ch7); on Blair, John, 152; on Bryan ("bloody shirt"), 84–85, 95; on the cakewalk, 65; on the Catholic Church, 42, 43–44, 45, 48; against the Democratic Party, 28; Emancipation Day rally, 1891 ("sun of our perfect freedom . . ."), 29–30; gubernatorial election, 1890, 28; at his testimonial dinner, 1911, 191; on Jack Johnson, 184; on Morris-Wheaton bill, 56–58; to the NAAC Chicago meeting, 72–73; to the National Negro Democratic League, 85–88, 93–94; on the Niagara Movement, 132, 166; oratorical skills, 15, 23, 53–54, 93, 144, 152; on Protestantism, 42, 47–48; against the Republican Party, 85–89, 93–94, 95; on school segregation, 174; speaking engagements, frequency of, 151–52; in St. Paul Democratic politics, 93; on Washington's takeover of NAAC, 109–10

McGhee, Matthew, 6, 155–56, 219n1
McGhee, Mattie Crane: background of, 147; and the cakewalk controversy, 64–65; child of (*see* McGhee, Ruth Lamar); later life of, 205–6; marriage to Fredrick, 9, 147, 206n13; McGhee's reliance on, 153; in music and theater, 49, 149, 150–51; at NAAC St. Paul convention, 105; photographs of, 48, 151; at St. Peter Claver, 48, 49, 149; and the Summers (Harry) case, 78
McGhee, Ruth Lamar, 33, 147, 151, 155, 205–6, 212n15
McGhee, Sarah, 5, 6, 9, 210n11
McKenzie (Jennie) case, 169
McKinley, William, 83, 85, 86. *See also* presidential elections
Merriam, William, 18, 28, 29
Metropolitan Hotel (St. Paul), 57–58, 75
migration from the South: Carnegie Conference on, 126; NAAC on, 69, 70, 99, 100
Miller, Charles, 48
Miller, Kelly, 76, 126, 149, 216n8(ch 7)
Minea (George) case, 50
Minneapolis, black community in, 4, 108, 148
Minnesota, civil rights in: civil rights law and amendments, 26, 55–58, 60; lack of support for the NAAC, 107–8; lynching, 53–54, 78, 213n7(ch 5); race relations, 26, 54–55
Minnesota Civil Rights Committee, 32–33, 38. *See also* Hardy, Samuel
Minnesota Supreme Court, 59, 79
Minton (Hattie) case, 14
Mitchell, William, 59
Montgomery, Isaiah, 101
Moore, George, 133
Morgan, Clement G., 129, 130
Morris, Edward Hopkins, 8; and the Carnegie Conference, 125, 126; civil rights law, second amendment to, 60; at Lincoln Day, St. Paul, 1908, 163, 164; McGhee as protégé of, 4, 7, 9, 11
Morris, William R., 56; background of, 11, 149; and the Haynes (James) case, 170; and the LEL, 66, 70–71, 75; later life of, 207–8; Minnesota civil rights law amendment, 55–56; in the Republican Party, 35; at testimonial dinner, 186
Morris-Wheaton bill, 56–58, 213n10(ch 5)
Moy Hee, 172

NAAC. *See* National Afro-American Council (NAAC)

NAACP. *See* National Association for the Advancement of Colored People (NAACP)

NAAL. *See* National Afro-American League (NAAL)

National Afro-American Council (NAAC): Bookerites vs. Trotterites, 1903, 109–11; Chicago convention, 1899, 72–74; civil rights litigation, 107, 108, 217nn23, 24; demands from, 68–70, 72–74; formation of, 68–69; Indianapolis convention. 1900, 76–77; Louisville convention, 1903, 108–11; McGhee in, 72, 74, 77, 111 (*see also* National Afro-American Council (NAAC), St. Paul convention, 1902); media attention to, 77, 105–6, 217n18; Philadelphia convention, 1901, 77–78; weaknesses of, 100, 107–8. *See also* American Law Enforcement League (LEL)

National Afro-American Council (NAAC), St. Paul convention, 1902, 96–106, *98*; entertainment, 98, 100, 104–5; illegal election of Fortune, 101–4; McGhee's challenge to, 102, 103, 106–7, 108–10; McGhee's preparations for, 96–98, 106; media attention to, 105–6, 217n18; Walters' speech to, 99–100

National Afro-American League (NAAL): demise of, 31, 32, 38; formation of, 26–27; and the Hardy (Samuel) case, 31–32; Hazel's criticism of, 30–31; McGhee in, 26, 27

National Association for the Advancement of Colored People (NAACP), 25; Chicago convention, 1912, 199; as cross-racial alliance, 167; origins of, 167, 193; Twin Cities Protective League affiliation, 198–99

National Negro Business League, 77

National Negro Committee "Appeal to Europe" letter, 194, 199

National Negro Conference, 1909, 167, 193

National Negro Democratic League, 85, 93–94

National Negro Suffrage League, 110

Negro American Political League, 164

Negro Catholic Congresses, 43–47; address to the Chicago World's Fair, 1893, 45–46; Baltimore, 1894, 46–47; Chicago, 1893, 45–46; Philadelphia, 1892, 43–45

Neumann's restaurant, 172

New York Freeman, 26

newspapers, African American: competition between, 10; on the NAAC, 77, 105–6, 217n18; on the Niagara Movement, 159, 165. *See also specific newspapers*

Niagara Movement, 129–32, 157–67; Boston meeting, 1907, 161–62; demands and aims of, 129, 131, 157–59, 164, 165; demise of, 167; financial problems of, 161; founding of, 129–32, *130*; Harper's Ferry meeting, 1906, 157–59, *158*; internal conflict in, 162, 164; legal work by, 160, 161, 166; McGhee's role in founding, 131–32; Oberlin meeting, 1908, 165; and the Pope (Barbara) case, 160, 161; Sea Island meeting, 1909, 166, 174; state affiliations of, 161; on violent self-defense, 165; weaknesses of, 165–66, 167; women in, 163

O'Brien, C. D., 23, 201

O'Connor, John, 135

Orr, Grier, 75, 136, 145

Osborn (Houston) case, 54–55, 213n7(ch 5)

Ovington, Mary, 167

Parker (George) case, 195, 197–98, 208

Peavey, F. H., 70, 71

Philosophy Literary Society, 7, 210n10

Pilgrim Baptist Church Men's Sunday Club, 150, 160

Pioneer Press. See St. Paul Pioneer Press

Pitts, Mary, *48*

Pledger, William A., 101, 110

Plessy v. Ferguson, 37, 69

Pope, Cora, 61

Pope (Barbara) case, 160, 161

Poppenburger, Henry, 138, 144

Porter, Emma, *48*

presidential elections: 1892, Cleveland vs. Harrison, 36, 37, 81, 82, 215n1; 1896, McKinley vs. Bryan, 82–85; 1900, McKinley vs. Bryan, 85–91; 1904, Roosevelt vs. Parker, 91–94, 216n15; 1908, Taft vs. Bryan, 216n18, 94–95, 165; 1912, Roosevelt vs. Wilson, 95

prison conditions, Southern, 69

Protestant Church, and African Americans, 39, 40, 42

Pugleasa, Joseph, 133, *134*, 136–37. *See also* Raverty (Peter) case

Quinnehan, Tom, 188–89

Ransom, Reverdy, 108
Raverty (Peter) case, 133–46; closing arguments, 143–45; crime, 133–35; jury selection, 136; McGhee's defense, 139–43, 144–45; prosecution, 136–39; verdict, 145
Reconstruction, 80
Reid, J. C., 63, 65
Republican Party: blacks' support of, 28–29, 35, 69, 80–81; civil rights, interest in, 28–29, 35, 36; dominance in Minnesota, 82; national convention, 1892, 33, 36; Scandinavians in, 36. *See also* presidential elections
Rhone v. Loomis, 58–59
Rice (Philip) case, 53, 208
Roberts (Mary) case, 178–79
Roman Catholic Church: and racial justice for blacks, 39–40, 42–43, 45, 46, 48–49; segregation of black Catholic churches, 46. *See also* McGhee, Fredrick L., as Catholic; Negro Catholic Congresses
Roosevelt, Theodore: and blacks in Spanish-American War, 86–87; and the Brownsville incident, 94, 159–60; invites Washington to White House, 91; McGhee's support of, 91–93; Niagara Movement on, 157. *See also* presidential elections
Ross, James, 51
Rudd, Daniel, 43, 44, 45, 47
Rudd, John, 43
Rudwick, Elliot, 162

St. Joseph's Advocate, 45
St. Paul: black Catholics in, 40; black community in, 4, 10, 108, 148, 215n4; city elections, 1892, 81, 215n1; Courthouse, Fourth and Wabasha, *14, 20*; Democratic dominance in, 82, 93; late 19th-century, 11–12; public employee salaries, 153
St. Paul Dispatch: on McGhee and the Morris-Wheaton bill, 56–57; on McGhee in the Shenk case, 22; on NAAC St. Paul convention, 105
St. Paul Globe: on the cakewalk, 64; on McGhee in the Emancipation Day speech, 30; on McGhee's denied patronage job, 82
St. Paul Pioneer Press: on black represen-

tation, Republican Convention, 1912, 95; on the Emancipation Day rally, 29, 30; on McGhee in *Cuba,* 62; McGhee's frequent appearance in, 3; on McGhee's gift to Bryan, 90–91, 212n11(ch 7); on NAAC St. Paul convention, 105–6
St. Peter Claver Sodality, 40–41, 46, *48*, 98, 149
St. Peter Claver's Benevolent Loan Association, 43–45
St. Peter Claver's Catholic Union, 45, 46
St. Peter Claver's Choral Association, 75, 98
Samuel Hardy v. East Tennessee, Georgia, and Virginia Railway Company, 31–35, 37, 170, 211n14
Scandinavians, in the Republican Party, 36
Schiff, Jacob, 167
Scholls, Maria Kapplinger, 16–19
school segregation issues, 174–75
Scott, Emmett J., *67*; at the Carnegie Conference, 126; exults at rout at NAAC, 111; at NAAC St. Paul convention, 97, 101, 105, 106
Scrutchin, Charles, 60, 173, 217n23
Sheehan, Ellen, 20
Shenk (Ida) case, 20–24
Shepard, Hattie, *48*
Shepherd, Harry, 97, 102
Slattery, Joseph, 40, 45
Sleet, Mrs. George, 200
Smith, Brown S., *130,* 186, 198, 202
Smith, Charles Summer, 198. *See also Twin City Star*
Smith, Harry, 76, 101, 129
Smith, Robert, 98
Smith, William Sooy, 5
Snider, Samuel P., 16, 18, 33, 36
A Social Glass, 74–75
The Souls of Black Folk (Du Bois), 124
Spalding, David, 47
Spanish-American War, blacks in, 60–62, 86–87
Spencer, James, 45
Springfield (Ill) race riot, 166–67
Stafford (William) case, 13
Stone, Horace, 3
Strong, Joseph, 186
suffrage: Carnegie Conference on, 126, 127; destruction of, post-War, 81; education requirements, 99; LEL call to action on, 67–68; McGhee on, 89, 95;

NAAC on, 69, 99–100; Niagara Movement on, 158
Sullivan, Mark, 63
Summers (Harry) case, 78–79, 172–73
Sussman (Henry) case, *177*, 177–78, 208

Taft, William Howard, 157, 164, 165. *See also* presidential elections
Theobald, Stephen, 49, 200
Thomas, W. Hannibal, 150
Thompson, H. A., *130*
Thompson (Samuel) case, 171, 222n5(ch 14)
Tillman, Ben "Pitchfork," 81
Tobie, Adda, *48*
Tolton, Augustus, 41–42, 44, 152
Trotter, William Monroe, *108*; background of, 149; in the Boston Riot, 125; at the National Negro Conference of 1909, 167; in the Niagara Movement, 129, 162, 164, 215n7; and Washington, Booker T., 109, 110
Turner, Mrs. Lillian, 175
Turner, Mrs. Val Do, 163, 201
Turner, Val Do, *187*; abortionist charges against, 187–89, 208, 223n3(ch 16); background of, 187, 221n18, 219n2(ch 16); and the Calderone (Antonio) case, 112, 114–15, 119; and the Hardy (Samuel) case, 78; in the LEL, 75; at Lincoln Day, St. Paul, 1908, 164; McGhee's friendship with, 154, 187; and the Parker (George) case, 197–98; at testimonial dinner, 186
Tuskegee Institute, 76, 124, 128
Twin Cities, black community in: Minneapolis, 4, 108, 148; St. Paul, 4, 10, 108, 148, 219n4
Twin City Star: on Jack Johnson, 184–85; on McGhee's support of Du Bois, 191; on NAACP affiliation, 198–99

Union Depot restaurant, 171
United Brotherhood of Friendship and Sisters of the Mysterious Ten (UBT/SMT), 182–84
Urban League, 25

Van Sant, Samuel, 78–79, 98–99, 108
Vanderbilt family, 63
Villard, Oswald, 193

Waldron, J. Milton, 161
Walker, George, 63
Walker, John A., 5
Walling, Wright, 167
Walters, Alexander: and the NAAC, 68, 74, 99–100, 101, 110; at the National Negro Conference of 1909, 167; and the Niagara Movement, 132, 164
Washburn, William D., 70, 71
Washington, Booker T., *67*; approach to black progress, 66, 71, 75–76, 87, 88, 99–101; approach to black progress, failure of, 159–60, 167, 194; "Atlanta Compromise" speech, 47, 214n1; at Carnegie Conference, 1904, 122, 124–28; Du Bois' relationship with, 122, 124–25, 128 (*see also* Carnegie Conference); European tour, 1910, 194; LEL luncheon speech, 75–76; at Lincoln Day, St. Paul, 1908, 163–64; McGhee's relationship with, 75, 76, 96–97, 127; at the Metropolitan Hotel, 57–58, 75; NAAC, takeover of, 77, 96–111; at NAAC convention, St. Paul, 99, 103, 216n6; and the Niagara Movement, 157, 159; and Roosevelt, 91, 92
Washington-Du Bois Conference. *See* Carnegie Conference
Watkins, W. F., 200
Watson, David. *See* Shenk (Ida) case
Webster (John) case, 178
Weir, Mayme, 61, 72
Weir, W. A., 98
West (Henry) case, 50–51
The Western Appeal. See The Appeal (St. Paul)
Wheaton, J. Frank, *56*; and the LEL, 66; Minnesota civil rights law amendments, 55–56, 60; Summers (Harry) case, 173
White, Clarence Cameron, 151, 198
White, Mrs. J. A., 183
Wilkins, Roy, 203
Williams, Alec "Hotfoot," 64
Williams, Bert, 63
Williams, Daniel, 200
Williams, Fannie Barrier, 102, 105

Yardley, William Francis, 9
Yates, Josephine Silone, 100, 105
Young, Florence, 50

Picture Credits

Fredrick L. McGhee: A Life on the Color Line was designed by Will Powers at the Minnesota Historical Society Press. The typeface is Clifford, designed by Akira Kobayashi. The book was set in type by Judy Gilats at Peregrine Graphics Services, St. Paul, and printed by Maple Press, York, Pennsylvania.